Exploring the Divided Self

David G. Richards

Exploring the Divided Self

Hermann Hesse's
Steppenwolf
and its Critics

CAMDEN HOUSE

Copyright © 1996 by
CAMDEN HOUSE, INC.

Published by Camden House, Inc.
Drawer 2025
Columbia, SC 29202 USA

Printed on acid-free paper.
Binding materials are chosen for strength and
durability.

ISBN: 1–879751–77–1

Library of Congress Cataloging-in-Publication Data

Richards, David G., 1935–
    Exploring the divided self : Hermann Hesse's Steppenwolf and its
critics / David G. Richards.
        p.   cm. – (Literary criticism in perspective)
    Includes bibliographical references and index.
    ISBN 1–879751–77–1 (alk. paper)
    1. Hesse, Hermann, 1877–1962. Steppenwolf.   I. Title.
II. Series.
PT2617.E85S737   1996
833'. 912—dc20   95–52417
                                                                          CIP

Acknowledgment

I thankfully acknowledge my indebtedness to Suhrkamp Verlag, Frankfurt am Main, for its friendly permission to reproduce the portrait of Hesse from 1927 which appears on the dustjacket, and for permission to quote from Hesse's works. In particular I wish to express my appreciation to Volker Michels, editor of Hesse's works for Suhrkamp and frequent contributor to scholarship on Hesse, for publication information and other assistance.

I am grateful to Professor Eugene Stelzig and especially Professor Steve Dowden, editor of the series in which this volume appears, for their valuable and helpful critique of my manuscript, to James Walker for his expert copy-editing, and to Dean Kerry S. Grant of the Faculty of Arts and Letters, University at Buffalo, for support from the Faculty's Research Initiative Fund.

For Stephanie

Contents

Preface

It was apparent in the early sixties when I was studying in Munich that Hermann Hesse was not highly regarded by German professors or literary critics. Nor were his books readily available to students and the general public in cheap paperback editions, though his collected works, published in 1957 by Suhrkamp in seven volumes, were. After Karlheinz Deschner had tried to demonstrate in his book *Kitsch, Konvention und Kunst* (Kitsch, Convention and Art, 1957), which had sold 78,000 copies by 1961, that Hesse's art is "epigonic," "conventional," third rate and definitely in the category of kitsch, and after a cover story in *Der Spiegel* the following year scorned and belittled him, almost no one wanted to risk revealing poor taste and judgment by speaking positively of Hesse.

When I returned to America to complete my studies at the University of California at Berkeley, I learned about a professor who was out of phase with his German colleagues: Joseph Mileck had spent years collecting material on and by Hesse for the Berkeley archives and had published in 1958 the first and still only review in English of Hesse scholarship: *Hermann Hesse and His Critics*. Not long after my arrival in Berkeley, the campus and the entire San Francisco Bay area became immersed in the countercultural turmoil of the Free Speech Movement and antiwar demonstrations on the one hand and the hippies and the drug culture on the other, both of which groups found a guide, a teacher, and a guru in Hermann Hesse. As a result of this boom in reception, which spread throughout the world, Hesse, in many ways a quintessentially German writer, became an international phenomenon whose sales far exceed those of any other twentieth-century German author.

The most popular, most influential, most controversial, and most innovative of Hesse's novels is *Der Steppenwolf*, which is why I have chosen it as the subject of my investigation. In keeping with the format of the series Literary Criticism in Perspective of which it is a part, this study will trace the development of criticism on *Steppenwolf* and, where relevant, on Hesse in general in order to reveal how critical approaches and methods have changed over time, what the particular contributions of the various approaches have been, and how extraliterary factors have influenced the critical and popular reception and interpretation of Hesse's novel. I have deviated from strict chronology in some cases to bring together studies which are closely connected by theme or methodology. In particular, I have collected in a separate chapter most of the investigations based on the application of Jung's archetypal psychology, which, beginning in the sixties, became the predominant approach to *Demian, Steppenwolf,* and other works from the critical period in Hesse's life that included his ongoing Jungian analysis.

Quotations from *Steppenwolf* in my text are identified by the abbreviation St followed by the page number; I have used the 1980 printing of the Bantam Book translation by Basil Creighton as updated by Joseph Mileck. Quotations from *Demian* are indicated by D and the page number of the Bantam Book paperback edition. Quotations from and references to Hesse's other writings are from Suhrkamp's twelve volume paperback edition of the *Gesammelte Werke,* which is known as the *Werkausgabe* and abbreviated WA. Also cited are letters from the four volume *Gesammelte Briefe* (GB) and the 1957 edition of Hesse's *Gesammelte Schriften* (GS). Citations from secondary sources are identified by author and year of publication. Complete information on these works can be found in the alphabetical listing at the end of the chapters in which they are cited and in the chronologically arranged bibliography following the text. Unless otherwise indicated, all translations except those from *Steppenwolf* and *Demian* are my own. Citations of Jung's writings are from the twenty volume *Collected Works of C. G. Jung* published by Princeton University Press.

Introduction: The Hesse Phenomenon

Writing just before the beginning of the Hesse boom in America, Joseph Mileck does not include *Der Steppenwolf* among the three Hesse novels he thinks most likely to achieve lasting fame (1958, 30–31). Two decades later Egon Schwarz concludes from his review of the reception of Hesse's works during half a century that *Steppenwolf* must be considered the author's main work. Only *Narziss und Goldmund* and *Das Glasperlenspiel* (The Glass Bead Game) can be seen as challengers, "but the majority of experts and the great mass of readers appear in this case to be united in giving precedence to *Steppenwolf*" (1980, 11). Hesse's German publisher, Siegfried Unseld, identifies *Steppenwolf* as the work that sparked Hesse's reception in postwar Germany and in America (1985, 113, 115).

Mileck's view is indicative of the early response to *Steppenwolf*: many of Hesse's friends and most contemporary critics were disappointed and embarrassed by the author's frank presentation of intensely personal problems, both in the novel and in the even more revealing and unrefined "Crisis" poems which immediately preceded it in composition, though not in publication. As is now apparent from the surprising history of its reception, the novel has appealed to readers precisely because it deals in an honest and forthright manner with the author's problems and conflicts, which, as he states in the book's preface, are also symptomatic of the times. Mileck's assessment that the novel lacks "the more universal implications inherent in all truly great art" (Mileck 1958, 30) has by now been refuted by the responses of several generations of readers. The boom has subsided, but students are still being drawn to Hesse and especially to *Steppenwolf*.

Hesse's biographers and critics identify a series of waves in the popular and critical reception of his works. These waves depend to some extent on the changes in Hesse's art during his lifetime but even more on external circumstances: his works have consistently appealed to youth in chaotic times and when traditional authority is questioned and resisted, and certain of his novels and stories have appealed especially to young people who are attempting to find and define themselves as individuals in rigid and authoritarian societies. Brief consideration of the phases of Hesse's artistic development and the waves in the reception of his works will provide a useful background for the detailed survey of the critical reception of *Steppenwolf* which follows.

Dividing Hesse's works into an early and a mature period has become a commonplace among critics and is sanctioned by the author's own evaluation. Hesse attributes the beginning of the "completely new and perhaps the most productive creative period" of his career to his psychoanalysis with the Jungian analyst Dr. J. B. Lang from May 1916 to November 1917 (*Tages-Anzeiger Zürich*, 8 March 1940). Through the prolonged suffering and stress caused by the breakdown of European civilization in the Great War, the deterioration of his marriage and the worsening mental derangement of his wife, the death of his father, and the long and serious illness of his youngest son, Hesse's own mental and nervous state had become sufficiently precarious for his physician to recommend psychoanalysis. By undertaking an "infernal journey" through himself, Hesse made the discovery that helped him out of this crisis and changed his life and art.

In his "Kurzgefaßter Lebenslauf" (Life Story Briefly Told, 1925) Hesse identifies this experience as the second great transformation of his life, the first one being his decision to become a poet. Now as then he finds himself in conflict with a world in which he had lived in peace. He has failed at everything, he claims, and feels alone, miserable, and maliciously misunderstood. He faces a hopeless abyss between reality and his ideal of what is desirable, reasonable, and good, but, unlike in the past, he now becomes introspective and finds the source of his suffering not outside in the world but inside himself, in his own internal disorder.

> I found all the world's war and thirst for blood, all its frivolity, all its coarse sensuality, all its cowardice in myself too. I had first to lose my self-respect, then my self-contempt, had to do nothing else but continue my glance into chaos to the end, with the now awakening, now extinguishing hope of again finding nature, again finding innocence. (WA 6:402)

The importance for Hesse of this transformation is manifest in his adoption of a pseudonym, Emil Sinclair, for the publications immediately following it and in the corresponding repudiation of his earlier work. He recognizes that his attempt to live in peace with the world and to please the public with his works was "just as foul as the external peace in the world." In his desire to be admired by the public, he has paid too dearly: by delivering what the public wants to read, he has sacrificed the poet in him to the *Unterhaltungsschriftsteller*, a designation that agrees with the tendency of contemporary reviewers to see him as a *Heimatdichter* (regional author) or *Idylliker*, whose entertaining tales are reminiscent of German Romanticism. That he refused to allow a five volume Italian edition of his selected works (1961–66) to include anything published before 1915 (Gummerer 1977, 71) indicates that he continued near the end of his life to distinguish between early and mature works and to distance himself from the former.

The works of Hesse's mature period may be divided into two groups, those written during the critical period of his life when he was intermittently in psychoanalysis, that is, from *Demian* (written 1917, published 1919) to *Steppenwolf* (1927), and those which follow the catharsis he achieved by writing *Steppenwolf* and the "Crisis" poems.[1] In the period following his second transformation, Hesse was no longer willing to cater to the tastes and desires of the public. As he tells his friends in a preface to "Krisis: Ein Stück Tagebuch," (Crisis: Pages from a Diary, 1928), he had constantly vacillated through most of his life between periods of intense sublimation and ascetic striving for spirituality, and periods of yielding to naive sensuality, to what is childish and foolish, and even to what is mad and dangerous. Yet he had unconsciously suppressed or glossed over most of this dark side of his life in his earlier works because he felt inferior in that realm (Michels 1972, 161). With increasing age, when writing "pretty things" no longer gave him any pleasure and "only a late awakening, passionate love of self-knowledge and sincerity" drove him to write, he had to deal with the part of life he had previously suppressed, no matter how difficult or unpleasant that might be (Michels 1972, 161–62). Hesse insists that his "ideal of sincerity" leaves him no choice but to express his dark as well as his light side. As he writes in response to Heinrich Wiegand's criticism of the "Crisis" poems: "Years ago I gave up aesthetic ambition, and I don't write fiction (*Dichtung*) but rather only confession, just as someone drowning or someone poisoned isn't concerned with his haircut or intonation but simply screams" (Michels 1972, 97). In short, Hesse had resolved to write primarily for himself, to examine and attempt to come to terms with his being in all its complexity.

The novels from each of Hesse's major periods have continued to find admirers. The early works are favored by readers who seek entertainment and escape and who share the author's strong feelings for nature and his romantic, idyllic sensibility, but they are also read by the youth who face problems similar to those encountered by Hesse's young protagonists, especially the stifling and stultifying effects of an authoritarian educational

---

[1]While there is much to recommend this subdivision, one should bear in mind that the separation between *Steppenwolf* and subsequent works is not of the same order as the break between *Demian* and earlier ones. *Siddhartha* (1922), for example, which falls within the critical phase, has at least as much in common with *Die Morgenlandfahrt* (Journey to the East, 1932) and even *Das Glasperlenspiel* (1943) as with *Demian* or *Steppenwolf*. Likewise, the elite group bearing the mark of Cain in *Demian* and the Immortals and the Magic Theater in *Steppenwolf* anticipate the "Bund" in *Morgenlandfahrt* as well as some elements of "Kastalia" in *Glasperlenspiel*.

system. Decades before American readers discovered Hesse, his early works were popular with Japanese youth, whose educational system has much in common with the German system portrayed in them (see Watanabe 1977, 222–33).

In America, on the other hand, it was the mature works which had the greatest impact, especially those from the middle period, "the most dramatic and most critical years of his life" (Mileck 1958, 20). These are the works in which Hesse is most critical of the times, most radical in his attack on traditional authority, most torn by the conflict within him of seemingly irreconcilable polarities, and most engaged in the process of individuation, in striving to find and understand himself. The novels of this critical period appealed both to the activist segment of the American youth movement of the sixties and seventies, which opposed the Vietnam War and rejected the military-industrial complex, big business, middle-class values, and the authority of parents, church, and state, and to the hippies, who were following Timothy Leary's encouragement to "Turn on, tune in, and drop out," and who sought to expand consciousness and to practice an ethic of peace and love.

Before the boom of the sixties, which began in America and reached Germany in the early seventies, there were four previous waves in Hesse's reception in Germany (see Baumer 1977). The first began in 1904 with the publication of *Peter Camenzind*, Hesse's first novel. Because of its emphasis on individual development and its criticism of modern culture, this novel appealed especially to members of the youth movement, who were dissatisfied with Wilhelminian Germany.

The second wave came with the publication in 1919 of *Demian*, which, as Thomas Mann wrote, had an "electrifying" influence on postwar youth and was praised by a number of contemporary writers. As noted above, this novel, published under the pseudonym Emil Sinclair, begins the period of Hesse's mature works. *Demian* and the essay "Zarathustras Wiederkehr. Ein Wort an die deutsche Jugend. Von einem Deutschen" (Zarathustra's Return: A Word to the German Youth by a German, 1919), which was published the same year, provoked a reaction against Hesse by former readers who did not like his new tone and by nationalists who had been offended by his pacifist position during the war. Anticipating even stronger disapproval of *Steppenwolf*, Fischer published only 15,000 copies in the first edition but soon had to print another 10,000. The third wave of Hesse's popularity initiated by this novel was cut short, however, by the National Socialists' antipathy to Hesse and his internationalism, pacifism, and anti-authoritarianism. From 1939 to 1945 his works were considered "undesirable literature" (*unerwünschte Literatur*), and no paper was allotted for reprints or the publication of new works (Michels 1972, 319).

Following the war many young readers turned again to Hesse and other authors who had warned against the coming disaster and whose books had been anathema to the regime that had led Germany to its destruction. Others, having seen Hesse's books on their parents' bookshelves, considered him part of the romantic inheritance that had led to National Socialism and from which they wanted to free themselves (Schwarz 1974, 57). As Hesse noted, he was continually attacked from both political extremes.

The recognition that accompanied the awarding of the Nobel prize for literature and the Frankfurt Goethe prize, both in 1946, initiated a fourth wave in Germany and the beginning of Hesse's international reception. Less than a decade after it began, this surge in popularity gave way in Germany to critical attempts to diminish Hesse as a writer and to a lack of interest on the part of German scholars and critics. As the German demand for Hesse's works fell to an all time low (see Pfeifer 1977, 12; Baumer 1977, 30) the totally unexpected and unprecedented boom began in America and quickly spread through most of the world, clearly establishing Hesse as the most widely read German author of the twentieth century.

The extraordinary increase in Hesse's popularity in America was unanticipated by scholars and little influenced by them. The novels that had previously appeared in translation had attracted few readers and minimal critical attention. Even his receipt of the Nobel prize did little to stimulate curiosity. The first of his novels to achieve moderate success was *Siddhartha*, which was published by New Directions in 1951 upon the recommendation of Henry Miller. The hardcover edition sold 13,000 copies in four printings; a paperback edition appeared in 1957 and soon became the publisher's best seller (Koester 1977, 157).

In *The Outsider* (1956), which was especially popular among rebellious youth, Colin Wilson maintains that Hesse's "novels of ideas have a vitality that can only be compared to Dostoevsky," because Hesse is himself a participant in the lives and events he recounts rather than an observer like Thomas Mann, who surpasses Hesse in his power to bring people to life, but whose ideas are less alive than Hesse's (63). It is not surprising that Wilson gives pride of place to *Steppenwolf* as "one of the most penetrating and exhaustive studies of the Outsider that has ever been written" (57).

Among Wilson's readers were the beatniks, led by Jack Kerouac, Allen Ginsburg, and Lawrence Ferlinghetti, themselves unconventional outsiders, who shared Hesse's interest in Eastern thought, his tendency to mysticism, and his antiauthoritarian, antimaterialist position, and the hippies, who may be seen as a populist offshoot of the beatniks. Even more important for the hippies and for the boost he gave to Hesse's popular reception was the drug guru Timothy Leary. Leary identifies Hesse as the author who best expresses the transpersonal, unitary consciousness that he and his followers were attempting to tune in to through the use of LSD and other drugs. While critics have been eager to claim that Leary misread and misinterpreted Hesse, his recognition of Hesse's use of symbols to capture an esoteric message which exists behind exoteric form reveals precisely the kind of insight and understanding Hesse did not find among his friends and critics.

Leary sees LSD as an instant and easy way to the *unio mystica*, the experience and state of being which true mystics achieve only after a long and arduous spiritual journey, one of the stages of which is the frightening and nearly unbearable "dark night of the soul." (Haller's despair and thoughts of suicide may be seen as manifestations of this stage, which generally precedes the mystical experience or illumination.) Thus Leary equates the LSD experience with the unitary perception Govinda achieves at the end of *Siddhartha* and with Haller's experience of the Magic Theater (Leary 1963, 170, 172). He advises his followers to read *Siddhartha* and *Steppenwolf* before their LSD trips: especially the last part of *Steppenwolf* is a "priceless manual" (181). Following the psychedelic trip they should read *Morgenlandfahrt* and *Glasperlenspiel* to see how they can avoid the negative consequences of the drug-induced experience, such as degeneration into priestly ritual or anarchy, by forming close support groups analogous to the "Bund" in the former and "Kastalia" in the latter. Noting that Pablo gives Haller drugs to prepare him for the descent into his soul, Leary wonders if Hesse might have used drugs and speculates that the members of the covenant (*Bund*) in *Morgenlandfahrt* may be based on an actual community of drug users to which Hesse belonged but which he left in order to develop his rational side and to write (175–77), a supposition Hesse's biographers have been eager to refute.

It was not long before the author many had thought too German for Americans became a cult figure and a primary component of popular culture. Berkeley had its "Steppenwolf" bar and "Magic Theater," Philadelphia its "Magic Theater" coffee house, Chicago its "Steppenwolf Theatre Company." The members of a rock musical group called "Steppenwolf" dressed like figures from the novel and performed the kind of music Hesse considered to be a symptom of the breakdown of Western civilization. Hesse's other novels have inspired similarly ironic incongruities such as "Demian's Rathskeller," "Siddhartha's Pad," and "The Bead Game" boutique. Also attempting to ride the Hesse wave were adaptations of his novels *Siddhartha* and *Steppenwolf* into films in 1973 and 1974 respectively, which runs contrary to Hesse's repeated refusal to allow his books to be transformed and distorted by this technological medium. By the time these films reached the market place, however, the Hesse wave had subsided, destroyed in large part by the commercial exploitation it spawned, and neither film was a commercial success.[2] Now a new wave may be forming, one that can be surfed via the Hesse news group on the Internet.

While Hesse's uncompromising criticism of bourgeois mercantile values, nationalism, militarism, authoritarianism in all its forms, and the destructive influence of technology has been a major source of his appeal to youthful readers, especially in the sixties and seventies, the primary factor in his popular success may be his uncompromising commitment to the discovery and development of the self. The intensely personal and confessional nature of his works appeals directly to readers who can identify with him and his heroes and for whom the texts provide a stimulus for introspection, readers for whom Hesse's texts are "relevant," a key word in the sixties and seventies, and have a therapeutic quality. Hesse not only deals with the young generation's particular conflicts, he also "leads them through discovery of themselves back into the midst of a newly structured life in which they derive their own identities, create their own universe, and establish its order" (Timpe 1969, 42). His works have consistently appealed to young people who are striving to find and define themselves in opposition to prevailing collective values and institutions.

Finally, "against the opposition of the cultural establishment," the fifth wave in Hesse's reception reached Germany from America in the seventies (Baumer 1977, 32). Beginning with the appearance in 1970 of Hesse's *Gesammelte Werke* (Collected Works) and the publication of inexpensive paperback editions, the sales of Hesse's books increased steadily. Between 1970 and 1977 nearly three million books were sold, which is three times the number sold in the previous seventy years (Pfeifer 1977, 12). The paperback edition of *Steppenwolf* sold 420,000 copies between 1969 and 1977, which is six times the total of all previous sales (Baumer 1977, 35). The current total is close to 2,000,000 copies. In America the Bantam paperback edition of *Steppenwolf* had sold 1,600,000 copies by 1976; the current total exceeds 3,000,000.

I do not mean to suggest with these figures that the number of books sold is an indicator of an author's stature. On the contrary, data on German bestsellers from 1915 to 1940 indicate that popular books are not generally the ones scholars identify as being artistically important and deserving of in-

---

[2]Theodore Ziolkowski identifies three stages in Hesse's reception in America. In the first Hesse is seen as a saint and guru, the source of secret wisdom, the knowledge of which sets his readers apart from the uninitiated. In the second stage Hesse is discovered as a cultural phenomenon by critics and journalists and is discussed in numerous articles in the scholarly and popular press. This is also the period when he is made into an institution and exploited commercially. The *coup de grace* is delivered by the pedagogical establishment, when it includes him in the curriculum of high school and college classes on English literature. At this point reading Hesse can no longer be a mark of distinction (1980, 7–17).

clusion in the official canon, though there are a few exceptions. Of the fourteen books with sales over 500,000 listed by Donald Ray Richards in his extensive compilation of German publications, only two are novels that are still read: Thomas Mann's *Buddenbrooks* (1901) stands in first place with 1,305,000 copies, and Erich Maria Remarque's *Im Westen Nichts Neues* (All Quiet on the Western Front, 1929) is in third place with over 900,000 copies sold. Among the fifteen books listed with sales of 400 to 500 thousand, Rilke is the only major writer represented. Not a single major author or work is found in the list of 28 books with sales between 300 and 400 thousand. The names that recur in these categories are Rudolf Herzog, Hedwig Courths-Mahler, Hermann Löns, Ludwig Ganghofer, and the like. Ludwig Finckh, known to us now primarily as Hesse's friend, has two books on the list with higher sales than Hesse's top seller, which is *Unterm Rad* (Beneath the Wheel, 1905) with 149,000 copies (1968, 55–57).

From these statistics as well as from numerous historical examples one might cite, it would appear that critics and literary scholars generally go against popular taste in their choice of writers and works they consider worthy of inclusion in the literary canon. And given the uncertainty and disagreement that prevail in the assessment of contemporary writers, time, rather than the opinions of critics and scholars, tends to be the major decisive factor in determining canonicity: if an author is read by at least three successive generations he or she is likely to gain a lasting place in the canon. It is apparent that Hesse now qualifies under this criterion.

The Hesse phenomenon is unusual, perhaps unique, for several reason: the reception of his works proceeded with minimal leadership from critics and scholars, who, on the contrary, have been motivated by Hesse's unexpected popularity to discover why his works have such powerful and apparently lasting popular appeal; Hesse's foreign popularity has greatly exceeded his popularity in his own country, a distinction he shares with Franz Kafka; and a relatively large proportion of the most important criticism and scholarship has likewise come from outside German-speaking countries, primarily from American scholars.

Like his popularity, the critical reception of Hesse's works has also proceeded in a series of waves. Writing in 1957, Joseph Mileck identifies a first period of critical literature which extends to 1926, a second from 1927 to the end of the war, and a third from 1946 (1958, xi). Seen from the nineties I think it makes sense to combine Mileck's first two periods into one and to extend it to about 1950. The period to 1926, which in any event is irrelevant for *Steppenwolf*, includes mostly short reviews of Hesse's works in newspapers and periodicals. The small number of dissertations on Hesse produced during this entire period — nine in Germany, three in Austria, three in Switzerland, and one in the United States (as listed in Mileck 1977,

1151–58) — indicate how slight the academic interest was before the fifties. As suggested by the title of my first chapter, the few monographs published during this period place greater emphasis on the author than on the works.

Scholarship on Hesse came to an abrupt halt when Hitler and the Nazis assumed power and critical writing on the arts was forbidden. It was resumed following the war by a generation of young scholars, who, like their counterparts in 1918, had discovered and turned to Hesse because he represented the antithesis of, and had warned against, the prevailing ideology and the country's leaders. These young scholars were more concerned with the content and, albeit to a lesser degree, the form of Hesse's works than their predecessors had been; the relevance of biographical details for them lies in their contribution to understanding the texts. As will be seen in chapter 2, these scholarly investigations provided a good foundation for the subsequent interpretations of individual texts.

Apparently resentful of Hesse's postwar success, some critics proclaimed that his art was irrelevant, epigonic, and second or third rate. Following these attacks in the late fifties, German scholarship on Hesse diminished to almost nothing. As noted above, however, Hesse's falling star in Germany corresponded with his rising popularity in America and with a dramatic expansion of the critical literature. In keeping with the tenets of New Criticism, which were predominant at the time, the majority of these studies, like the dissertations of the fifties, paid close attention to the works' content and form. They differed from the dissertations, however, in their focus on individual works. The first and primary phase of this so-called Hesse boom, the decade of the sixties, is treated in chapter 3. Chapter 4 deals with the second phase of the boom, a period noteworthy for the publication of numerous commentaries and collections of essays and documents designed for use by teachers and students. It begins in the seventies when the international Hesse wave reaches Germany, giving rise to a resurgence of popular and scholarly interest.

Because the relevance of Jung's psychology for understanding and interpreting some of Hesse's works, especially *Demian* and *Steppenwolf*, has been made increasingly evident by the scholarship on this subject and by the increase in the number of studies based on or including the application of Jung's concepts, I have departed from a strict chronological approach in my final chapter in order to consolidate my review of the conflicting arguments and the findings of these investigations.

Works Cited

Baumer, Franz. "Deutschland." In *Hermann Hesses weltweite Wirkung: Internationale Rezeptionsgeschichte*, ed. Martin Pfeifer, 15–38. Frankfurt am Main: Suhrkamp, 1977.

Gummerer, Gottfried. "Italien." In *Hermann Hesses weltweite Wirkung: Internationale Rezeptionsgeschichte*, ed. Martin Pfeifer, 69–84. Frankfurt am Main: Suhrkamp, 1977.

Koester, Rudolf. "USA." In *Hermann Hesses weltweite Wirkung: Internationale Rezeptionsgeschichte*, ed. Martin Pfeifer, 155–71. Frankfurt am Main: Suhrkamp, 1977.

Leary, Timothy and Ralph Metzner. "Hermann Hesse: Poet of the Interior Journey." *The Psychedelic Review* 1 (1963): 167–82.

Michels, Volker, ed. *Materialien zu Hermann Hesses "Der Steppenwolf."* Frankfurt am Main: Suhrkamp, 1972.

Mileck, Joseph. *Hermann Hesse and His Critics: The Criticism and Bibliography of Half a Century.* Chapel Hill: U of North Carolina P, 1958.

Mileck, Joseph. *Hermann Hesse: Biography and Bibliography.* 2 vols. Berkeley: U of California P, 1977.

Pfeifer, Martin, ed. *Hermann Hesses weltweite Wirkung: Internationale Rezeptionsgeschichte.* Frankfurt am Main: Suhrkamp, 1977.

Richards, Donald Ray. *The German Bestseller in the 20th Century. A Complete Bibliography and Analysis: 1915–1940.* Bern: Herbert Lang, 1968.

Schwarz, Egon. "Ein Fall globaler Rezeption: Hermann Hesse im Wandel der Zeiten." *Zeitschrift für Literaturwissenschaft und Linguistik* 15 (1974): 50–60.

Timpe, Eugen F. "Hermann Hesse in the United States." *Symposium* 23 (1969): 73–79.

Unseld, Siegfried. *Hermann Hesse: Werk und Wirkungsgeschichte.* Revised and expanded version of 1973 edition. Frankfurt am Main: Suhrkamp, 1985.

Watanabe, Masaru. "Japan." In *Hermann Hesses weltweite Wirkung: Internationale Rezeptionsgeschichte*, ed. Martin Pfeifer, 222–33. Frankfurt am Main: Suhrkamp, 1977.

Wilson, Colin. *The Outsider.* Boston: Houghton Mifflin, 1956.

Ziolkowski, Theodore. "Hermann Hesse in den USA." In *Hermann Hesse heute*, ed. Adrian Hsia, 1–24. Bonn: Bouvier, 1980.

1: The Author in His Works: Criticism to 1950

Prewar Criticism

Critical writing on Hesse prior to 1950 was primarily positivistic and biographical. It was characteristic of monographs from this period to consider an author's work as the product and reflection of his or her state at the time of composition and of the circumstances in which the work arose. First and foremost among such monographs on Hesse is Hugo Ball's *Hermann Hesse: Sein Leben und sein Werk* (Hermann Hesse: His Life and Work, 1927). Commissioned by Hesse's publisher Samuel Fischer to celebrate the poet's fiftieth birthday in July 1927, it was completed shortly before Ball's death the same year. Ball, Hesse's friend and a fellow poet, was aided in his project by information provided by Hesse and members of the Hesse family. The biography was written quickly and contains some errors but was not surpassed for many years. As befits the occasion for which it was commissioned, it tends to be more informative and appreciative than analytical and critical, and it treats the works primarily as documents of the author's biography. It is analytical and innovative, however, in the application of psychoanalytic theory: one contemporary reviewer considered it to be a first attempt in the application of psychoanalysis to the writing of biography, and it provoked some discussion and controversy among critics as to the validity of this approach (Werner-Birkenbach 1992, 177).

In just two pages of general comment on *Steppenwolf*, which he had seen only in typescript and galleys (Freedman 1978, 309), Ball anticipates the public's negative reaction to the new, darker, and more disturbing side of Hesse's "most powerful incarnation," and he attempts to direct attention to the positive benefits that could result from seizing and controlling the enemy within. He also sees the novel as a telling product and document of the times: "That such a mythological beast allows itself to be seen in the midst of our modern life points to a time in which the art of love and conciliation, the understanding human art, can only be found in print, only in black and white." A negative Romanticism appears in this "manly and serious" book. No matter how much one may moan and groan, "here is the attempt to repel the demonism of our time, which has been condensed and

THE AUTHOR IN HIS WORKS

reduced to a fitting formula, in order to gain space for all goodness and unimpeded eminence" (213).

At a time when German chauvinism was on the rise, Ball foresees an especially strong negative response to *Steppenwolf* from nationalistically oriented readers, just as Hesse's pacifism in the war and his persistent criticism and disparagement of the German educational system evoked journalistic attacks and scholarly silence following the publication of *Demian*. The professor in *Steppenwolf* both represents and anticipates the author's experience with this element of society.

Ball's biography was the primary source of information on Hesse for more than two decades, and though it has been superseded by more accurate and detailed biographies such as Zeller's (1963), Mileck's (1978), and Freedman's (1978), it remains a valuable source. Subsequent reprints were updated by the inclusion of Anni Carlsson's chapter "Vom Steppenwolf zur Morgenlandfahrt" in 1933 and another entitled "Hermann Hesses 'Glasperlenspiel' in seinen Wesensgesetzen" (The Fundamental Principles of Hermann Hesse's *Glasperlenspiel*) in 1947. For a Swiss edition published in 1947 by Fretz und Wasmuth, the final chapter, "Der Weg zum Glasperlenspiel" (The Path to *Glasperlenspiel*), was provided by Otto Basler. These essays differ from Ball's study in that they focus on Hesse's works rather than on his biography. The various changes which had been made in Ball's text were omitted in editions from 1956 on, by which time other biographical works had superseded it, and Ball's original text became more appreciated in its own right as part of his own *oeuvre*.[1]

Carlsson begins her discussion with a description of a three-phase development that Hesse supposedly underwent and that recurs in his works, a development he describes in "Ein Stückchen Theologie" (A Bit of Theology, 1932), from which she quotes without identifying her source:

> It is the path that leads from the innocence of the child to the adult's despair, to that often recurring puberty of the spirit, in which all values must seem doubtful, because the laws that support them are chimerical, because a final realization of the spirit's demands proves to be impossible. "This despair now leads either to destruction or else to a Third Kingdom of the Spirit, to the experience of a state beyond morality and law, a penetration to grace and salvation, to a new higher kind of irresponsibility or, briefly stated: to faith, to a new kind of innocence." (1947, 236; WA 10:74–75)

---

[1] For a detailed account of changes made in Ball's text see Sabine Werner-Birkenbach, "Hugo Balls 'Hesse-Biographie': Zur Wechselbeziehung von Rezeption und Edition," *Hugo Ball Almanach 1992*, 157–236. The author discusses changes made in response to the criticism of his unflattering treatment of Ludwig Finckh. (The pacifist Ball was strongly opposed to Finckh's immoderate nationalism and patriotism.) She also lists twenty-three minor textual revisions made by Hesse.

This development begins in Hesse's works with Peter Camenzind's child-like, mythical "Naturreligion" and progresses through Demian's demonic, Protestant avowal of the necessity of individuation, of finding one's self, to the Steppenwolf, who, in his suffering from guilt and despair, is inclined to abandon the path of individuation and to sink into dissolution, to return to the mother, to God, to the universe. With the guidance of Hermine and Pablo, Carlsson concludes, Haller comes close to achieving the state of mind characteristic of Hesse's Third Kingdom, which is represented in the novel by humor, the Immortals, and the proper use of the Magic Theater. And though Haller fails, there is still some hope for the future, as there was indeed for Hesse, who depicts the attainment of the goal in *Morgenland-fahrt*. Carlsson thus identifies the positive elements in the novel, which, to Hesse's dismay, had escaped most reviewers and friends (238–43).

In his study *Hermann Hesse*, published in 1928, Hans Schmid uses bio-graphical information and passages from Hesse's works to develop a psychological portrait of the artist. German literature of our century, he writes, is essentially literature of the soul, often the sick soul, and Hesse is a typical representative, observer, and recorder of the disturbed Occidental soul. Citing Freud and other psychoanalysts, Schmid asserts that love or libido withdrawn from objects and not redirected to others may be redirected inward to the self, and preoccupation with the self may awaken self-pity, sentimentality, and melancholy. He defines sentimentality as an "attitude of the soul that derives from a hypertrophy of the egocentric emotional life. The sentimental person tends to pity himself or to torment himself, which implies both autoerotic and autosadistic impulses." These derive from primitive self love, which is connected to a deficiency in one's sociability. The self pity of a discordant soul is made manifest in the sentimental attitude of the adult (112–13).

Schmid considers melancholy to be the passive side of sentimentality. A person suffering from melancholy lacks interest in the external world but is also saddened by the emptiness of his ego. A melancholy person lacks shame and obtains satisfaction from revealing and communicating his condition. The compulsion to communicate also derives from the need to illuminate and try to understand one's confused soul. "With Hesse both sentimentality and melancholy probably derive from the multiplicity of his feelings, from the weakness of his will, from his social inadequacy, and from his lyrical love of his own ego" (113–14).

According to Schmid, Hesse's works to *Demian* are dominated by longing for the mother and the wish to be a child again. In *Demian* he takes possession of his mother following his father's death, exhausts that theme, and turns to his own feminine self. In *Kurgast* and *Steppenwolf* he reveals his inner feelings as never before and in so doing overcomes his sentimentality. Writing in 1928, Schmid cannot know how Hesse's development will continue, but his claim that "*Steppenwolf* is an orgiastic self-destruction," though considerably overstated, does appear to anticipate the transformation which followed the completion of *Narziss und Goldmund* and is manifest in his sustained emphasis on *Geist* (156–57, 181).

The earliest treatment of Hesse in an American journal is W. Dehorn's "Psychoanalyse und neuere Dichtung" (Psychoanalysis and Recent Literature, 1932). Following a discussion of the importance of literature as a "psychographic document" that can be used to good advantage by the psychoanalyst, the author claims that artists have two paths for building a bridge from the demonic unconscious to the harmony of conscious mastery of life: he can proceed as what Dehorn calls a "hygienist" and therapist, who is concerned with obtaining and preserving health, or as a mystic and advocate of ethics, who seeks salvation in a moral and religious life (254).

In Dehorn's view, Hesse is a hygienist. In his early novels he deals with the crises of young men struggling to come to terms with their sexuality. What in those works was the product of dream life and fantasy becomes a true problematic in *Roßhalde*, because now Hesse and his protagonist are married. *Demian* deals with the Oedipal fantasy, with Demian supposedly representing the father and the Apollonian principle of form, a peculiar interpretation given the many indications in the novel that Demian represents the totality of the Self in which the opposites are united. As Sinclair's daimon, fate, and goal, Demian is the inner voice guiding Sinclair along the path from the guilt and despair of the fallen child to the Third Kingdom of unitary consciousness (Dehorn 340–42).

Just as he does not recognize the deeper meaning of Demian, Dehorn fails to recognize the importance of the Immortals, who, as Hesse wrote in a letter of 15 February 1954, have exactly the same function in *Steppenwolf* as the eponymous figure does in *Demian*. Dehorn is therefore unjustly dissatisfied with the novel because it contains no sign of deliverance or recovery from the fundamental dualism from which Harry Haller and his time suffer. "*Steppenwolf* is a completely unsuccessful masquerade of self irony" he concludes. "It ends in stupidity and horror." Dehorn's negative evaluation is reinforced by the novel's contrast with *Siddhartha*: "The puzzling sequence of *Siddhartha* and *Steppenwolf* fill us with radical doubt in the artistic practical wisdom of the Swiss writer. Until now Hesse has been incapable of reconciling drive and spirit." He knows what the goal is, but "he lacks the force of will and the light of love to demolish the world of delusion and, in the motherly source of things, to seize and experience anew nature and culture" (344).

In the conclusion of his cursory discussion, Dehorn faults Hesse's works for not being better psychoanalysis. He thereby departs from his beginning assumption, which is that literature provides psychiatrists with psychographic documents. His study is more judgmental than analytical.

Postwar Criticism: A New Beginning

Hesse's books were not among those burned in May 1933, and his name was not included on the "official black list" of forbidden authors. Because of his ambiguous situation, however, one after the other of the periodicals to which Hesse had frequently contributed book reviews dropped him, until only *Die neue Rundschau*, an organ of Hesse's publisher Samuel Fischer, would risk publishing them. In the invitation to review books of his choice for the Swedish *Bonniers Litterära Magasin*, Hesse saw the opportunity to continue his advocacy of books that could not be reviewed in Germany. Because of the prominence he gave to works by Jewish and communist authors, German critics accused him of betraying contemporary German literature and of thereby giving support to Germany's enemies and the Jews. "The German poet Hermann Hesse takes on the role of yesterday's Jewish criticism in his betrayal of the people," writes a journalist in *Die neue Literatur*. "For the sake of Jews and cultural Bolsheviks he helps to spread abroad ideas that are damaging to his fatherland" (cited by Abret 1992, 126 and Michels 1992, 94–95). Even more vitriolic and hysterical assaults followed this one, until it was decreed by the cultural ministry in May 1937 that such attacks should cease and that the distribution of Hesse's works should not be obstructed (Abret 134).

Despite this decree, however, distribution of Hesse's books was subjected to some control. Works containing passages critical of the times were not reprinted. This included even *Narziss und Goldmund*, in which a pogrom is mentioned. And Hesse's final novel, *Das Glasperlenspiel*, with its depiction of an ideal society which is completely contrary to the Third Reich, was not allowed to be published. Later attempts to forbid all Hesse's works were successfully prevented by the courageous intercession and mediation of Peter Suhrkamp, Fischer's successor as Hesse's publisher (Michels 1992, 101).

As was the case during and after the First World War, Hesse was attacked from both political extremes. At the same time his reviews were being denounced by Nazis, emigrants blamed him for continuing to publish in German periodicals, to which Hesse responded: "I feel obligated not to abandon this messed up [versaute] and brutalized Germany, but to preserve in my sphere the tradition of propriety and justice. Furthermore, I am now the only German critic who announces books by emigrants and Jews" (Michels 1992, 92). Emigrants and communists also blamed him for not publicly condemning Hitler and National Socialism, as Thomas Mann and others had done, and for living in aristocratic seclusion in Ticino. This was his home, of course, which he opened to many fleeing emigrants, and, as Michels points out, it was in Hitler's back yard, whereas Thomas Mann and the others were writing from safer havens in Europe and then in America.

By decreeing in November 1936 that criticism of the arts was to be replaced by appreciative reports about art, Goebbels eliminated true literary criticism during the Third Reich. And since Hesse had not yet attracted much attention abroad, there is a hiatus of more than a decade in the criticism of his works.

Critical writing resumed when the end of the conflict was in sight and Richard Matzig, a Swiss Germanist, was drawn to the author who had repeatedly warned the Germans about the coming catastrophe and who had spoken out against militarism and nationalism in general and against Hitler and his program in particular. Matzig begins his book *Hermann Hesse in Montagnola: Studien zu Werk und Innenwelt des Dichters* (Hermann Hesse in Montagnola: Studies of the Works and the Inner World of the Poet, 1947), with an account of his visit with the author in November 1944. He thus attempts to reintroduce Hesse to German readers in a time of crisis analogous to the one following the First World War. Considering this goal and the great happiness Hesse's books had given him, as he states in his afterword, it is not surprising that his study is respectfully appreciative and more descriptive than analytical.

Ball's authorized biography enables Matzig to dispense with biographical information, but he does recapitulate some of the themes, tendencies, and subject areas which Ball identifies and which form a foundation for Matzig's subsequent discussion of Hesse's works from *Demian* through *Glasperlenspiel*. By frequently making comparisons between Hesse and other authors and by identifying the Indian, Chinese, Greek, Gnostic, Romantic, psychoanalytic, and other sources of Hesse's thought, he attempts to go beyond Ball in establishing Hesse's place in the context of intellectual history.

Matzig's basic approach resembles what the French call "critique créatrice," a creative criticism that intends to convey to a receptive public the critic's appreciative sentiment, understanding, and love of an author or a work. This is one of several approaches that arose when criticism, reacting against positivism and its focus on facts and external details, took a turn inward, both to the subjective or impressionistic response of the critic, as with Matzig, and to a phenomenological analysis of the genre, structure, and style of the text.

Matzig differs from earlier writers in the greater attention he gives to *Steppenwolf*. Like Ball, he is aware that even Hesse's friends thought that he had gone too far in this novel and in the "Crisis" poems which preceded it, that he had revealed too much of the dark side of his inner self, and that he had been too negative, pessimistic, even cynical in his evaluation of his own condition and the condition of society. Matzig's discussion sometimes sounds like an apologia for the author:

> Far be it from us to blame the poet for his despair and the shrill sounds it forces upon him. Disgusted with life, this spiritually strong man plunged into intoxication, into jazz, which has become a ventilator for the fantasy [*Wahn*] and desires of an entire generation. Suppressed until now, this half of life, too, had to be thrust into the light of his consciousness. (59)

Following the lead of the fictional editor of Harry Haller's manuscript, Matzig emphasizes its importance as a "document of the times," for Hesse's sickness of the soul, like Haller's, "is not the eccentricity of a single individual, but the sickness of the times themselves, the neurosis of that generation to which Haller belongs, a sickness, it seems, that by no means attacks the weak and worthless only but, rather, precisely those who are strongest in spirit and richest in gifts" (St 23–24).

As the story of a modern artist who suffers from personal problems which reflect the times in which he lives, *Steppenwolf* stands in a tradition of German confessional literature and of novels dealing with artist figures: Matzig mentions Goethe, Mörike, Keller, and Spitteler. Like a seismograph, the sensitive artist registers and records vibrations that otherwise go unnoticed but that may forecast catastrophe, as Hesse did in registering the Germans' unwillingness to learn from the Great War and to avoid the attitudes and behavior that caused it (60).

Haller lives in a transitional period in which the old style of life and old beliefs and values have been lost, and nothing new has yet emerged to replace them. Matzig sees parallels in the breakdown of late antiquity and in the tensions of the Reformation. Haller also shares the anguish of Nietzsche, who foresaw by decades the deadly crisis of the twentieth century and in whose voice Hesse, in his essay "Zarathustras Wiederkehr" (1919), addressed the postwar German youth, attempting to lead them away from nationalism and other collective ideals to themselves. According to Matzig, "Harry Haller, too, feels that new worlds, new constellations glow up from destruction: in this process of becoming, pregnant with death, fearful in uncertainty, the poet gropes his way now forward, now in circles, a sufferer to whom one thing is given: to relate what he is suffering" (61).

The importance for Hesse of the desire to express his suffering, which he felt his friends did not sufficiently appreciate, and of the God-given ability to do so cannot be overestimated. As he states again and again in letters to his friends, his suffering is the source of his art, and his confessional self-expression is the essence of all his works beginning with *Demian*. Though the reception of *Steppenwolf* was much more positive than Hesse anticipated, he was nevertheless deeply disappointed that no one commented on the novel's new form or recognized the careful artistry of its style and construction. Matzig's few general observations did nothing to correct this situation.

Two books on Hesse were published in 1947, a year after he received the Nobel and Goethe prizes. Gotthilf Hafner's undertaking is best defined by its subtitle, *Ein Dichterbildnis* (A Poet's Portrait). He claims to correct "stillschweigend," that is, without calling attention to them, a number of biographical and bibliographical errors that had found their way into literary histories and articles on Hesse. His treatment of the works is brief — slightly more than one page on *Steppenwolf* — and consists of little more than plot outlines.

Max Schmid's *Hermann Hesse: Weg und Wandlung* (Hermann Hesse: Journey and Transformation, 1947), on the other hand, is the first study to deal in some detail with all the major works from *Demian* through *Glasperlenspiel*. Schmid identifies Hesse's fundamental problem as the conflict between consciousness and experience. In Hesse's earlier works this problem is directly expressed in his representations of childhood and his relationship to nature; from *Demian* on, however, it becomes the subject matter of his art (20).

Schmid's view of this dichotomy is based on Ludwig Klages's *Vom kosmogonischen Eros* (On Cosmogonic Eros, 1929) and *Der Geist als Widersacher der Seele* (The Spirit as Adversary of the Soul, 1929–32). As Klages describes it, the spirit, which in the course of man's development became a part of his nature, has destroyed his original state of harmony and has come into conflict with the older part of his nature, which exists in a world of images beyond or outside of space and time and is equivalent to soul. Hesse's struggle in his mature period is between these principles: at times he wants to sink back into the world of images, which is the world of the mother, the unconscious, and of death, and at other times the reawakened spirit struggles against the soul to achieve its higher goals and its own form of timelessness and spacelessness in the frigid realm of pure spirit, which is equivalent to Fichte's "absolutes Ich" (absolute ego). This is the realm represented in *Steppenwolf* by the Immortals, and it is the goal of Haller's striving and development (42–46).

According to this scheme, Maria and Pablo are counterparts or adversaries of the Immortals rather than guides or stations along the path to them. They attempt to lead Haller into the world of images, that is, into nature and the soul, a goal identical to the one achieved by Siddhartha. This assumption poses interpretive problems for Schmid: since Pablo and Maria were sent by Hermine, their function, or at least their goal, would presumably be similar to hers, yet Schmid sees Hermine as a guide into an eternity beyond time and space, a *spiritual* realm in which her saints and Haller's artists meet. She introduces him to Pablo and Maria in order to rejuvenate his soul, which is a prerequisite for overcoming the conflict in him between spirit and soul; then, like Hermine's saints, he must transcend his nature and become sinless and spiritualized (85–87).

Similarly, Schmid struggles to resolve his uncertainty concerning the function of both the Magic Theater and Pablo's transformation into Mozart. To that end he postulates a vaguely defined "double layer of symbolism," on the basis of which he then concludes: "because of this double layer, the symbolism of *Steppenwolf* is capricious and not easily accessible" (94), which is to say that he finds the source of the inconsistency in the novel rather than in the postulates of his interpretation.

Likewise, Schmid's imposition of Klages's ideas and metaphysical approach on his analysis of Haller's love-hate relationship with the bourgeoisie and his disgust with his times results in some peculiar conclusions, for example, that modern music lacks soul and that it cannot be experienced but only comprehended by the spirit. As rigid and unconvincing as the main scheme of his interpretation may be, however, Schmid's study is nevertheless valuable and deserving of recognition as the first major attempt to move beyond the mostly superficial observations of earlier writers. It establishes a new level of discourse that subsequent studies must match to be worthy of consideration.

Works Cited

Abret, Helga. "Schlechte Zeit für Literaturkritik: Hermann Hesse als Literaturkritiker zwischen 1933 und 1938." In *Hermann Hesse und die Politik*, 7th International Hermann-Hesse Colloquium in Calw, ed. Martin Pfeifer, 107–140. Bad Liebenzell: Verlag Bernhard Gengenbach, 1992.

Ball, Hugo. *Hermann Hesse: Sein Leben und sein Werk*. Berlin: Fischer, 1927. Rpt. Berlin and Frankfurt am Main: Suhrkamp, 1963.

Carlsson, Anni. "Vom Steppenwolf zur Morgenlandfahrt." In *Hermann Hesse: Sein Leben und sein Werk*, Hugo Ball, 237–58. Revised and expanded ed. Berlin: Fischer, 1933.

Dehorn, W. "Psychoanalyse und neuere Dichtung." *Germanic Review 7* (1932): 245–62, 330–58.

Freedman, Ralph. *Pilgrim of Crisis: A Biography*. London: Cape, 1978.

Hafner, Gotthilf. *Hermann Hesse: Werk und Leben. Umrisse eines Dichterbildes.* Reinbeck bei Hamburg: Parus, 1947. 2d ed., rev. Nuremberg: Carl, 1954.

Matzig, Richard B. *Der Dichter und die Zeitstimmung: Betrachtungen über Hermann Hesses Steppenwolf.* St. Gallen: Verlag der Fehr'schen Buchhandlung, 1944. Revised version in *Hermann Hesse in Montagnola. Studien zu Werk und Innenwelt des Dichters.* Basel: Amerbach, 1947.

Michels, Volker. "Zwischen Duldung und Sabotage: Hermann Hesse und der Nationalsozialismus." In *Hermann Hesse und die Politik*, 7th International Hermann-Hesse Colloquium in Calw, ed. Martin Pfeifer, 87–105. Bad Liebenzell: Verlag Bernhard Gengenbach, 1992.

Mileck, Joseph. *Hermann Hesse: Life and Art.* Berkeley: U of California P, 1978.

Schmid, Hans Rudolf. *Hermann Hesse.* Frauenfeld and Leipzig: Verlag von Huber & Co., 1928.

Schmid, Max. *Hermann Hesse: Weg und Wandlung.* With a biographical appendix by Armin Lemp. Zurich: Fretz & Wasmuth, 1947.

Werner-Birkenbach, Sabine. "Hugo Balls 'Hesse-Biographie': Zur Wechselbeziehung von Rezeption und Edition." *Hugo Ball Almanach 1992* (1992): 157–236.

Zeller, Bernhard. *Hermann Hesse in Selbstzeugnissen und Bilddokumenten.* Reinbeck bei Hamburg: Rowohlt, 1963; Translated as *Portrait of Hesse: An Illustrated Biography.* New York: Herder and Herder, 1971.

2: Content and Form: Criticism from 1950 to 1958

The decade of the fifties is remarkable for the number and depth of critical studies of Hesse's texts written by the young doctoral candidates
who discovered and turned to Hesse after the war. Since they took the form
of mostly unpublished dissertations, these enlightening explorations of the
content and form of Hesse's works reached only a small audience of spe-
cialists. The number of dissertations produced in German-speaking countries increased from only fifteen before 1950 to thirty-two in the fifties. This
was also a decade of awakening interest in English-speaking countries,
where the number of dissertations increased from one before 1950 to
eleven in the fifties, ten in the United States and one in England. While the
number of German dissertations then decreased sharply to eleven in the sixties, eight in the seventies, and even fewer in the eighties, the number in the
USA continued to increase, with twelve in the sixties and twenty-seven in
the seventies. Then, reflecting a general decline of scholarly interest, the
number dropped to nine, including one Canadian, in the eighties.

The best of these studies explore and analyze specific facets of Hesse's
works in greater detail and depth than had the previous, predominantly
biographical surveys. Their goal is not to interpret individual works but to
investigate such topics as Hesse's use of nature and landscape, music, magical thinking, and religion, or the influence on him of German Romanticism,
Goethe, Gnosticism, and Indian and Chinese thought. A predominant
theme of these studies is Hesse's ongoing attempt to overcome polarities
and to find unity. In this chapter I will review relevant arguments and conclusions from the best and most frequently cited dissertations and from the
few articles and books published during this period.

The first and still the best treatment of Hesse's use of magic and magical
thinking is Franz Baumer's 1951 dissertation "Das magische Denken in der
Dichtung Hermann Hesses" (Magical Thinking in Hermann Hesse's
Works). Baumer identifies and discusses in the context of Hesse's *oeuvre* a
number of the author's references to magic and magical thinking and his
use of magician figures as psychopomps, that is, guides of or into the soul.
He also demonstrates how magical thinking relates to Hesse's primary
problem, his suffering from the tension of polarity, and how it constitutes
one of his attempts to find unity beyond polarity. Because of the importance of this topic, especially in connection with Hesse's peculiar concept of

humor, and because it has not received adequate attention in subsequent studies, I will discuss Baumer's dissertation in some detail.

In Baumer's view, magic is part of a central complex in Hesse's thought and world view, a complex which also includes mysticism, pantheism, music, alchemy, Gnosticism, and children or primitives. What all the elements in this complex have in common is freedom from the tension of opposites that accompanies individuation (as with children and primitives), the striving to transcend polarity, to bring the poles together in a greater and higher unity, not the unity that precedes but the one that follows individuation, the one that was identified in the previous chapter with Hesse's Third Kingdom.

Magic, like astrology and alchemy, is based upon an assumed correspondence between microcosm and macrocosm, between the inner world and the outer world, and between all vital forces. It is related to mysticism in its postulate of the inherent unity of all being. If God is in all things (pantheism), then the unity can be called God (8). Hesse's inward journey ("Weg nach innen") is a search for God, for the divine spark contained in the soul, for the original unity that exists before and beyond individuation. It is also a search for the *Urgrund*, the *Urmutter* or Faustian "Mothers," the source of all creativity. It could be identified as the unconscious. It is an eternal realm or state in which time and space are "aufgehoben," that is, dissolved or transcended. In this greater and richer context, the possible influence of Ludwig Klages noted above becomes irrelevant.

For the most part, Hesse's use of magic differs from tradition in that his "magicians" use their magic to transform the inner world rather than to influence external objects and forces, albeit with the assumption that internal changes can effect external ones. Baumer is therefore correct in referring to Hesse's magical *thinking*; Hesse calls it a "magical conception of life" (WA 6:407).[1] Magic for Hesse is the feeling that the external world is at one with his inner self (WA 6:406). This way of thinking is first manifest in *Demian*: Sinclair presupposes such a congruence of inner and outer world when he asserts that "if the outside world were to be destroyed, a single one of us would be capable of rebuilding it" (D 88). Also characteristic of magic is the sense that a higher unity exists beyond every apparent antinomy in a realm that transcends time and space; this magical unity of opposites is represented in *Demian* by the god-devil Abraxas and is also important for *Steppenwolf* (Baumer 44, 93).

---

[1]This reference is to Hesse's "Kurzgefaßter Lebenslauf," in which he imagines the continuation of his biography beyond the present and envisions himself resorting to the *practice* of magic, black and white. He uses it at the age of seventy to seduce a young girl. Then, in his prison cell, he shrinks himself in order to enter a train and to disappear into a picture he has painted on the wall.

The magical realm beyond polarity is found in the unconscious, in the soul, and can be reached only through introversion, that is, by following the "Weg nach Innen," by traversing the hell of one's inner being, not just once, but many times, as Haller discovers (St 248). And since there are no polarities in this magical realm, the way "down" through hell may lead "up" to the Immortals (Baumer 125). Those who undertake this journey are the "madmen" who are allowed entry into the Magic Theater, that is, into the soul, the unconscious. They stand in marked contrast to the "normal" or average people, whom Haller both admires and despises (51).

After Harry Haller reads the "Treatise on the Steppenwolf," which he obtains through a mysterious series of "chance" events, and which contains a penetrating analysis of his condition, he feels ambivalent, "now submitting gratefully to an invisible magician because of his wise conduct of my destiny, now with scorn and contempt for its futility, and the little understanding it showed of my actual disposition and predicament" (St 81). Harry is suffering too much from the despair of individuation that characterizes the second stage of development noted above, and he has already experienced too many encounters with himself, too many painful and futile dissolutions of his personality to be willing to accept the challenging positive message and task of the Treatise to liberate himself by "going back to the mother, back to God, back to the all" (St 55) and by confronting the "chaos of his own soul," thereby learning to know himself (St 64). This is expressed metaphorically, according to Baumer, through his fear of drowning and his unwillingness to enter the water.

Against his conscious will, however, Haller is guided to the Magic Theater by the magician who is his daimon, his Self, his fate, and who speaks and acts through Hermine, Maria, and Pablo, who are "split-off, personified powers of the poet's own soul" (Baumer 84). Through Maria and "the magic touch of Eros" Haller had already begun to experience many images from his past and to realize "how rich was the gallery of my life, and how thronged the soul of the wretched Steppenwolf with high eternal stars and constellations" (St 160). He concludes from this insight "that I had only to snatch up my scattered images and raise my life as Harry Haller and as the Steppenwolf to the unity of one picture, in order to enter myself into the world of imagination and be immortal" (St 162). As the embodiment of the magician whose guidance Haller was ready to accept after reading the Treatise, Pablo gives him access to the inner picture gallery of his soul: "I can give you nothing that has not already its being within yourself. I can throw open to you no picture gallery but your own soul. All I can give you is the opportunity, the impulse, the key. I can help you to make your own world visible. That is all" (St 200).

From Baumer's perspective, entry into the world of images means "penetrating to the foundation of being, to the magical whole of life, to the magic center" (125). In this magical realm beyond space, time, and polarity, including the polarity of inner and outer worlds, Haller can relive — not repeat — the past and experience any of the countless possibilities inherent in him. And above all, he can meet the Immortals and learn to see and relate to the world as they do: through humor. To accomplish this would be an "awakening," which is the state achieved on entry into Hesse's third stage or kingdom of human development, when the ego has become the Self (121).

After reviewing Hesse's use of magic in a number of works, Baumer concludes that, beginning with *Demian*, Hesse's use of "humor" includes laughter, irony, and scorn, and is an "expression of intellectual superiority and a magical view of life" (122). In his *Nürnberger Reise* (Trip to Nuremberg, 1927) Hesse writes that magic corresponds to a psychic state in which the eternal self in us observes the mortal ego with sympathy, scorn, and neutrality. Since this definition of magic is very close to his definition of humor, the two can be seen as analogous. The whole meaning of the Magic Theater, then, according to Baumer, is to show "the experience of becoming one's self [Selbstwerdung]" of following the path to the magic center, which is equivalent to recognizing the spiritual unity of all being (132).

Haller gains considerable insight in the Magic Theater, but he is not able to break through to humor. In the end he confuses the illusory picture world with reality, and continues to take the latter seriously, as demonstrated by his killing of Hermine in the arms of Pablo. And while he recognizes his own participation in the faults and guilt of others, he does not achieve the unitary consciousness suggested to him by the quotation he finds in the pocket of the first victim of his hunt of automobiles: "tat twam asi." "That is you," or, as Hesse translates the phrase from the Upanishads in *Kurgast* (Guest at a Spa, 1925): "Love your neighbor, for he is you yourself." Haller is determined, however, to begin the game afresh and to repeat it often, and this, we know from the Treatise, is the prerequisite of achieving true manhood.

In his discovery of Hesse following the war, Siegfried Unseld may be representative of the generation whose dissertations are being discussed in this chapter. He reports that an elderly teacher gave him Hesse's works when he returned from the war in 1946. While reading them he experienced what Hesse calls an "awakening," which motivated him to study literature and to write his dissertation on Hesse (26). Hesse had an even more dramatic influence on his life when, at their first meeting in 1951, he suggested that Unseld contact Peter Suhrkamp, who was looking for a young successor. Unseld began working for Suhrkamp in January 1952 and took over the directorship of the Suhrkamp Verlag following Suhrkamp's death in 1959, thus becoming Hesse's publisher. Besides editing some of Hesse's works, Unseld has written several books on Hesse including a useful brief account of the origins and reception of Hesse's works (*Hermann Hesse: Werk und Wirkungsgeschichte* [Hermann Hesse: The Works and their Reception, 1973; expanded edition 1985]).

Like Baumer, Unseld recognizes the importance of magic for Hesse, but, in keeping with the focus of his dissertation "Hermann Hesses Anschauung vom Beruf des Dichters" (Hermann Hesse's Concept of the Poet's Profession, 1951), his concern is limited to the role of the poet as *homo magus*, who "creates images from his unconscious, archetypal images of the divine, which his word conjures up." An authentic poet must be able to recreate the totality of the world, and that is possible only when his poetry is based on a belief in a higher order, as Hesse's is (126–27). Indeed, Hesse sees poetry as a manifestation of the divine: he was inspired to become a poet by Hölderlin's "magic of the seer" which is the "secret of poetry." Or, as Heidegger put it: "Dichter sein in dürftiger Zeit heißt: singend auf die Spur der entflohenen Götter achten" [To be a poet in deficient times means: observing in song the track of the departed gods: 8].

As he states in his essay "Kindheit des Zauberers" (Childhood of the Magician, 1923), Hesse wanted from the beginning of his career to "enchant, transform, and intensify" reality. In this essay he describes a three-stage process that anticipates his subsequent development. In the first stage the author attempts to take images from the external world into himself and transform them. In the second stage the self is itself transformed by the images from the external world that are introverted. This characterizes Hesse's "inward journey" that begins with *Demian*. Finally, the knowing poet becomes invisible by taking a position "behind his figures," as Hesse does in *Morgenlandfahrt* and, by the interposition of another narrator, in *Glasperlenspiel* (10).

The goal and original contribution of Unseld's study is his attempt through a phenomenological approach to understand Hesse's literary works as literature, to put, as Hesse does, the quality of craftsmanship above all ideas and feeling content as the element in art that cannot be faked. This is the first study to use consistently a "werkimmanente" or "new critical" methodology, which Heidegger calls "das-Sich-an-ihm-selbst-Zeigende" [showing the thing by means of itself: 7]. Unseld analyzes some poems in considerable detail, but the inclusive scope of his study does not permit such close reading of the larger works. His relatively short, eleven page discussion of *Steppenwolf* focuses on the tripartite structure that constitutes Hesse's primary organizing principle, from the macro level of the novel as a whole to the micro level of individual sentences and the rhythm of Hesse's language.

Unseld notes that each of the three major parts of *Steppenwolf* is characterized by a different narrative point of view and a different style. Though written in the first person, the editor's preface presents an objective or epic description. The second and largest part consists of Haller's first person subjective report of his experiences. This is interrupted by the Treatise, which constitutes a recapitulation with supporting evidence. It contains the whole plot in concentrated form and provides a map or plan for the subsequent development (117).

The Treatise is likewise divided into three sections, two of which are subdivided further into three sections each. The first part shows Haller's fragmentation: he is (1) a night person ("ein Abendmensch"), (2) a lonely person ("ein Einsamer"), and (3) an independent person ("ein Unabhängiger"). The second major part presents the Steppenwolves' possibilities for existence and their position in space and time. They can (1) live in confinement with the bourgeois, (2) die tragically, or (3) gain entry into the Third Kingdom, an imaginary, sovereign world of humor, a realm in which the poles are united and even the bourgeois can be included. The third major section shows how the Steppenwolf can save himself: he must look into the chaos of his own soul and come to full consciousness of his Self. He will then discover that his split into two parts was a fiction, that he consists of a multitude of parts and is a bridge between nature and spirit (116–21). Like Carlsson, Unseld bases his analysis of the structuring principle of Haller's developmental process on Hesse's "Ein Stückchen Theologie."

Two complementary dissertations by students of Günther Müller may be mentioned for their historical interest as demonstrations of the morphological method of analysis developed by Müller in the early forties and systematically presented in his *Die Gestaltfrage in der Literaturwissenschaft und Goethes Morphologie* (The Question of Form in Literary Studies and Goethe's Morphology, 1944). At a time when foreign influences were unwelcome in Germany and when art "criticism" was required to be appreciative rather than evaluative and judgmental, this method had the advantage of being based on Goethe and his study of the morphology of plants: just as Goethe sees a plant's organic unity and growth as a product of opposing tendencies to grow both vertically and in a spiral, and as he recognizes the importance for human and animal life of the polarity of systole and diastole as observed in the contraction and dilation of the heart and in breathing in and out, so Müller and his students see the literary work of art as an organic unity whose form and content are based on the law of polarity. In her 1951 dissertation "Das Polaritätsgesetz in der Dichtung: Am Beispiel von Hermann Hesses 'Steppenwolf'" (The Law of Polarity in Literature: Exemplified in Hermann Hesse's *Steppenwolf*), Maria Liepelt-Unterberg finds an appropriate text on which to demonstrate the validity of her critical presuppositions.

The novel's preface, for example, reveals a polar contrast between the editor and Harry Haller, which exemplifies the tension and contrast between Harry and the bourgeois world in general. Here and elsewhere in the novel the presentation of such contrasts is reflected in the style by polarized adverbs of time ("*At first* his gait didn't please me at all . . . *only later* did I notice and learn that he was sick."), contrasting pairs of adjectives, epithets, and nouns (One hears "laughter sounding, unusually bright and gay laughter, yet nevertheless a terrible and strange laughter, a laughing like crystal and ice, bright and radiant, but cold and implacable"), syntactic peculiarities in the use of multiple conjunctions which connect opposing modes of action or states ("I remember one such demand, which *however* was *not even* a demand, *but* consisted *rather* in a glance . . . ") (12, 65, 64; author's emphasis). Liepelt-Unterberg concludes from her study, which includes more abstract speculation and historical review of the philosophical concept of polarity than empirical analysis of the text: "The organization of the material, the arrangement of the parts, the content of metaphysical thoughts and images and the criteria of the style reveal, each in its own element, the polar vital consciousness *(Lebensgefühl)* of *Steppenwolf* to a degree that this vital consciousness — in the form developed in the Treatise — is to be seen as the constructing principle of the novel" (66).

Liepelt-Unterberg indicates the need for a further study that would apply her findings to other works by Hesse, and that need was soon met by the dissertation of a fellow student, Marianne Wagner: "Zeitmorphologischer Vergleich von Hermann Hesses 'Demian', 'Siddhartha', 'Der Steppenwolf', and 'Narziss und Goldmund' zur Aufweisung typischer Gestaltzüge" (Time-morphological Comparison of Hermann Hesse's *Demian, Siddhartha, Der Steppenwolf,* und *Narziss und Goldmund* to Reveal Typical Structural Elements, 1953). Using elaborate graphs, Wagner charts the relation of narrational time (*Erzählzeit*) to narrated time (*erzählter Zeit*) in order to establish a typical pattern within the various segments of each novel and, if possible, between the novels. For *Steppenwolf* she identifies a regular alternation between segments of expansive and concentrated narration, which corresponds to and reflects a balance between, respectively, reflexivity and event. Event is represented primarily through conversation and summary and through some retrospective sequences of a scenic-imagistic nature; reflections, on the other hand, mainly emphasize events in Harry's soul. Wagner finds some areas of contact between the novels, such as in the centrality of polar contrast, but concludes that they do not reveal a common morphological type or genre.

While these dissertations contribute little to our understanding and interpretation of *Steppenwolf*, they are of some interest as a parallel to and anticipation of a phenomenological or "new critical" analysis of the unity of content and form as a criterion for evaluating the success and stature of literary works of art.

In one of the first major articles on Hesse to appear in English ("Hermann Hesse: The Exorcism of the Demon," 1950), a study that marks the beginning of serious scholarship on Hesse in America, Oscar Seidlin considers Haller's goal to be dissolution of the ego. Unlike Sinclair, he does not want to find and know himself, but rather to escape the self, to dissolve it into nothingness (339). According to Seidlin, Hesse's approach is existential rather than psychoanalytic. Whereas Freud points to curable diseases and attempts to repair the disturbances of man's functional existence in the world, Hesse identifies a malaise inherent in the human condition: the disturbance of his authenticity, or what the existentialist philosopher Heidegger terms "Eigentlichkeit." Hesse's three stages of development can be identified with Heidegger's sequence of *Eigentlichkeit, Geworfenheit,* and *Zuhandenheit* as follows:

> The true (and incurable) plight of man began with his individuation, with his separation from the All-ness, with the beginning of time. Time is the horrible proof that paradise is lost, that man is no longer living in his "Eigentlichkeit," but in the all-powerful and tormenting sequence of moments (this is what Heidegger calls "die Geworfenheit"), the permanent transience of all things and of his own existence. It is man's curse that he can no longer live in the simultaneousness of his experience, that he is suspended between eternity which knows only past and future, and time which knows only the transitory moment. Now it becomes evident that the great exorcism . . . means more than the schism in the individual soul: it is the paradoxical attempt to mobilize all the powers, actions and reactions of the soul into an ever-present simultaneity (Heidegger calls it a "Zuhandenheit") which will be capable of outwitting the deadening course of time. (340)

Hesse bravely attempts in all his major works to find a solution to the insoluble problem of attaining eternal simultaneity, which is equivalent to his Third Kingdom. In Seidlin's view, the solution seems to be reached in music. Especially in *Glasperlenspiel* but also in *Steppenwolf* "music appears as deliverance from the curse of the one-after-the-other." Haller considers music to be "something like time frozen to space" above which a "superhuman serenity, an eternal divine laughter" is suspended. To live in humor and to live in music is "to live in the world as if it were not the world," and that, according to Seidlin, is what Thomas Mann defines as the attitude of irony (341).

Yet another goal of the inward journey is identified by Kurt Weibel in his 1952 dissertation "Hermann Hesse und die deutsche Romantik" (Hermann Hesse and German Romanticism; published 1954): it is spirit (*Geist*), which Weibel also calls the "magical spirit." But spirit, as Weibel defines it, is not the polar opposite of nature or matter but the essence of what "understands, loves, forgives and therefore unifies and propitiates and stands above all oppositions" (8). In the course of his discussion, which sometimes lacks consistency, Weibel equates this spirit at one time with God and at another with the mother or "motherly" principle, which was the goal of the Romantics' inward journey. And since spirit derives from soul or, as stated by Novalis, is "crystallized soul," the soul becomes the unifying element, the place where the inner and outer worlds come together and where time and polarities are transcended.

According to Weibel, *Steppenwolf* contains a compressed summary of Hesse's development as a poet and also reveals the attitude that is evident in all his subsequent work. This attitude is determined by "the new experience of eternity in the perception of an orderly, bright, unchangeably constant opposite" (77). Haller resembles his predecessors such as Camenzind, Sinclair, Klein, Klingsor, and Siddhartha in his recognition of the "eternity of the expanded soul, eternity in the remembrance of the unity of nature, which is the whole in the attachment to the inexhaustible source of a transitory, chaotically changing world." He differs from them, however, in that he also sees "the firm, serenely unchangeable contours of the spiritual being that is hidden behind all appearances" (77–78).

A major part of Weibel's discussion follows up on Hugo Ball's reference to Hesse's great admiration for Romantic poets and the parallels that exist between their works and his. Such similarities and parallels are of particular interest insofar as they elucidate the text. This may be the case with Jean Paul's "Vorschule zur Aesthetik" (Introduction to Aesthetics, 1804), which describes theoretically the path to humor that Haller follows and the "ladder of fantasy" he climbs to reach the realm of the absolute. The ascent begins, according to Jean Paul, with a conception or receiving (*Empfangen*), which is accompanied by acts of creation. The second rung is characterized by talent, in which a number of traits stand out, for example, wit, reason, cleverness, and mathematical historical imagination. These talents exercise a tyrannical influence and must be overcome, just as Haller must suppress his reason in order to achieve a musical unity of forces on the level of genius, the highest level of fantasy. The genius is guided by instinct which represents the heavenly, divine, eternal element that survives in man as his partial possession (83–84).

In Jean Paul's scheme, according to Weibel, it is humor that sustains the fantastic genius's hovering in the heavenly heights. Humor relies on the contrast between idea and appearance, the same contrast Mozart points out to Haller in connection with the distorted radio broadcast of Handel's divine music. "Romantic humor," as defined by Weibel, "means the recollection of the infinite in the objectivizing perception of the risible contradiction of the world . . . . Humor makes a whole out of the finite world, in order to rescind it as such" (85–86).

Another illuminating comparison pertains to the Greek god Hermes, who came to Hesse's attention in Hölderlin's use of centaurs in his poem "Chiron," and who relates to a problem Hölderlin shares with Haller, namely, the need to accept and affirm his inferior, animalistic aspect. According to Weibel, Hesse's understanding of Hermes anticipates some of the conclusions later published by Karl Kerényi. As a psychopomp or guide of souls, Hermes has a function similar to that of Demian and other figures in Hesse's works who represent the inner fate or daimon of the heroes they teach and guide. That role is assumed in *Steppenwolf* by Hermine, Pablo, and Maria, who together with Haller constitute a quaternity, an archetypal symbol of totality that corresponds to the four-sided herm (a statue of Hermes) and to the representations of Hermes with three nymphs, which symbolize fertility (91–94).

Hermes is the god of meetings and fortuitous discoveries, such as those that guide Haller to Hermine and the Magic Theater,[2] and he is the controller of dreams. He guides souls into the underworld, as Hermine does in attracting Haller to "hell," and as Pablo does when he introduces him to the Magic Theater. As the god of thieves and deception, Hermes is associated with the night and darkness, the times Haller prefers. Sometimes represented in an ithyphallic form, Hermes is identified with active, procreative masculinity, and, like Pablo, he is associated with shamelessness and forbidden love: Pablo offers to sell Maria to Haller for a night and proposes to celebrate with him a "love orgy for three" (St 165). Like Demeter and Persephone, the mother-daughter unity, he is both the begetter and the begotten.

A further manifestation of Hermes's unifying role is his close relationship to Dionysus and the Sileni, in whom, according to Kerényi, "the hermetic-spiritual aspect exists in friendly harmony with the other, the animalistic-divine" (Weibel 92), a synthesis also embodied by Hölderlin's

---

[2]The fact that the god's name is contained in his own and hence in the figures who represent the male and female sides of himself, Hermann and Hermine, is such a fortunate find or coincidence for Hesse. It is probably no coincidence that Haller is reading *Sophia's Trip from Memel to Saxony* by J. T. *Hermes*: this, together with Haller's interest in mythology, might well be a hint to readers. Compare also the Steppen*wolf*'s great admiration for *Wolf*gang Amadeus Mozart and Johann *Wolf*gang Goethe.

centaurs. Unity is also represented by the hermetic androgyny or *herm*aphroditic constitution of the soul, which finds expression in *Steppenwolf* in the doublet of Hermann and Hermine, and which is represented, one might add, by Hermine's appearance at the masked ball in male attire. Weibel interprets the murder of Hermine as the incorporation of the feminine or motherly principle into the manly. The Steppenwolf has therefore relived the Greek mystery rite of Hermes (93–94).

In his *Hermann Hesse: Biographie* Edmund Gnefkow provides a biographically oriented analysis that may be seen as an update and expansion of Hugo Ball's study. Gnefkow identifies four phases in Hesse's life to 1952, of which the first two are of interest here. In the works to 1916 Gnefkow sees the influence of Romanticism's postulated unity of the individual, nature, and God. In the critical period preceding his psychoanalysis, Hesse realized that this unity cannot be taken for granted and that the Romantic assumption of such a unity conceals the polarity of existence (1952, 36, 55).

In the second phase of his development, from 1916 to 1926, Hesse was able through psychoanalysis to achieve a provisional unity of the self. He learned that the polar tensions he experienced derive from the conflict between the conscious and unconscious. This insight provided the foundation for the development of his thinking about unity and polarity. What he had previously only intuited now became the material for conscious representation. Moreover, Hesse's search for new answers to the central questions of his existence led him through the cultural history of Europe and Asia. According to Gnefkow, the real impact of Eastern thought on Hesse occurred only after his psychoanalysis. It was also more instrumental than the psychoanalysis in enabling him to find a lasting unity of the self and to obtain momentary glimpses into a more comprehensive unity of self and world and even of self, world, and God, albeit still from a Romantic perspective centering on the ego (50, 58, 79).

The psychoanalytic path to unity was problematic for Hesse, Gnefkow continues, because it did not include a striving for unity with the world and with God. On this path the curse of individuation is intensified rather than reduced. If followed consistently to the end, this path would lead to suicide, as it does for some of Hesse's heroes and as it nearly does for Haller. Consequently, Hesse abandoned the psychoanalytic path in favor of the Asiatic-meditative path, which raised the problem of polarity to a higher level by including union with the world and with God.[3] "But this, too, proved to be

---

[3] In claiming that Hesse abandoned psychoanalysis in favor of Asiatic wisdom, Gnefkow is apparently thinking only of the Freudian form of analysis. Jung finds confirmation of his theories in Chinese and Hindu thought. He was a friend of the Sinologist Richard Wilhelm and provided a commentary and forward for his translations of *The Secret of the Golden Flower* and *I Ching*, both of which books Hesse read.

a path to self-redemption," Gnefkow concludes, "in that the Maya-world is denied as an illusion and God is taken into the ego. This path, too, if exclusively followed, would lead to the destruction of the personality; for Hesse as a Western man the drive to be active in the world is a necessary complement to the via contemplativa" (84–85).

Through Lao-Tzu's wisdom of inner vision or Tao and through the Christian-mystical concept of Grace, Hesse nevertheless gained the certainty that belief in the unity in himself could enable him to live through the polarities of the world. He considered Tao and Grace, along with the Hindu Atman, to be equivalent expressions for a unity above polarity. (Hesse was aware of, and sometimes practiced, Yoga, but he found it overly intellectual in comparison to Lao-Tzu's Taoism [85]). For Lao-Tzu there are two paths to unity: one leads through being to meaning, the other leads through non-being. Whoever would follow the first path has to recognize the opposites in the world of appearances and behave with inner freedom toward them. This will enable one to act without desire in inconspicuous accord with Tao. Through the path of non-being, on the other hand, as Wilhelm writes, "one arrives at an inner vision of secret forces, at union with the mother. It is the path of loneliness and of silence; it leads out of multiplicity to unity" (quoted by Gnefkow 89). The path to the mothers is also the path to the children, to nature, to the sources of all being, to the archetypes, and this is the path Hesse had intuitively followed. In his vacillations, he also followed the path through the world, and both paths, the one inward and the one through and above the world, are right, as he learned from Lao-Tzu, because both lead to unity (89).

Dschuang Dsi, a great interpreter of Lao-Tzu, recognizes that, because of the relationship between the oppositions in the world, the I is also the Not-I and the Not-I is also the I. He calls the state in which they no longer form an opposition "the pivot of meaning, which he considers to be the middle point around which the oppositions can revolve, so that each finds its justification in infinity" (90). Gnefkow identifies Hesse's rather idiosyncratic use of humor with Dschuang Dsi's "pivot of meaning": the laughter produced through the grace of humor could unite the polar opposites in Haller just as it does the guest and the observer in Hesse's *Kurgast*. And time is overcome in such a state, as it is in the realm of Hesse's Immortals or later in *Morgenlandfahrt*.

To make his case for the previously overlooked importance for Hesse of Chinese thought and literature, Gnefkow discusses several other Chinese poets and thinkers. He identifies parallels and possible influences, but he does not attempt to analyze and interpret Hesse's texts according to these

Gnefkow also fails to recognize the role in Jung's psychology of striving for unity of the Self with God and the world.

insights. He claims, for example, that Hesse was stimulated by the use of magic in Taoism to investigate medieval alchemy, but he makes no attempt to identify magical or alchemical elements in Hesse's works.

In the first British dissertation on Hesse, "Hermann Hesse as Humanist" (1954), John Christopher Middleton identifies eight sections in the complex design of *Steppenwolf.* He divides Haller's own account, which Unseld sees as a single unit, into six parts. Analogous to the questing heroes in a number of expressionist "Stationendramen" (station plays, as in the stations of the cross), the suffering Haller progresses through a series of stations which lead him to, and prepare him for, the self-discovery provided by the Magic Theater, a theater of chance, death, and the soul that enables him to see reality *sub specie mortis* (235–36).

Middleton claims that each station or section marks a stage in Haller's progress toward "Selbstschau" (seeing and knowing his self), but he does not demonstrate this development in his analysis. In some cases he focuses on a motif or motif-complex, but since the motifs tend to recur throughout the novel, and since every section has a number of different ones, they do not for the most part constitute discreet structural units. This shortcoming detracts little, however, from what is a valuable study, whose primary contribution lies in the attention given to the novel's interwoven images and motifs, some of which had not previously been identified by the novel's interpreters.

For example, Middleton considers the second section, which includes the part of Haller's narrative that comes between the preface and the Treatise, to be dominated by water imagery. As Unseld observed, Haller hesitates to cross the wet, muddy street on a rainy night to read the letters that have appeared magically on a stone wall. According to both authors, this represents his resistance to the call that will lead him to the Magic Theater: he does not want to get wet or dirty. Yet he does overcome his inner resistance and crosses over to read the invitation, and, when he returns that evening to the same place, he receives the Treatise. Middleton sees Haller's hesitation to cross the wet street as analogous to his later resistance to Hermine's attempt to teach him how to dance, even after she has told him: "You're dying just for the lack of a push to throw you *into the water* and bring you to life again. You need me to teach you to dance and to laugh and to live" (St 126, emphasis added). Throughout his works, from the drowning of a number of his early heroes to Knecht's drowning at the end of *Glasperlenspiel,* Hesse consistently uses water both as a symbol for the death of the self, which is decreed for Haller in the Treatise, and for rebirth to a new life. As another in a series of Hesse's self-representations, Haller has already endured a number of repetitions of the death-rebirth cycle, and, as we have seen, he is determined at the end to begin afresh (Middleton 240–42).

Middleton finds the rhythm of the second section more or less repeated in the fourth, which immediately follows Haller's reading of the Treatise. At a funeral, a place of death and of contrast between body and spirit analogous to that represented by the hospital and the church which were connected by the stone wall of section two, Haller once again meets a representative of the "invisible magician" who is conducting his destiny, at this point by directing him to the Black Eagle, where he meets Hermine (248). The meeting itself is framed by scenes involving Goethe, around whom a number of interlocking motifs cluster. It is preceded by Harry's disastrous evening with the professor and his wife, whom he insulted by his tactless disapproval of their treasured engraving of Goethe. Just before going to the professor's house, he had been reading *Sophia's Journey from Memel to Saxony*. As noted by Weibel and as Middleton also observes, this novel is connected through the name of its author, Johann Timotheus Hermes, to Hermes, Hermine, and Hermann. But it also connects to Goethe, whose Werther and Lotte admired it. And like Haller, Sophia lived in an age of transition and was out of step with her times and its conventions (Middleton 248–49).

Following his meeting with Hermine, Haller has a dream about Goethe in which a scorpion tries to crawl up his leg. Haller thinks the scorpion might betoken something friendly, that it might be a messenger from a woman, "dangerously and beautifully emblematic of woman and sin" (St 107). And after he berates Goethe for his shortcomings, Goethe shows him a small leather or velvet box in which lay a diminutive effigy of a woman's leg on the dark velvet. When Haller reaches for it, the leg moves, and he thinks it might be the scorpion. Seeing Haller's struggle between desire and dread, Goethe, whom Haller has taken too seriously, teases him "with the charming and dangerous thing" (St 112). To further emphasize the association of the scorpion and its sting to woman and sex, Haller thinks the scorpion's name might be Vulpius, the name of Goethe's controversial long-time mistress and later wife (Middleton 250–52). Molly, who is also mentioned in the dream, resembles Christiane Vulpius in the unconventionality of her non-marital relationship with the poet Gottfried August Bürger, who was married to her sister.

Each of the motifs in this complex recurs in the novel and relates to other motifs. For example, the appearance of Goethe and the reference in the Treatise to Faust and his fragmented personality prepare the reader to see Haller, with his need to expand his soul or take his own life, as a Faust figure, and the actors in the Magic Theater, who are "children of the devil" playing out their roles in the revelry of a Walpurgis Night and in hell, as associates of Mephistopheles. The bare leg on a bed of velvet in the dream relates to Maria, who appears to Haller in a velvet dress and is called by him his "velvet girl." She helps Haller overcome his dread and give in to his desire. In contrast to the dark rainy night of the beginning, she represents a summery source of light, warmth, and Eros; she appears to Haller not as a potentially deadly scorpion but as a flower and as the bird of paradise which the Treatise foretold he would find in his own psychic potential (242, 251–53, 258).

The power of Eros reaches its climax in the Magic Theater: Haller loses his identity in the crowd, as is indicated by the loss of his identifying number, and he experiences a further opening and expansion of his soul when he is led into the realm of the Faustian Mothers, where all the components or possibilities contained in his unconscious become accessible to him. Those components are like chess pieces that can be rearranged and redeployed in an unending sequence of different games. He goes against the pacifism and *bel-esprit* of his conscious persona, for example, in his war on machines and the people who use them, and he is able to recreate past relationships so that all girls he failed to win in the past now become his (263–65).

Middleton provides evidence for the relationship between the Magic Theater and alchemy which Gnefkow mentioned without elaboration. Pablo appears dressed in the primary alchemical colors of red (*rubedo*), white (*albedo*), and black (*nigredo*). Even more than magic, alchemy has transformation as its goal, the transformation of substances, which, as indicated by a number of alchemists and as interpreted by C. G. Jung, represents a projection or symbolic representation of the transformation of the alchemist himself. When he opens the last door of the Magic Theater, Haller fails to recognize the embracing Pablo and Hermine as the alchemical *rebis*, the symbolic *conjunctio oppositorum*, the creative union of the male and female principles in himself to form the unitary hermaphrodite in his own soul. As Haller learns from Mozart, his failure to distinguish between a psychic event and a material one has prevented him from gaining the distanced, cosmic perspective of the Immortals. He has not achieved "Selbstschau," has not succeeded in knowing himself (264–71).

At the same time Middleton discovers some previously overlooked examples of Hesse's artistic use of interconnecting motifs and symbols, he also identifies what he considers to be weaknesses in the narrative. On occasion the novel seems facile and superficial, he writes, because of the privacy of Hesse's symbolism, which sometimes cannot be understood without knowledge of previous works. And the book is limited in depth and scope by Hesse's continuing use of the "decorative word" rather than the "symbolic word" (272–73).

Furthermore, the story's hero appears more as a zealot than as the penetrating and sophisticated mind, which, according to the introduction, he is supposed to be. His observations on music, for example, are based more on emotional reactions than on true understanding. And with the novel's monologic form "there is the danger that no adversary may question the hero, and that the hero's inner enemies are never rational beings" (272–73). Middleton also objects to the work's Romantic assumption that the soul is a dynamic unitary design, that everything which happens to the individual is part of that design, and that the evolution of character depends on the realization of that design in action and experience (277–79).

In his 1958 dissertation on symbolism as an expression of Hesse's inner world, Peter Baer Gontrum continues the investigation begun by Middleton; he identifies four groups of symbols that are of central and recurring importance in Hesse's thought and art and that parallel his view of human development through three kingdoms or stages, to which Gontrum adds a fourth.

Characteristic of the first stage is the symbol of the garden, which is connected with childhood and paradise, a time of unity, innocence, happiness, and harmony, when the child is in a magical relation to the secrets of nature. It is the world of the mother. In this realm flowers symbolize harmony and eroticism. The motif of stealing fruit or flowers, which recurs in Hesse's works, is analogous to eating from the tree of knowledge; it is the sin that marks the loss of innocence and banishment from the garden and that initiates the journey which ultimately leads inward to the Self (5–24). It is accompanied by a sense of loss and the need to search for a new *Heimat* and by the agony and despair caused by the internal conflict between polarities. As Hermine tells Harry, who, like her, is in this stage, homesickness (*Heimweh*) is their only guide as they attempt to "stumble through so much dirt and humbug before we reach home" (St 175).

Gontrum identifies three groups of images which are associated with the journey: first, clouds, sail boats, birds, and wind invite the wanderer to set out and encourage him on the way; second, streets, trains, and boats serve as symbolic vessels; and third, the forest provides encouragement and represents the goal itself (27). Despite their presumed centrality in Hesse's writing, not many of these symbols occur in *Steppenwolf.* Gontrum mentions the wind in connection with Haller's loneliness and need to keep on the move. Haller meets Hermine in the Black Eagle hotel; the eagle symbolizes sovereignty and domination, and Harry immediately and willingly submits to her commands. Hermine and Harry eat duck and chicken together, which, as Middleton observed, may be seen as analogous to Sinclair's eating of the heraldic sparrow hawk. Although Gontrum intends to avoid psychology in his study as much as possible, he refers in this context to Middleton's

Jungian interpretation of this symbolic act as a fertilization of the unconscious: it clearly is so for Sinclair, whose imagination immediately becomes
activated following his dreamed consumption of the sparrow hawk. According to the Jungian interpretation, the consumption or assimilation of
the raptor, which eats animals, symbolizes the sublimation of animal instincts in the soul and the transfer of unconscious drives to the life of the
spirit (33). Harry, on the other hand, does not consume and thus assimilate
a powerful bird of prey, as Sinclair does, but rather domestic birds which
feed on seeds and plants.

Gontrum's third group of symbols is associated with Hesse's Third
Kingdom of internal and external harmony and unity. Images from the
childhood level such as plants, flowers, and the garden recur on this level as
reminiscence or evocation of that early period. Such is the case with the
araucaria and azalea plants in the "little garden of order" in the first floor
vestibule of the house in which Haller has a room. He realizes that this sa-
cred place, which he uses as a temple, is connected to his yearning for
something homelike, for the bourgeois security and harmony of his childhood (St 32–33). Connection is made to his childhood through odors,
tastes, and sounds as well as through images. When all the girls become his
in the Magic Theater, for example, Rosa Kreisler is evoked or conjured up
by the taste and smell of a spring bud, and each of the girls he re-
experiences, this time with confidence and success, are associated with flowers or, in the case of his first erotic experience, a tree. The imagined enjoyment of these "blooms," each having her secret and the bouquet of her soil,
makes him ripe for Hermine, who rises as "the last figure in my populous
mythology" (St 231). After having been carried like a child by the unifying
"stream of sex," he is deposited on shore and proceeds to his last meeting
with Hermine. Other motifs cited by Gontrum which may express unity
and harmony are trees, the wind, water, fire, and birds. Also mentioned but
little developed is the motif of the mirror, which may be used, as it is in the
Magic Theater, to transcend time and reflect the past and future self (69–
82).

Hesse uses a fourth group of symbols to express the unity and eternal
becoming one may occasionally sense in special moments of illumination.

> The symbols which give the believing person the feeling of taking part in
> the eternal are infrequent with Hesse, but they are the crowning of his
> creation of symbols. The first symbols of this kind are fire, water, and the
> cave. They constitute a threshold to another world beyond nature, in
> which the dying person gives his bodily existence to the destructive but
> also comforting secret of nature. (116)

Other symbols are not clearly manifest in images but must be intellectually
construed: in this category are "forms of water and all other forms of nature

in their totality, their unity and eternal transmutability, and . . . the eternally revolving stars" (116).

As a thinker, Haller sees himself under the sign of Aquarius. Thinking and water are connected in the comparison of taking a bath while reading old books. Haller once remarked to the editor of his papers that the difference between the thinker and those who are created for the active life is that the thinker must swim in his unconscious, for it is there that the origins lie (124–25). Concerning Novalis's statement that "most men will not swim before they are able to," he says:

> Is not that witty? Naturally, they won't swim! They are born for the solid earth, not for the water. And naturally they won't think. They are made for life, not for thought. Yes, and he who thinks, what's more, he who makes thought his business, he may go far in it, but he has bartered the solid earth for the water all the same, and one day he will drown. (St 17–18)

Hermine tells Haller that he needs her because he is desperate and dying "just for lack of a push to throw you into the water and bring you to life again" (St 126). This is like a response to his early unwillingness to cross a wet and seemingly bottomless street to read the neon sign announcing the Magic Theater. Wet earth is connected with death and burial in the cemetery scene. Just before the masked ball Harry watches a film in which the red sea parts and the Egyptians are drowned. These and other events involving water, death, and rebirth culminate in the Magic Theater, where he experiences a vision of death, gains distance from his earlier life, and recognizes the proximity of his desiccated intellect to death. The insight he gains enables him to overcome his hubris and prepares him for dissolution in a greater unity (Gontrum 124–25).

Stars, according to Gontrum, are the most significant and direct images we have of cosmic life and eternal unity. In *Steppenwolf* the stars are identified with the Immortals. Goethe wears a medal in the form of a star (*Ordensstern*), and Mozart is transformed into a comet. Given its cold and rarefied atmosphere and its association with cheerful serenity and humor, the cosmic realm would seem to represent the side of intellect and spirit in the polarity of nature and *Geist*, yet Goethe and Mozart combine both principles in themselves (Goethe's star appears to be composed of flowers) and instruct Harry that he should do likewise (137–38).

Hesse's eightieth birthday was celebrated in 1957, as his seventy-fifth had been in 1952, by a number of articles on various facets of his life and works, not a few of which praised the simplicity, musicality, and striking ef-

fectiveness of his language.[4] Attracting more attention than all of these trib-
utes, however, was Karlheinz Deschner's very different evaluation in *Kitsch,
Konvention und Kunst* (Kitsch, Convention and Art), which was widely reviewed and became something of a bestseller for "a literary polemic," as it
was subtitled. Deschner claims that Hesse at his best is only second rate and
that his pseudo-art is conventional, epigonic, and mediocre.

Deschner differs from most of the authors discussed in this chapter in his
assumption that the artistic merit of a literary work is determined not by its
subject matter or content, but by the way it is written, by its artistry, craftsmanship, style, and technique. "Decisive is not the meaning of the subject
but the way it is presented, not the theme but the representation." "What
affects us decisively," Deschner admits, "is the content, *is* the substance. But
this substance, and this is extremely important, is only able to work through
the form, and its effect is all the more intense the more perfect the form is in
which it appears" (12–13; author's emphasis). Popular success means
nothing, for, as Schopenhauer recognized, the masses are not able to appreciate the formal elements of art; they accept and affirm what supports their
own Weltanschauung (13–14).

Deschner is especially critical of epigonic art, that is, art that consciously
or unconsciously imitates great art of an earlier time, and of kitsch, which he
defines as "derailed, degenerate, and pseudo-art" (23). One is aware of the
artist's ambition but also of his complete failure and incompetence. The
author may attempt to express authentic experience and feelings but lacks
the technical mastery to do so. Kitsch is therefore an "artistic weakness, an
aesthetic derailment, a decorative failure." One can recognize kitsch only if
one is familiar with and able to recognize authentic art, with which it can be
compared (24–25). Through this clever ploy Deschner effectively disarms
all but the boldest and most self-assured of his potential opponents, those
who do not fear running the risk of appearing unable to recognize true art
and who are able to make a sound argument for the *artistic* merit of
Hesse's works. Few critics were willing to accept the challenge.

From a comparison of several poems by Hesse with finer examples by
Trakl and Rilke, Deschner concludes that Hesse is decidedly third-rate as a
poet. "That Hesse published so devastatingly many verses completely without stature," he insists, "is a regrettable lack of discipline, a literary barba-
rism" (168). Although Deschner's carefully selected examples from among
the great number of Hesse's poems do reveal some lapses in taste and tal-

[4]In *Hermann Hesse: Vom Wesen der Musik in der Dichtung* (Hermann Hesse: Concerning the Essence of Music in Literature, 1957) Werner Dürr considers music to
be at the center of Hesse's quest for unity. One can experience God or the divine in
music, as Haller does in the music of Bach and Mozart, or one may experience life
and sensuality in it, as he does in jazz.

ent, a more objective and fair treatment should also include some analysis of the craftsmanship and artistry of some of Hesse's finest poems. As a poet, Hesse may not bear comparison with Trakl and Rilke, but some of his best poems will no doubt be anthologized along with theirs for years to come.

Closer to our concern is Deschner's almost equally devastating belittlement of Hesse's prose, which he presents in a cascade of vituperative formulations. Dismissing claims to the contrary by Thomas Mann and by an unnamed critic, Deschner declares that the style of *Narziss und Goldmund*, the only novel he discusses, is completely unoriginal and stale and that it "clearly borders on the sugary-Romantic, foolishly-sentimental, the silly and the tasteless" (115). It is the most blatant kitsch and reveals "an overly simplified manner, a black and white technique of the cheapest sort" (117–18). Hesse's language is "conventional and hackneyed"; everything is not only "forcefully exaggerated" but also "stuck in leached-out shells of words." Grammatical mistakes abound; meaningless repetition is commonplace (118–19). "There is in this book no image, no formulation, which one hasn't already read often and often (*sic*) in earlier writers. *Narziss und Goldmund* is the expression of a typically epigonic art." Deschner cites Hesse's own modest disclaimers of his artistic stature to bolster his argument that "Hesse is in most of his works, I say this without hesitation, not even second-rate, because, as he says himself, he is an 'epigone'" (122).

Deschner's book was followed in 1958 by an equally deprecating cover story in *Der Spiegel* entitled "Hermann Hesse in his Vegetable Garden," which, according to Volker Michels, "so determined our image of Hesse in the sixties, that not only was the author subjected to ridicule, but so too for years were all those who still had the courage to become seriously involved with Hermann Hesse" (1976, 8). Deschner's book and the *Spiegel* article appear to represent and to have released a form of reaction against Hesse similar to the one that followed the First World War. One cannot know to what extent they simply reflect a developing trend or to what extent they influenced critics and scholars, but they do mark a turning point, following which Hesse disappeared from the curriculum and was no longer considered worthy of critical study. The situation which then prevailed in German universities is aptly described by Adolf Muschg, a young scholar who, like Unseld, had devoured Hesse's works following the war: "But when I began to study German literature, it was considered chic not to pay attention to a writer like Hesse" (1992, 11). (Muschg's lost interest was revived by the new insight he gained through the publication in 1977 of two volumes of Hesse's political writings.)

Works Cited

Baumer, Franz. "Das magische Denken in der Dichtung Hermann Hesses." Ph.D. diss., Munich, 1951.

Deschner, Karlheinz. *Kitsch, Konvention und Kunst: Eine literarische Streitschrift.* Munich: Paul List Verlag, 1957.

Dürr, Werner. *Hermann Hesse: Vom Wesen der Musik in der Dichtung.* Stuttgart: Silberberg, 1957.

Gnefkow, Edmund. *Hermann Hesse: Biographie.* Freiburg i.Br.: Gerhard Kirchhoff Verlag, 1952.

Gontrum, Peter Baer. "Natur- und Dingsymbolik als Ausdruck der inneren Welt Hermann Hesses." Ph.D. diss., Munich, 1958.

Liepelt-Unterberg, Maria. "Das Polaritätsgesetz in der Dichtung. Am Beispiel von Hermann Hesses 'Steppenwolf.'" Ph.D. diss., Bonn, 1951.

Michels, Volker, ed. *Über Hermann Hesse.* Vol. 1. Frankfurt am Main: Suhrkamp, 1976.

Middleton, John Christopher. "Hermann Hesse as Humanist." Ph.D. diss., Merton College, 1954.

Muschg, Adolf. "Hermann Hesse und das Engagement." In *Hermann Hesse und die Politik,* 7th International Hermann-Hesse Colloquium in Calw, ed. Martin Pfeifer, 11–24. Bad Liebenzell: Verlag Bernhard Gengenbach, 1992.

Seidlin, Oskar. "The Exorcism of the Demon." *Symposium* 4 (1950): 325–48.

Unseld, Siegfried. "Hermann Hesse: Einmal wirklich dienen." In *Hermann Hesse und die Politik,* 7th International Hermann-Hesse Colloquium in Calw, ed. Martin Pfeifer, 25–41. Bad Liebenzell: Verlag Bernhard Gengenbach, 1992.

Unseld, Siegfried. "Hermann Hesses Anschauung vom Beruf des Dichters." Ph.D. diss., Tübingen, 1951.

Wagner, Marianne. "Zeitmorphologischer Vergleich von Hermann Hesses 'Demian', 'Siddhartha', 'Der Steppenwolf', 'Narziss und Goldmund' zur Aufweisung typischer Gestaltzüge." Ph.D. diss., Bonn, 1953.

Weibel, Kurt. "Hermann Hesse und die deutsche Romantik." Ph.D. diss., Bern, 1952. Winterthur: P. G. Keller, 1954.

3: Hesse Scholarship in America: The Beginning of the Boom

In the same year the *Spiegel* article appeared, Joseph Mileck's *Hermann Hesse and His Critics* and Theodore Ziolkowski's analysis of the sonata form of *Steppenwolf* were published on this side of the Atlantic. Both scholars had written their doctoral dissertations on Hesse, Mileck at Harvard in 1950 and Ziolkowski at Yale in 1956, and both have made numerous contributions to scholarship on Hesse. Also in 1958, an article by comparatist Ralph Freedman on Hesse as a modern novelist was published in the widely distributed *PMLA*. With the appearance of these and other contributions, the center of scholarship on Hesse shifted from Germany to North America.

Mileck's book contains a short biography of the author; an extensive bibliography of works by Hesse, including stories, essays, and poems that appeared in periodicals and newspapers; a bibliography of books, articles, and dissertations about him, most of which are in German; and a critical review of that secondary literature. The latter is divided into units on (1) books, (2) pamphlets, and (3) articles in books, pamphlets, and periodicals arranged by topic, for example, "Hesse and his Age," "Hesse and Youth," "Hesse and Nature," and so on. It also includes a section on poetry and one on *Glasperlenspiel*, which at that time had "already occasioned more criticism than any other single work" (178). Mileck discusses some of the more important secondary material in some detail, but for the most part he provides little more than a general description of a study's content and approach. He includes only one of the dissertations treated in the previous chapter, namely Weibel's, which also appeared as a book. The unpublished German dissertations are listed; Middleton's is not.

Considering the dramatic increase in readership that was about to take place and the primacy of *Steppenwolf's* contribution to it, it is noteworthy that Mileck considers *Siddhartha*, *Narziss und Goldmund*, and *Glasperlenspiel* to be the works most likely to survive, because in them "Hesse seems to have managed to extricate himself sufficiently from this engrossment with his own immediate, personal problems to enable him to mold his art with that care necessary to insure it, beyond all doubt, against the wear of time and to give it some of the more universal implications inherent in all truly great art" (30–31). Mileck speculates that "Hesse is not likely to attract many readers here [in America] except for a few kindred spirits in our university circles, and for the German speaking intellectuals who have emigrated to America in the past two decades" (199). This view was shared by other American critics and by Hesse, who never expected to be understood and accepted by what he considered to be unsophisticated readers.

In 1977 Mileck published an updated and expanded biography and a comprehensive bibliography in two volumes. The bibliography consists of just under 1300 pages and lists everything known to have been written by Hesse — letters, articles, reviews, poems published in newspapers, and translations of his works into 34 languages — and everything written about him. It also lists recordings made by Hesse and other miscellany. This monumental work remains unsurpassed for its listing of Hesse's writings and is still a valuable source for secondary literature to 1975. The biographical portion was superseded in 1978 by Mileck's own *Hermann Hesse: His Life and Art* and by other biographies, including especially Ralph Freedman's *Hermann Hesse: Pilgrim of Crisis*, also from 1978.

Apparently unaware of the dissertations by Unseld and Middleton, Theodore Ziolkowski claims in the preface of his essay "Hermann Hesse's *Steppenwolf*: A Sonata in Prose" (1958) that "little or nothing has been done to demonstrate that his [Hesse's] insistence upon the structural quality of the book is valid" (115). Ziolkowski attempts to demonstrate the literal accuracy of Hesse's claim that "purely artistically *Steppenwolf* is at least as good as *Goldmund*; it is structured around the intermezzo of the Tractat as strictly and rigidly as a sonata and develops its theme purely" (115; letter of 13 November 1930). (Hesse also compares the structure of the novel to a fugue or canon [letters of 8 July 1927 and October 1932]. Werner Dürr refers to these statements in his study of music cited in chapter 2, but he does not think they are to be taken literally [1957, 54].)

In Ziolkowski's view, the internal structure of the novel is divided into three main sections: the preliminary material, the action, and the Magic Theater. The preliminary material is further subdivided into the introduction, Haller's narrative which begins the book itself, and the Treatise (115). All this is introductory and not part of the plot, which occupies the second section. Separating Haller's preliminary material from the rest of the plot development might be seen as an artificial division of a continuous development, but it is a prerequisite of Ziolkowski's comparison of the three different segments of the introduction with the three parts of the sonata form.

The three sections of the introduction are narrated from the different perspectives of the three types of beings described in the Treatise, who are "differentiated relatively according to their degree of individuation" (118). Haller's subjective report is located in the middle between the objective narratives of the editor, who represents the bourgeois ego, and the Immortals, whose perspective is cosmic. Each section contains two themes corresponding to the polar opposites in Haller: "The [editor's] introduction states the two themes theoretically; the second section brings the development in which the significance of these themes for Haller's life is interpreted; and the 'Tractat' recapitulates the themes, theoretically again, and proposes a resolution to the conflict." Ziolkowski considers this scheme, which consists of exposition, development, and recapitulation, to be the sonata or first movement form (120). One might object that this ABA structure suggests a greater similarity between the mundane perspective of the bourgeois editor and the cosmic perspective of the Immortals than is warranted by their shared objectivity and theoretical approach. Insofar as they occupy opposite poles of a continuum, they would seem, rather, to represent polar opposites, with Haller closer to the bourgeois editor than he is to the Immortals.

Ziolkowski may indeed be attempting "to force one art form willfully into the Procrustean bed of another" (121) — a criticism he anticipates — by taking the formal analogy too literally and by pushing it too hard, but the effort is nevertheless valuable for the insight it provides into Hesse's craftsmanship. In a more general and less controversial way Ziolkowski also finds musical analogies for the other two parts of the novel: he considers the Magic Theater to be a theme with variations, the theme being Haller's multiple personalities as described in the Treatise (132–33), and he compares the second part with its "double perspective" to musical counterpoint, in which distinct melodic lines or parts are combined into a single musical fabric (123–24).

The concept of double perspective or double perception was first applied by Margot Böttcher in her 1948 dissertation "Aufbau und Form von Hermann Hesses *Steppenwolf*" (Structure and Form of Hermann Hesse's *Steppenwolf*) and is related to Max Schmid's postulate of two levels of symbolism in the novel, which was mentioned above (Schmid 1947, 95–96). As developed and systematically applied by Ziolkowski in connection with his analysis of musical counterpoint, this concept becomes a widely accepted but also controversial tool for explicating the sometimes puzzling and problematic interplay of reality and fantasy in the novel. An alternative approach, which is based on Jungian psychology and Hesse's claim that all his figures are parts of himself, will be considered below, especially in chapter 5.

From the time Haller reads the Treatise, it becomes necessary, Ziolkowski maintains,

> to make a clear distinction between two levels of reality: the everyday plane of the Bürger or the placard-bearer, and the exalted, supernal plane of the Immortals and the magic theater. Haller might be called an eidetic, that is, "an individual capable of producing subjective (visual or other) images or 'Anschauungsbilder' of virtually hallucinatory vividness." Accordingly, his

experiences on the upper level of reality assume fully as much intensity for him as the action on the level of mundane reality. (123)

Ziolkowski attempts to find a plausible realistic explanation for the seemingly unrealistic events that precede this moment: because Haller is depressed and "willing to grasp eagerly after any ray of hope which would alleviate his desperate condition . . . his overwrought mind reads an imaginary message" in some marks on a wall; and later, in an inebriated and rhapsodic state, he meets a man who shoves a pamphlet into his hand, "*any* pamphlet — which Haller's acrobatic and stimulated mind converts, at home, into the 'Tractat'" (author's emphasis). In moments such as this "a remote and more perceptive area of Haller's intelligence — an area which is usually blocked by the problematics of his dual personality and the exigencies of his existence," is able to manifest itself (123). It is this interplay or simultaneity of the real and the imagined that Ziolkowski identifies as double perspective or double perception. "By means of double perception almost any given action of the book may be interpreted on two distinct levels, and this produces the effect of simultaneity or concomitance of the two planes or melodic lines" (123).

The application of double perspective becomes more problematic when it must account for the importance of Hermine, who on the real level is simply a prostitute. Haller considers her insights and remarks to be almost preternatural, but, according to Ziolkowski, "any reader will recognize that most of Hermine's remarks, like the utterances of the Delphic oracle, are open to two interpretations." What she says to Haller on the occasion of their first meeting is "precisely what one would expect from a prostitute with long experience in handling drunks and mothering would-be suicides. Only Haller's lonely and despondent state allows him to ascribe any higher significance to her casual remarks" (125). The prostitute can teach him how to dance, to laugh, to live, and to love, but her meaning for Haller goes beyond that. She becomes a symbol for him, and, on a higher level of reality, she and Pablo are important "as reflections of his own thoughts! For occasionally these two representatives of the sensual world utter deep and significant statements which ill conform to the very realistic picture drawn of them" (126).

By clearly expressing the central tenet of the novel, which Haller is unable to articulate for himself, Hermine confirms his incipient belief in the eternal spiritual kingdom of the Immortals. She also tells him what Steppenwolf-natures like themselves live for, namely, eternity and the kingdom of God (126). Significantly, she includes herself among those humans "who ask too much and have a dimension too many" (St 174). It seems to Haller that the clairvoyant girl has read his thoughts and returned them to him in a new and different form. As with his reading of the Treatise, it is supposedly

Haller's double perspective that enables him to see a symbolic meaning in Hermine. He transplants his own thoughts into her words (126–27).[1]

The culmination of the development of Haller's double perspective comes in the Magic Theater: in what is nothing more than an opium fantasy on the realistic level, Haller, like the Immortals, is able to transcend the *principium individuationis* (105). At the same time, what takes place there has symbolic meaning and has been prepared for by symbolic events such as Haller's descent to "hell" in the basement of the ball followed by his ascent to the room in which he experiences the Magic Theater, a movement Ziolkowski considers to be symbolic for Haller's acceptance of the cosmos. Interrupting that progression is Haller's nuptial dance with Hermine, which symbolizes the "imminent marriage of the two poles of existence in his soul: the intellectual or spiritual with the sensual or natural" (127).

Ziolkowski's interpretation based on dual perspectives and two levels of reality appears to falter and become unconvincing in the attempt to account for Hermine's death and the role of the Immortals. "On the dream level," he writes,

> Haller seems to take a knife and kill Hermine. Yet the actual event probably amounts to no more than an exclamation of jealousy and disgust when he realizes that the woman whom he had elevated to symbolic stature, rather than being the ethereal personification of an ideal, is indeed very much of the flesh. It is, to be sure, a murder on this level of reality also, for in his mind he eradicates the idealized image of Hermine which had obsessed him. As he contemplates her (imagined) corpse [!], he meditates: "Nun war ihr Wunsch erfüllt. Noch eh sie ganz mein geworden war, hatte ich meine Geliebte getötet" [Now her wish was fulfilled. Before she had become completely mine, I had killed my beloved]. (131)

But Haller would have to be completely mad on the real level, one might object, in order to be contemplating her *imagined* corpse and to think that he has actually killed her, when in *reality* he has merely expressed his jealousy and disgust and removed her symbolically from his mind. Furthermore, Ziolkowski does not attempt to explain what is happening on which level when Pablo takes up Hermine, who shrinks in his fingers to the dimensions of a toy figure, and puts her in the same pocket from which he takes his potent cigarettes (St 247–48), just as Haller had pocketed the chess pieces which represent parts of his personality. And what is the situation of the real Hermine at the end of the novel?

[1]In a similar attempt to reconcile Hermine's philosophical, literary, and psychoanalytical insight with her status as a prostitute, G. W. Field suggests that one may "view her and the other characters as constantly flitting in and out of the real and surreal worlds — like Hoffmann's creation [in *Der goldene Topf*], who is at one moment an archivist, and at the next a salamander" (1970, 104).

Similar ambiguity prevails in Ziolkowski's explication of Pablo and Mozart. Because Mozart later turns into or is replaced by Pablo, Ziolkowski assumes that the Mozart who brings in a radio and reproves Haller actually is
Pablo on the first level, whom Haller takes for Mozart again on the second
level. Their conversation is therefore on the plane of dream or higher reality
(131). Haller supposedly comes to realize that Mozart and Pablo are two
aspects of a single person who represents the union of the poles of spirit and
nature (132), but this interpretation denies the wholeness of Mozart as an
Immortal and contradicts Ziolkowski's own definition of the Immortals as
those who "accept chaos as the natural state of existence, for they inhabit a
realm *where all polarity has ceased* and where every manifestation of life is
approved as necessary and good" (119; my emphasis). An interpretation
based on a double perspective or two levels of reality runs the risk of re-
peating Haller's error when he confused the "beautiful picture gallery with
reality and stabbed to death the reflection of a girl with the reflection of a
knife" (St 245).

In a revised and expanded version of his essay, which is included in *The
Novels of Hermann Hesse: A Study in Theme and Structure* (1965), Ziolkowski appears to respond to an interpretation by Egon Schwarz — discussed below — which implicitly counters his argument for double
perception. In a new section captioned "The Märchen," Ziolkowski mus-
ters historical support for his thesis. "To insist on a realistic basis for the surrealistic episodes of the novel in no way constitutes a deprecation of Hesse's
visionary powers," he begins.

> These symbolic projections of Haller's inner world, the imaginative expres-
> sion of higher reality, contain the true meaning of the work, as Hesse ar-
> gued in letters to readers who saw in the book no more than a paean to
> prostitutes and jazz musicians. All too often, however, critics have over-
> looked the realistic basis, thus ignoring the technique of double perception
> and missing precisely the ambiguous quality of "reality" that Hesse was so
> intent upon rendering. Only the interaction of the two levels of reality
> produces the characteristic tension of the novel, and the source of Haller's
> schizophrenic depression becomes understandable only when we see him
> enmeshed in the turmoil of everyday reality. For that reason Hesse comes
> closer to literary realism in many passages of this novel than anywhere else
> in his works. (200)

"If there is anything 'Romantic' about *The Steppenwolf*," Ziolkowski adds,
"it is precisely this pronounced juxtaposition of the real and the imaginary."

Ziolkowski identifies the Romantic *Märchen* as the literary form in
which such a juxtaposition is possible, and it is in this tradition that *Steppenwolf* can be located. Also possible in this genre is the reunification of
nature and spirit, which was the central theme of Romanticism, as it was for

Hesse. One of the most brilliant authors of such tales is E. T. A. Hoffmann, whose works Hesse greatly admired, and Hoffmann departs from the earlier tradition by situating his tales squarely in the present and by clearly establishing time and place. The fantastic elements of Hoffmann's tales thus "rise immediately out of the everyday life of contemporary bourgeois society" and constitute a "fantastic interpretation of reality and not a transposition into a fairy-tale realm" (203).

Hoffmann refers to the "chronic dualism" of his heroes: because they are able to experience reality as fantastic, to perceive the miraculous in everyday life, they appear demented to ordinary people. But these experiences are ambiguous and can be justified rationally, according to Ziolkowski, as visions inspired in the hero by something he sees in reality. Hoffmann makes clear that the "miraculous is a capacity for poetic vision in everyday life, and not a realm set apart by itself." The fairy-tale elements are "not to be dismissed as fantastic, but are to be understood as projections of the characters' own inner visions," as if they were "real in the ordinary sense." Likewise, the myths Hoffmann incorporates in his stories are recapitulated or symbolically fulfilled by the characters within the story's realistic framework (203–206).

Of course Ziolkowski's characterization of Hoffmann's tales is also meant to apply to *Steppenwolf.* The novel begins with a dualistic view of reality in a contemporary and realistic setting. The Treatise anticipates the "myth of reunification." During the course of the story inner vision assumes greater significance for Harry Haller than external reality, and he "interacts more naturally with the figures of his imagination than with those of external reality" (206). The imagined figures become corporeal, as it were, by being projected onto externally real figures. But which figures are imaginary and which real? All the important figures, unless one includes the professor and his wife in that category, are participants in the latter part of the story and may therefore, according to Ziolkowski's argument, be considered figures of Haller's imagination or "inner vision." According to Ziolkowski, the fairy tale requires a sound basis in reality because the entire tale is

> *an internal vision that is projected into everyday life.* Reality supplies the material from which the vision is constructed in the minds of Anselmus and Haller. Only the contrast between reality and vision makes possible the frustrations of their heroes and the irony in which the authors delight. We can thus conclude, somewhat paradoxically, that to deny the realistic basis of *The Steppenwolf* is to deny Hesse's most conspicuous debt to German Romanticism: his exploitation of Romantic forms and techniques. (206; my emphasis)

Thus Hermine, Pablo, and the other figures are both real and, on a higher level, reflections of Haller's own thoughts (212).

In *Dimensions of the Novel: German Texts and European Contexts*, Ziolkowski identifies criminal heroes in works by André Gide, Thomas Mann, and Hesse as metaphors for the artist. As Thomas Mann writes in an essay on Dostoevsky ("Dostoevsky — in Moderation," 1946), the artist is related to the criminal in his "intellectual separation and alienation from bourgeois respectability" and in his "independent and ruthless thought" (1969, 315). Thus Sinclair in *Demian* assumes the role of a thief in his encounter with Kromer, and under Demian's influence "he chooses as models for his behavior the 'criminals' of the Bible: Cain; the unrepentant thief of the cross at Golgotha; and . . . the Prodigal Son" (311). Friedrich Klein in Hesse's *Klein und Wagner* has committed a real crime and is a "clear instance of a criminal hero conceived purely as a metaphor for the conscience of the artist" (319). Ziolkowski refers to *Klein und Wagner* along with Kafka's *The Trial* and Thomas Mann's *Felix Krull* as "essentially the reification of a metaphor" (322). As the application of a Jungian approach will demonstrate, interpreting *Steppenwolf*, too, as the reification of a metaphor avoids the pitfalls of the clever but ultimately unsatisfactory theory of double perception and accords with Hesse's own remarks on the subject.

As authors of innovative or experimental works often do, Hesse has provided his readers with hints for interpreting his novel. Even the prosaic editor of Haller's manuscript recognizes that Haller's experiences are "for the most part fictitious, not, however, in the sense of arbitrary invention. They are rather the deeply lived spiritual events which he has attempted to express by giving them the form of tangible experiences" (St 22). From a perspective diametrically opposed to the editor's, the Treatise makes a similar statement by means of an actual discussion of literature. The belief that the ego is a simple "fixed phenomenon" is based on a false analogy, we are told. Even the most sophisticated literature has traditionally presented people as seemingly unified beings. "Of all literature up to our days the drama has been the most highly prized by writers and critics, and rightly, since it offers (or might offer) the greatest possibilities of representing the ego as a manifold entity" (St 68).

This possibility is undermined, however, by the physical presence of the actors, which creates the illusion of unity. The heroes of Indian epics, on the other hand, are "not individuals, but whole reels of individualities in a series of incarnations."

> And in modern times there are poems [that is, literary works], in which, behind the veil of a concern with individuality and character that is scarcely, indeed, in the author's mind, the motive is to present a manifold activity of soul. Whoever wishes to recognize this must resolve once and for all *not to regard the characters of such a poem as separate beings, but as the various facets and aspects of a higher unity, in my opinion, of the poet's soul.* If

"Faust" is treated this way, Faust, Mephistopheles, Wagner and the rest form a unity and a supreme individuality; and it is in this higher unity alone, not in the several characters, that something of the true nature of the soul is revealed. (St 68–69; my emphasis)

Just as Faust has "Mephisto and a whole crowd of other souls" in his breast, so, too, according to Hesse, does the Steppenwolf. Like Goethe in *Faust*, Hesse represents an internal drama in which the characters are all parts of the hero, just as the chess pieces in the Magic Theater, including the one Pablo pockets, represent different parts of Haller's personality and their dynamic, ever-changing relationship to each other.

In contrast to Ziolkowski and in accord with the hint provided by Hesse in the Treatise, Egon Schwarz interprets Hermine as "*nothing other* than a fragment of Harry's personality, a part of his spiritual structure," and he adds that recognizing this fact is a "presupposition for understanding the whole allegory" (1961, 193; my emphasis). It is not by accident that she bears the feminine form of the author's name, just as Harry Haller bears his initials, for she is the sensual element of his being, the Steppenwolf become human and externalized through projection, the part of him that has been neglected in his pursuit of culture and in the development of his intellect. She represents the "grace of regeneration" he is allowed to experience on the "brink of despair." Through her he learns how to love himself and others (194). The goal of the developmental process Haller undergoes is to fall in love with Hermine and then to kill her. "That is the meaning of the book: he is to learn to develop his sensual self, to integrate it with the core of his being, and finally to eliminate it as a separate entity" (195). Noting Pablo's ambiguous criticism of Haller for not knowing what to do with the figure of Hermine, Schwarz concludes nevertheless that Harry has succeeded in identifying her with a part of his own being (195).

Schwarz considers Goethe along with Nietzsche's cultural pessimism and the psychoanalysis of Freud and Jung to be the major influences on the novel. The parallels to *Faust* are so abundant and significant, he observes, that "one could justifiably call *Steppenwolf* Hesse's *Faust*" (192). Like Faust, Haller is an aging man who has absorbed the whole intellectual learning of the time and who is disgusted with life and on the verge of committing suicide. Both figures are saved from death by the intervention of supernatural beings with whom they enter into agreements that border on the forbidden and are reminiscent of the traditional pacts with the devil. Both are then led by their new companions into areas of life, including love and sensuality, which until then they had ignored. The relationship between Haller and Maria is reminiscent of that between Faust and Gretchen, and the masked ball resembles the Walpurgis Night (192).

As a novel of education or development, *Steppenwolf* also has much in common with Goethe's *Wilhelm Meister*. The *Entwicklungsroman* generally has a strong autobiographical element, Schwarz notes, since it gives expression to the poet's most intimate, concrete life experiences (193). The parallels between Haller and Hesse have been well established, and, as seen above, Hermine, too, is a part of their personality. She is also connected to the "second large sphere, which, along with the autobiographical, is peculiarly incorporated in the basically realistic composition of the *Entwicklungsroman*: the realm of the supernatural" (195).

The model for the Magic Theater, according to Schwarz, is the Society of the Tower in *Wilhelm Meister*. Both represent a kind of supernatural order beyond the logic and understanding of the limited individual. Like the members of that secret society, Pablo and the Immortals have inexplicable knowledge of the secret recesses of the hero's mind. Both figures are guided along their paths by mysterious figures and events, and the "Tract of the Steppenwolf" can be compared to Wilhelm's "Lehrbrief" (certificate of apprenticeship). Both the Society of the Tower and the Magic Theater represent a higher reality and a new perspective from which to view the "groping, erring, goalless searching of the central figures." Without that perspective, the heroes' lives would be meaningless, if not absurd; with it, even their mistakes may be seen to fit into a developmental scheme (195–96).

Unlike the usual hero of such novels, however, Haller already has his education and maturation behind him, from which Schwarz concludes that *Steppenwolf* can be seen as an inverted *Entwicklungsroman*. It is noteworthy in this connection that Goethe's novel comes at the beginning of the bourgeois era, when the nobility still represented a higher social level and greater refinement and freedom of mind, and when the bourgeois hero had the possibility to rise above the limitations of his class. No such noble class and no such possibility exists for Haller at the end of the bourgeois era. Although he has gained knowledge and experience comparable to that which Wilhelm Meister obtains during his development, there is no elect group at the end of the path to raise him into a higher sphere and give meaning to his experiences and accomplishments. Instead, his knowledge and maturity are the sources of his despair and despondency. What he needs is a reverse development, a regression, in order to recover the part of himself he has denied and neglected. If he can do that successfully, he will be receptive to the teachings of the Immortals: he will achieve the inner unity and harmony that is manifest in humor and laughter, and he will recognize, as Goethe's Faust did, that we have life in its colorful reflection ("Am farbigen Abglanz haben wir das Leben"). There is little hope for contemporary culture, but there is a way out for the gifted individual (197–98).

In *The Lyrical Novel: Studies in Hermann Hesse, André Gide, and Virginia Woolf* (1963), Ralph Freedman offers an enlightening explanation for the lack of epic action and event in Hesse's novels and provides a useful perspective on the relationship of real and symbolic content. Hesse was well aware of the strong tradition of the lyrical novel in German literature and of his own contribution to it:

> Narrative as a disguised lyric, the novel as a borrowed label for the experimentations of poetic spirits to express their feeling of self and world; this was a specifically German and romantic matter, here I felt immediately a common heritage and guilt (WA 11:10).

Characteristic of the lyrical novel, according to Freedman, is a shift of emphasis from men and events to formal design: action becomes subordinate to imagery, portraiture to a more effective rendering of the mind with its awareness, feeling, and perception. The causal and temporal movement of traditional narrative and the usual scenery of fiction are replaced by symbolic patterns of imagery. The experiencing self is not separated from the world experienced but combined with it "in a strangely inward, yet aesthetically objective, form" (2). The world is conceived as a

> poet's vision fashioned as a design. [It] is reduced to a *lyrical point of view*, the equivalent of the poet's 'I': the lyrical self. In the masquerade of the novel, this point of view is the poet's *mask* as well as the source of his consciousness, whether it appears as one or more disguised *personae* or in the more direct function of the diarist, the confessor, or first-person narrator." (8; author's italics)

The poet-hero represents and experiences parts of himself in objects and other figures, and by this act he transmutes those objects into manifestations of his "infinite self," the visible work of art. By mirroring the poet's inner state, the objects lose their separate, independent identity and become manifestations of the poet's spirit and features of his self-portrait (20). The world thus becomes the hero's mirror, but, as described by Friedrich Schlegel and Novalis, it is a *magic* mirror that can show the past, the future, or what is hidden in the unconscious. It transcends time and unites it with eternity.

The world as a magic mirror reflects the eternal self, and that eternal, archetypal self is ever present in Hesse's mind and art. "I know better than anyone," he writes, "the condition in which the eternal self in us observes the mortal I and appraises its leaps and grimaces, full of pity, full of scorn, full of neutrality" (WA 7:156–57). Hesse repeatedly projects his inner schisms and conflicts into a hero who "raises his inadequate sensual self to the state of a harmonious or symbolic self . . . . the conflict between self and world is projected into an ego that can unify them only in mystical revelation or in the illusion induced by art" (Freedman 49).

Freedman identifies several methods Hesse employs to depict the relation between the time-bound experiences which his protagonists encounter and their reflections in timeless art. One method is the use of the poetic symbol, through which the timeless ideal can be portrayed as a dimension of events in time, as the sparrow hawk and Abraxas in *Demian*, for example, and the flowers in *Steppenwolf* are used to represent the union of opposites toward which the heroes are striving. A second method "posits a wanderer through space and time who acts as a perceiving eye, that is, as the passive romantic hero, in whom encounters and dreams are mirrored as art." Like Goethe's Wilhelm Meister and Novalis's Heinrich von Ofterdingen, Haller and Goldmund "wander through the world of sense and symbolic dream, their sensibilities modified by events and encounters," but, unlike their predecessors, "Goldmund and Haller move through worlds which mirror, directly and allegorically, their internal states of mind, that is, disintegrations and resolutions occurring beneath the ordinary level of conscious and even unconscious experience" (51–52).

Like other writers of his generation, Hesse suffers from the inability of language to render the higher reality he intuits, to describe or express the higher unity that exists beyond polar opposites. He envies the musician's ability to create harmony within dissonance, to present simultaneously the harmony and dissonance of opposing motifs, and to reconcile the opposites, which is what he wants to accomplish in his writing.

> If I were a musician I could write without difficulty a melody in two voices, a melody which consists of two notes and sequences which correspond to each other, which complement each other, which condition each other, which in any event stand to one another in the closest and liveliest reciprocity and mutual relationship. And anyone who can read music could read my double melody, could see and hear in each tone its counterpoint, the brother, the enemy, the antipode. Well, and just this double-voiced melody and eternally moving antithesis, this double line I want to express with my own material, with words, and I work myself sore at it, and it doesn't work. (53; Quotation from *Kurgast*, WA 7:111)

Painting, too, has certain advantages over literature: "if music deepens the melody of life and catches it in art, the effect of painting works precisely in the opposite direction: it freezes the fluid manifold of experience in timeless portraiture" (54). Whereas Sinclair in *Demian*, Klingsor in *Klingsors letzter Sommer* (Klingsor's Last Summer, 1920), and some of Hesse's other heroes represent themselves in painted images, Haller's portrait *appears* to be drawn by others in the editor's preface, the Treatise, and the Magic Theater, but it is also reflected in the narrative's primary figures and symbols.

Here we confront once again the hermeneutic problem that Ziolkowski tried to solve with his postulate of a double perspective or double perception, namely, what is to be considered "real" in the narrative, what symbolic, and how do the two interrelate? Freedman characterizes the protagonist or symbolic hero of the lyrical novel as being analogous to the lyrical "I" in poetry. The novel's world and figures have their source in him and are transmuted into imagery through his perception and point of view. But as the protagonist, he unifies not only symbolic images but also the novel's scenes. "The relationship between these two roles played by an identical figure constitutes an important dimension of lyrical fiction. In most lyrical novels, this tension is reflected in an ambiguous world composed simultaneously of a texture of images and of the linear movement of narrative." The symbolic protagonist is "self-reflexive," because his own psyche is mirrored in the world, which thus becomes symbolic. A typical strand in the lyrical novel is therefore allegorical, not, as a rule, in the consistent correspondence between the hero's encounters and representative ideas or concepts outside himself, but in the relation of events to himself. "The figures and scenes he confronts signify ideas, which, in turn, symbolize his own inner condition" (72–73).

While Freedman recognizes that "the novel's world, its landscapes and stylized textures of faces and events" are the creation of the protagonist and reflect his psyche, he stops short of a reading that is entirely allegorical, symbolic, or metaphoric. He does not interpret the figures as nothing other than parts of the author, because he considers the figures and scenes that signify ideas and symbolize the hero's own inner condition to be objectively real as well. Thus he sees tension "reflected in an ambiguous world composed simultaneously of a texture of images and of the linear movement of narrative" and in the mirroring of one level of reality or one perception by the other in a complex texture of reciprocal reflections of external and internal figures, images, and events (72).

Despite Hesse's claim that his figures are all parts of himself, Freedman believes that he is following the author's lead in assuming the objective reality of figures and scenes, since Hesse himself locates internal events in external reality. Using Haller's notebook to describe the hero's mental and spiritual disintegration enables Hesse to "render a hero's inner life yet to remain, on the surface at least, within the conventions of the realistic novel" (74). Furthermore, the way Hesse presents the hero's disintegration precisely as he experiences it implies the identity of Haller's inner life and the novel's world. And part of that world consists of a universal, transcendent reality represented by the Immortals, who intervene in Haller's life and attempt to guide him toward the goal of finding humor and pure detachment in the impersonal magic of art. The symbolic hero thus faces himself in an ultimate self-encounter (75–76).

This self-encounter or self-reflection is manifest in the many examples of mirroring, real and metaphoric, that occur in the novel. In Freedman's view, the symbolic mirror becomes "the center around which the novel is built," just as the *blaue Blume* (blue flower) was the center of *Heinrich von Ofterdingen* (76–77). Mirrors are frequently used and discussed, and they become a primary means of self-discovery in the Magic Theater. The Treatise, too, functions as a magic mirror, which reflects the true nature of Haller's fragmented personality and foresees his confrontation with the chaos of his soul. In their function as Haller's guides toward his goal, Hermine, Maria, and Pablo resemble Demian, Pistorius, and Frau Eva, the allegorical figures who guide Sinclair's development. But in *Steppenwolf* the relationships are more complex. "These figures portray not only different aspects of the hero, or particular stages in his growth or decline, but also different types of mirroring which are unified in the concluding scenes" (82–83).

The alleged reality of the figures who are allegorical and a mirroring part of the hero is lost sight of in Freedman's discussion of their function. Hermine, for example, "exemplifies a direct correspondence between self and ideal." She identifies herself as Haller's mirror: "Don't you understand, my learned friend, that I please you and am important to you, because I am a kind of mirror for you?" (St 123; Freedman's translation). Haller agrees that her face is like a magic mirror for him (St 124), and he acknowledges again and again that she is his double or his sister and that she reflects significant parts of him and speaks to him with his own voice. From the beginning she knows what is in his mind as well as or better than he does. He equates her with his soul and merges with her in the final dance. As a prostitute, an "artist of the body," she mirrors Haller's profession as a writer, "an artist of the intellect" (83).

What is more, Hermine is a projection not only of the hero's precise image but also of the personality he aspires to be. As his reflection she contains masculine qualities and reminds him of his childhood friend Hermann, with whom he identifies. "She is a formed image of the self, a new creation of its being." Like Demian, she becomes the hero's "eternal self" (83–84). Her androgyny symbolizes the wholeness he lacks and which is his goal, and she is his guide to that goal. But just as Maria is her instrument or puppet, she is Pablo's. According to Freedman, Pablo combines the roles of Hermine and Maria and also functions on the higher level of the Immortals. As the director of the Magic Theater he is also a master mirror, "an embodiment of his own *Spiegelkabinett*— in which all other figures, and hence all of Haller's aspirations, are joined" (86–87).

In keeping with his focus on mirrors, Freedman sees *Steppenwolf* as a structure of various triads which mirror one another and which center on and are interconnected through Harry Haller (77). The first triad is the obvious one represented by the external division into the editor's introduction, the Treatise, and Haller's notes. Each part of this triad mirrors a different element of Haller's personality: the first presents a realistic reflection from a standpoint outside Haller; the second offers a symbolic, universalizing reflection from the standpoint of the Immortals or Haller's eternal self; and the third reflects his own thoughts and perspective. The symbolic, universalizing function is most important because it subverts the bourgeois fiction that the self is a single entity and "seeks to replace a purely psychological outlook on man's divided state with a mystical and ideological rationale." Schizophrenia is thus transformed into a positive value for the spiritual rebel and a necessary transition to new self-discovery. The Treatise informs Haller that he can be saved "only if he is made to accept unequivocally his dual identity as a *Steppenwolf* and to project it playfully into the detached magic of art" (79–80).

The mirror in the Magic Theater exhibits a double nature: on one level it reproduces its subject in a symbolic design, but it also refracts a single object in multiple parts. It becomes a stage on which figures act as if they were performing a show of the imagination, and where actors and spectator are the same person (89). Freedman considers the movement of the narrative through a sequence of individual scenes or acts reflected in mirrors to be an important mode of lyrical progression, which, as Ziolkowski demonstrates in his discussion of the novel's musical form, has its analogy in the expansion of musical chords and in counterpoint.

> Within this musical and pictorial movement, the mirroring technique gives rise to a lyrical allegory in which the divided self is ultimately contracted with its ideal image. A book is composed in which all figures and events are reflections of the hero's soul, in which a magic disquisition and a Magic Theater are symbolic extensions of himself. (93)

Only in this ideal self with its humor, detachment, and magical imagination can the integration of the personality take place, and that can only be outside the social arena of our time. The real world Freedman sees juxtaposed with the hallucinatory in this novel has almost no part in his analysis; its postulated existence is not only irrelevant but actually detracts from the consistency of his sound argument.

Freedman returns to the problem of double perception in his contribution to a collection of essays published by Ziolkowski in 1973 ("*Person* and *Persona*: The Magic Mirrors of *Steppenwolf*"). The "persona" in this argument is the "other self" or "objectified self" of the writer as represented in the work of art. Freedman uses "person" to refer to the author, but also to the author's representative in the work of art. "But the artist who seeks to observe everything, including himself, sees and hears on two different levels — that of the person and of the persona — which are not always readily explained by one another." Freedman finds this relationship especially well developed in Thomas Mann's *Death in Venice*, where Gustav von Aschenbach,

> the *man*, views the object of his passion (the boy Tadzio) in ever higher degrees of sexual excitement. But Gustav von Aschenbach, the *artist*, converts this viewing into art . . . . The person's viewing has turned into the persona's vision and has become something distinct and detached. (155; author's italics)

Freedman identifies Harry Haller with Hesse, who repeatedly refers to himself in letters as a wolf from the steppe. "Hermann Hesse, who felt isolated and depressed, was the *person*. His Steppenwolf-protagonist Harry Haller, who played with these feelings in art, became the *persona* . . . . the *pathology* of the first became the *imagination* of the second" (160; author's emphasis). *Steppenwolf* is thus the record of a crisis transformed into art. The novel's arena "appears to be a mind in which space is created for God's voice (the 'immortals') to be heard. And Haller's pilgrimage resembles that of psychoanalytic education" (161).

By shifting from one level of insight to another, the novel also tests the internal against an external reality, and this, in turn, shifts the reader's attention from the reality of life to the reality of art (161). The interplay of life and art, person and persona, is analogous to Ziolkowski's double perception, which provides a "key to an understanding of the relationship between the biographical and formal levels of existence that Hesse juxtaposes in his novel." Yet Hesse's record of a crisis functions as a work of art precisely because "Hesse made the unconscious stratagems of the person conscious by means of various devices which replaced the external references of society and nature, familiar from so-called 'realistic' novels, with aesthetic and philosophical references." Freedman sees the tension and peculiar fascination of the book in the relationship between the person's crisis and the persona's reconstructed symbolic world (162). As seen above, that relationship between the two levels is established largely through the use of mirrors and mirroring.

The weak point in this astute and complicated argument is the presupposition based on Ziolkowski's argument of the existence of an external reality, a "real" world outside the fictional one, and the equation of the fictional Haller with Hesse, the "person in life." In my view it would be more accurate to speak of different levels of internal reality and to see Haller as a mask or "persona" of the author and part of his symbolic world, just as Hermine, Maria, Pablo, and Mozart are. All are parts of the same ideal totality, "the eternal I" or Self which Hesse believes exists beyond the "real" world. The author thus begins with his internal reality, which he projects onto, or mirrors by means of, seemingly real figures and events. These, then, are the fictive products of his imagination and symbolic representatives of the figures and forces that constitute his inner world. As Freedman argues, they reflect or mirror his inner world, or, as we saw in connection with Baumer's dissertation, they constitute a magical congruence of inner and outer worlds. Such an interpretation would agree with Freedman's statement that "psychoanalysis, which seeks to remold consciousness and explores various layers and levels of the self, fashioned many of Hesse's artistic strategies in the early 1920s and most noticeably in *Steppenwolf*" (161).

In an article appearing in the same special issue of *Monatshefte* as the essay by Schwarz discussed above, Ziolkowski considers Haller's development not as an educational process, as Schwarz does, but as a religious one. In agreement with Carlsson, Ziolkowski bases his analysis of Hesse's chiliastic vision on the three stages of development described in "Ein Stückchen Theologie." Haller is clearly in the second stage, in which the despair he suffers from the conflict of polar extremes has brought him close to taking his own life. His goal is to achieve entry into a Third Kingdom, which is analogous to the Kingdom of God or to Christ's millennial reign following his second coming, a realm in which the conflict between polar opposites will be resolved. Since this realm is eternal, it may be possible to gain access to it even now.

> It is an eternal realm of spiritual values that exists independently of the everyday world, a realm that occupies modally the same position as the Christian millennium. But instead of being a third stage in the future, it exists simultaneously with the second stage on a totally different level of being. In that realm Goethe and Novalis and Mozart still live, and by projecting himself into that other sphere Harry Haller can also enjoy the bliss of the spiritual millennium. (Ziolkowski 1961, 202)

Haller fails in the end to escape everyday reality into the eternal realm, for that is possible only in death, but in his awareness of its existence and promise he does find consolation and the determination to continue living and striving to attain it.

Two comprehensive studies dealing with Hesse and his works were published in the mid-sixties: Ernst Rose's *Faith from the Abyss: Hermann Hesse's Way from Romanticism to Modernity* (1965), and Mark Boulby's influential and often cited *Hermann Hesse: His Mind and Art* (1967). Both authors want to counter the predominantly biographical approach of earlier criticism by giving greater emphasis to Hesse's artistry. Rose writes of his study:

> Our narrative will clear up many otherwise obscure allusions and will prove beyond cavil the reality of the existential problem raised in Hesse's written works. But we also hope to make the reader aware at the outset of the essentially aesthetic context in which this problem is raised, and of the essentially artistic logic which prompted Hesse to make use of his personal experiences and reminiscences. (2)

And Boulby declares:

> The argument of this book proceeds from two premises: the first that there is in Hesse's work a more complex, and more coherent, set of structural patterns than has yet been shown; and second, that a satisfactory insight into these symbolic structures is possible only if the early writings, especially *Peter Camenzind* and *Beneath the Wheel*, are taken fully into account. (v)

Both authors combine the findings of previous scholarship with their own original insights. Since it is not feasible in the present study to consider every nuance of the interpretation of particular images, symbols, or figures, the identification of all possible influences or parallels, or every shift in emphasis or focus, I will limit my discussion of these and similar books and articles to elements that relate to basic interpretive problems or that constitute substantially new insights and possibilities for further development.

Both Rose and Boulby accept and make use of Ziolkowski's analysis of the musical form of *Steppenwolf*, though Boulby thinks Hesse's remark on the novel's musical form "leads to a deeper level of interpretation than this; the novel dances" (162). Both authors also appear to accept Ziolkowski's postulate of a double perspective, though some of their own arguments and conclusions qualify or contradict it. Rose asserts, for example, that "the world of Hesse's novels has no existence outside of the writer's soul" (158), and that Hesse departs from realism in his mature works (51–52). In his view, the proper designation for Hesse's contrapuntal style would be Surrealism, "if by Surrealism is meant the employing of real objects to express non-objective experiences" (55). The style of *Steppenwolf* and *Morgenlandfahrt* reminds Rose of paintings by Paul Klee or Marc Chagall: "we face here a world which is not fully obeying the laws of reality, but is rather moving in its own magic orbits. Whenever Hesse wanted to describe his vocation from this time on, he introduced himself as a 'magician'" (56). Rose's application of the double perspective to Hermine's functioning on a conscious and a subconscious level, however, reverts to the "real" perspective his previous argument had undermined.

Of the editor's preface, which is the most realistic part of *Steppenwolf*, Boulby writes: "Whether the existence of the introduction in *The Steppenwolf* actually results in an intensification of the novel's realism is open to doubt, as it is in the case of *Demian*; the introduction equally (or correspondingly) has a distancing, depersonalizing effect" (163). The Treatise goes much further than the introduction in "objectifying and universalizing" Haller's problems, and, finally, Haller's notes, which are "only for madmen," contain nothing from the same level of reality as that described in the prosaic introduction" (173). Boulby discerns not two but several levels of reality and, like Rose, a movement from the real to the "superreal." Concerning Hermine, Boulby writes: "Just how far one should go . . . in assigning the prostitute Hermine to the 'real' world and the ideal Hermine (and all her mantic utterances) to Harry's projective imagination is an uncertain matter." After considering her function on different levels, Boulby concludes that

> there is without doubt a great deal in the view, which Harry himself asserts, that many of the utterances of Hermine and Pablo are but projections of his own higher self; the constant emphasis [by Ziolkowski] upon the change of level . . . must charitably be interpreted as a deliberate pointer to the 'double perception' on which the novel is based and not as the uneasy effort to remedy a sensed weakness of composition. (187–88)

With the emphasis they place on psychoanalysis, and especially on Jung, Rose and Boulby come close to describing an approach or developing an explanation that would obviate the need to defend Hesse's craftsmanship by postulating a double perspective, but neither author quite reaches the conclusion that would in fact be consistent with their interpretations.

Despite his disparagement of attempts to interpret literature in half-understood psychoanalytic terms and his admitted lack of knowledge in this area, Rose recognizes the importance of psychoanalysis for Hesse and undertakes to use Jungian concepts in his interpretation. He identifies Hermine with Haller's "double and 'shadow,'" for example, though in Jung's psychology Haller's shadow would be masculine, and he sees her as the personification of Haller's suppressed lower self on the unconscious or symbolic level. More appropriate is his identification of Hermine with the Jungian "anima," but his equation of the anima with libido, which Haller unsuccessfully attempts to suppress when he kills her (92), is not accurate: the "mana" possessed by the Jungian anima is not the same as libido. (See Jung 1966, CW 7:227–241.)

With greater understanding of Jung's concepts, Boulby correctly states that the first stage in Jungian analysis or in the Jungian process of individuation is confrontation with the "shadow," which is represented here by the wolf part of Haller's personality, that is, the inferior, repressed counterpart of the conscious ego or persona. Boulby also connects the wolf to what he considers to be the masochism of a frustrated saint.

> Thus the wolf may be seen in his inverted aspect as a terrible perversion of the Pietist's will-to-God, his rending of Harry Haller as a satanic variant of the struggle to destroy the Natural Man; he is, maybe, the repressed world of the mother, but he is also a bestialization of the demands of the father in Harry's heart. In his savaging of Harry, the bourgeois, he tends to represent not one extreme, but *the* extreme. (180–81)

In Boulby's view, the dissociation of the personality that occurs in Hesse's works and especially in *Steppenwolf* has its roots in his Pietistic upbringing. "The problem of the novel's form, and hence the understanding of the work as a whole, turns really upon the nature and function of the tractate," which is analogous to the Christian tracts used by Protestant missionary societies, such as the one with which Hesse's parents were associated. "None of Hesse's novels," he writes,

> is so clearly indebted to his Pietistic heritage as is *The Steppenwolf*; the form is the imposition by faith of order upon chaos, the theme is the reflections of a Pietist upon the way of life of a profligate with aspirations to sainthood. The saint, in any case, Hesse defines as one "in whose soul-state the chaos of the world is turned into meaning and music." (164)

According to the Treatise and the Magic Theater, the chaos of the dissociated personality and the masochistic destructiveness of asceticism and inverted aggression can be overcome through non-attachment or depersonalization and by "eternal surrender of the ego to metamorphosis" (182). A person who has achieved that state can reconstruct the personality at will and can thereby achieve an infinite variety in of life (196).

As the "anima" or projected embodiment of the soul, Hermine's function is to lead Haller beyond the split between bourgeois and wolf to deeper layers of the unconscious. Boulby identifies the goal as the Third Kingdom of the Spirit, and he compares Haller's deep noetic state to the "world of the child and the *Märchen*, both of which are the sphere of the hermaphrodite" (191), which is to say, of Hermine, who is hermaphroditic. By awakening his sensuality and ability to love and play, Hermine frees him from his destructive asceticism and from the error of dualistic thinking, which derive from the delusion that the personality is a unity (180–81). His murder of her, which is committed in a dream, indicates that he has failed to achieve that higher level and has reverted instead to his bourgeois self (199). "The senses are denied by the very language in which the acceptance of sensual experience is enjoined." It is the "eternity of the father which here finds its form" (204).

Boulby sees parallels between *Steppenwolf* and Goethe's *West-östlicher Divan*: "both glorify the temporary resurgence of potency, both unite the mystical and the sensual in a peculiar blend and above all both are hermaphroditic in their innermost sense and structure" (191–92). If I understand his argument correctly, Boulby identifies hermaphroditism with the undifferentiated state of childhood and other states of potential transformation or metamorphosis. From Haller's statement:

> For she talked to me about Hermann and about childhood, mine and her own, and about those years of childhood when the capacity for love, in its first youth, embraces not only both sexes, but all and everything, sensuous and spiritual, and endows all things with a spell of love and a fairylike ease of transformation such as in later years comes again only to a chosen few and to poets, and to them rarely (St 190),

Boulby concludes that "transvestism is the Steppenwolfian form of metamorphosis" (191). If Haller is to undergo a metamorphosis, however, it cannot be through a regressive return to the world of childhood and Märchen, that is, through reentry into the First Kingdom, which is not possible in Hesse's scheme; it must take place through the overcoming of polarity on the higher level of the Third Kingdom through the attainment of humor.

Independent of Boulby, whose book is not included in his bibliography, and in agreement with Schwarz, whom he does cite, Henry Hatfield stresses the significance for *Steppenwolf* of psychoanalysis and Jung, who "was a far more appropriate guide for a romantic like Hesse than Freud would have been" (1969, 75). Like Schwarz and others, Hatfield also considers *Steppenwolf* to be in the tradition of the *Bildungsroman*, which Hesse and Thomas Mann revive by introducing parody, myth, and, in Hesse's case, Jungian symbolism. But since, as Schwarz pointed out, Haller must undergo a reverse development in an attempt to be rejuvenated and reborn, he is more like Faust than Wilhelm Meister (64).

Hatfield views the Treatise as the work of an astute physician or psychoanalyst, and the Magic Theater as a "carefully worked out allegory of psychoanalytic treatment: despite his resistance, the subject is led to relive his past, dramatize his aggression, and so forth" (65, 72). The many souls mentioned in the Treatise are equivalent to Jung's archetypes, of which Hermine, Maria, and Pablo are embodiments. Of the symbolic murder of Hermine, Haller's "anima," "other self," and, less accurately, "alter ego," Hatfield writes:

> Apparently the point is not so much that "each man kills the thing he loves," although it is relevant that killing Hermine is a form of partial suicide; it is rather that a man must "interiorize" his anima; that is, he must

come to understand its nature as an image, not an autonomous personality, and thus "overcome" it by dealing with it consciously and rationally. (76)

The hoped for outcome of the psychoanalytic treatment of the Magic Theater is catharsis, and Haller does seem purged at the end of the "performance," just as Hesse may have experienced a catharsis in writing it. Like Hesse, Haller had to learn "not to sulk like a child, not to brood but to find joy in the moment, and above all to laugh," and no longer to find masochistic satisfaction in isolation (69). Hesse's great talent is manifest in his ability to transform the impressions and reactions he describes and expresses in his "Crisis" poems into "the most challenging of his novels" (67).

In a study published the same year as Hatfield's, Dorrit Cohn analyzes the narrative technique used by Hesse to achieve this transformation. Because "external reality appears largely as a reflection or projection of the self," she writes, *Steppenwolf* might be considered a "mononovel" like Rilke's *Malte Laurids Brigge* and Sartre's *La Nausée*, though it differs from them in its use of a retrospective view rather than the immediacy of a diary. In *Steppenwolf* we have the "unusual case of a first-person narrator who is extensively involved in the narration of his own past thoughts." By "barring from the language all elements that draw attention to the verbal gesture of narration itself, and thereby to the temporal distance separating the past from the present self," and by introducing into the language elements of extreme tension and pathos, such as exclamatory phrases, rhetorical questions, repetitions, and parallel constructions, Hesse is able to capture Haller's "hyperactive consciousness as a 'presence' despite the continuous use of the past tense" (Cohn 1969, 121–22).

This style is similar to what is called in German *erlebte Rede*, which Cohn translates as "narrated monologue". The narrated monologue renders the immediate consciousness of fictional figures in a third person narrative. The analogous technique in a first person narrative might be called the "self-narrated monologue," according to Cohn. Where the technique of the interior monologue is used to express the figure's consciousness in past time, it must be located in the past by some introductory phrase such as "I said to myself." Through its consistent use of the past tense, by contrast, the self-narrated monologue does not require explicit introduction or quotation. Descriptions of outer reality can blend with subjective responses without any indication of self-quotation; scene, gestures, and thoughts conjoin continuously (122–23).

Another mode for rendering the consciousness of a fictional figure is the use of internal analysis. This is "the most indirect method, in that a narrating voice may be heard recounting and explaining the inner life of the character" (123). Cohn identifies several passages in which Hesse uses internal analysis in an analytic manner. By far the most extended example is the Treatise, in which Haller is analyzed from outside and above in the third person. "If we regard this treatise as a product of Haller's own mind — and Ziolkowski has shown that there are excellent reasons for doing so — then it would present the most extreme and extended example of the analytic point of view in the novel" (125–26).In the scene from the Magic Theater entitled "Wunder der Dressur [Marvelous Taming of the Steppenwolf], in which Harry is both spectator and dramatis persona, self-analysis in the third person attains symbolic representation (126). Other instances of internal analysis occur when the "narrator describes his mental situation over a long period of time, compressing a long 'erzählte Zeit' [narrated time] into a brief 'Erzählzeit' [narrative time]."

From the use of temporal indicators in the narrative, Cohn establishes that the narrator's

> temporal zero point . . . in self-narrated monologues and their surrounding context [is] not the day on which he records his past, but the past day he records: conclusive proof that this idiom — like its third-person analogue — plunges the reader into the here and now of the experiencing consciousness, transforming the past tense into a virtual present. (127)

The self-narrated monologue is also able to create within a text in the past tense the feeling of a true, unknown future. The devices used to this end are questions ("Must I really experience this yet again?"), the many uses of *würde* [would] constructions, and the conditional modal *mögen* [may] ("Whoever this clever and mysterious girl may be . . . ") (128). The use of these syntactic patterns indicates the persistence of the narrator in relinquishing his present vantage point and surrendering to his past self. According to Cohn, "the tone of this verbal empathy is marked by many of the stylistic traits associated with *Pathos*: overemphases, repetitions, exclamations, syntactical tensions and complicated rhythmic configurations" (129).

As Pablo and Mozart repeatedly tell him, it is precisely this pathos that Haller must overcome through humor. Haller's final sentences continue to be fraught with pathos; he has not changed.

In a study of "Hesse's Use of *Gilgamesh*-Motifs in the Humanization of Siddhartha and Harry Haller" (1969), Kenneth Hughes concludes that Haller does change, that he is humanized in the same way Enkidu, the wild man of the Babylonian epic, is: through the power and influence of a woman and sexuality. What is portrayed in the Bible as a "fall" that results in the loss of paradise is depicted in the epic as a positive development from an animal to a human state. In the introduction to a translation of *The Gilgamesh Epic*, which Hesse reviewed in 1916 (WA 12:15), Hugo Gressmann refers to Enkidu as a "Steppenwesen" who is transformed from a "Natur-wesen" (natural being) into a "Kulturwesen" (cultivated being). He is "raised to a higher level through his experience of sexual and moral knowl-edge," and he can now distinguish good from evil (132).

Haller and Siddhartha resemble Enkidu in the process of individuation they undergo under the influence of courtesans, but they differ from him and from the Biblical Adam in that these encounters are not their first and therefore take place on the second level of Hesse's tripartite pattern of de-velopment, in the Second Kingdom, rather than in the paradisiacal first. Ac-cording to Hughes, Hesse's heroes "achieve their higher innocence — indeed, their innocence *is* higher — only because they do not follow the path of traditional religious teaching, but rather the path of the *Gilgamesh* epic" (140). Perhaps "innocence" is not the right designation for what Hesse's heroes achieve on the second level, which is the level of knowledge and despair, a difficult and painful existential state that Hesse's heroes must endure but strive to transcend.

Works Cited

Böttcher, Margot. "Aufbau und Form von Hermann Hesses *Steppenwolf,* *Morgenlandfahrt* und *Glasperlenspiel.*" Ph.D. diss., Humboldt University, Berlin, 1948.

Boulby, Mark. *Hermann Hesse: His Mind and Art.* Ithaca: Cornell U P, 1967.

Cohn, Dorrit. "Narration of Consciousness in *Der Steppenwolf.*" *Germanic Review* 44 (1969): 121–31.

Dürr, Werner. *Hermann Hesse: Vom Wesen der Musik in der Dichtung.* Stuttgart: Silberberg, 1957.

Field, G. W. *Hermann Hesse.* New York: Twayne Publishers, 1970; New York: Hippocrene Books, 1972.

Freedman, Ralph. "*Person* and *Persona*: the Magic Mirrors of *Steppenwolf.*" In *Hesse: A Collection of Critical Essays,* ed. Theodore Ziolkowski, 153–79. Englewood Cliffs, N.J.: Prentice Hall, 1973.

Freedman, Ralph W. B. *The Lyrical Novel: Studies in Hermann Hesse, André Gide and Virginia Woolf.* Princeton: Princeton U P, 1963.

Hatfield, Henry. "Accepting the Universe: Hermann Hesse's *Steppenwolf.*" Chap. in *Crisis and Continuity in Modern German Fiction: Ten Essays.* Ithaca: Cornell U P, 1969.

Hughes, Kenneth. "Hesse's Use of *Gilgamesh*-Motifs in the Humanization of Siddhartha and Harry Haller." *Seminar* 5 (1969): 129–40.

Jung, C. G. *Two Essays on Analytical Psychology.* Vol. 7, *The Collected Works of C. G. Jung.* Princeton: Princeton U P, 1966.

Mileck, Joseph. *Hermann Hesse and His Critics: The Criticism and Bibliography of Half a Century.* Chapel Hill: U of North Carolina P, 1958.

Mileck, Joseph. *Hermann Hesse: Biography and Bibliography.* 2 vols. Berkeley: U of California P., 1977.

Rose, Ernst. *Faith from the Abyss: Hermann Hesse's Way from Romanticism to Modernity.* New York: New York U P, 1965.

Schmid, Max. *Hermann Hesse: Weg und Wandlung.* With a biographical appendix by Armin Lemp. Zurich: Fretz & Wasmuth, 1947.

Schwarz, Egon. "Zur Erklärung von Hesses 'Steppenwolf.'" *Monatshefte* 53 (1961): 191–98. Translated as "Hermann Hesse: *Steppenwolf (1927)*" in *Reflection and Action: Essays on the Bildungsroman*, ed. James Hardin, 382–414. Columbia: U of South Carolina P, 1991.

Ziolkowski, Theodore. "Hermann Hesse's Chiliastic Vision." *Monatshefte* 53 (1961): 199–210.

Ziolkowski, Theodore. *Dimensions of the Modern Novel: German Texts and European Contexts.* Princeton: Princeton U P, 1969.

Ziolkowski, Theodore. "Hermann Hesse's *Steppenwolf:* A Sonata in Prose." *Modern Language Quarterly* 19 (1958): 115–33; Rpt. in Liebmann 1977, 90–109. Rev. rpt. in Ziolkowski 1965, ch. 9.

Ziolkowski, Theodore. *The Novels of Hermann Hesse: A Study in Theme and Structure.* Princeton: Princeton U P, 1965.

4: Development and Consolidation

In 1970 Egon Schwarz wrote that the previous decades of literary scholarship on Hesse had been dominated by variants of a single approach variously identified as *"explication de texte, werkimmanente Strukturanalyse,* close reading, criticism, and interpretation" (1970, 980). His claim a decade later that a person would have to have unusual historical sensitivity to be able to recognize distinct periods in the academic reception of Hesse's work (1980, 113) implies the continuity of that scholarly perspective and methodological approach. With some exceptions, the statement still holds true. German scholarship in Germany and America has not followed the succession of critical fads in the same way critical writing on French, English, and comparative literature has. German scholars pioneered in the development of reception theory, but in general the German tradition of hermeneutics has remained predominant, able as it is to assimilate the findings of other approaches in an ongoing process of interpretation.

While the approach identified by Schwarz continued to prevail in the seventies and beyond, a distinction can nevertheless be made between criticism published in the sixties and that of the following period, beginning in the early seventies, when the heady freshness of exploding popular and critical reception gave way to official recognition and acceptance, when some critics subjected the entire Hesse phenomenon to critical scrutiny and students began to lose interest in a figure being co-opted by the establishment.

By this time Hesse had been included in the English curriculum of high school and college English courses; unlike the German professors who had offered courses on Hesse, usually at the request of students, the English teachers were not familiar with Hesse's background or with the tradition in which his work is imbedded. To provide them and their students with such information and to help with the analysis and interpretation of the texts, commentaries, interpretations, and collections of critical writings and documentary material were published. Monarch Press, for example, published seven titles, including one on *Steppenwolf* by John D. Simons (1972), in its series of Monarch Notes, which provide plot summary along with notes and bibliography. The two favorite novels of young readers were dealt with together in *Steppenwolf and Siddhartha: Notes* by Carolyn Roberts Welch (1973), which appeared in the series of Cliff's Notes, and in *Hermann Hesse's "Steppenwolf" and "Siddhartha"* by Ruth Goode, which was added to Barron's Educational Series in 1985. The more Hesse entered the cultural mainstream and became the object of commercial and academic exploitation, the more he lost his appeal to the rebellious members of the counterculture who had discovered him and made him into a cult hero.

By identifying authors who may have influenced Hesse or works that are similar to his, some critical studies from this period attempt to establish Hesse's position in the context of world literature. Taking their cue from his essays on Dostoevsky, for example, some writers compare figures from Hesse's critical period with similar figures in Dostoevsky's novels. Others compare Hesse's works with the German writers he admired such as Goethe, Novalis, Hoffmann, Jean Paul, and Stifter, or with contemporaries or near contemporaries who deal with similar themes such as Kafka, D. H. Lawrence, and Max Frisch.

Since Hesse's astonishing popular reception was as much a sociological and psychological phenomenon as a literary event, it was documented, described, analyzed, and criticized by journalists and critics in popular periodicals and scholarly journals. Hesse's publisher Suhrkamp was proud to document his international reception and to list the translations of his works into many languages. The first of three such volumes appeared on the anniversary of Hesse's hundredth birthday in 1977; others followed in 1979 and 1991. As will be seen in this chapter, some authors dealing with reception attempted to understand and explain Hesse's appeal, others sought to undermine and warn against it.

Some scholars have been impressed by the unity of Hesse's oeuvre taken as a whole and have investigated major themes and motifs that recur in them, such as the nature-spirit dichotomy, death, education, the role of women, and manifestations of Eastern religion and philosophy. Academic conferences have been devoted to particular facets of Hesse's thought such as politics, religion, and music. The results of these investigations will be included here only insofar as they contribute to the scholarship on *Steppenwolf*.

In a published Australian dissertation Marga Lange undertakes an existentialist interpretation, which is based on the "Heideggerian assumption that man exists only in terms of his relations to the world, and that man must be studied as a whole, as a 'Gestalt'" (1970, 3).[1] Because of the variety of forms it has taken, Lange does not attempt to define existentialism, but she does identify, some commonality among the existentialists, including Hesse, such as their individualism, their subjectivity, and their reflection about the meaning of human existence, freedom, and God (4). Lange's interpretation, which is based on close textual analysis, focuses on *Daseinsproblematik*, the problem of how one is to live in the world.

[1]Lange does not mention the earlier existentialist interpretations by Unseld, Seidlin, and others, but her study has a different focus and is more extensive and detailed.

According to Lange, Harry Haller suffers from an identity crisis or an existential crisis, just as Hesse did at the time of his psychoanalysis. He shares the existentialist's awareness of the absurdity of human endeavor, and he feels "ontological guilt" for having neglected his true "subjective self" in favor of his "false self system." His self is divided between the wolf in him, which represents his authentic self, and the bourgeois, which is existentially "unauthentic." The authentic part of Haller agrees with Nietzsche's condemnation of the herd as represented by the bourgeoisie and with his advocacy of self-transcendence, self-fulfillment, and subjective experience (7–17). The Treatise, which "may be regarded as a sophisticated piece of existential psychoanalysis of Haller and of 'the Outsider' in general," is the product of Harry's unconscious and foreshadows the course his development must take if he is to find a resolution for his crisis and achieve authenticity, which requires that he have the courage to be himself (22–23).

Existentialist psychoanalysis has a similar aim: its concern is not with the individual's successful adjustment to his culture, which requires the sacrifice of one's being in an attempt to relieve symptoms, but rather with enabling the patient to realize his being fully. Awareness is only part of the process, which must also include action if the individual is to achieve his full potential (30–31). Action also involves one's relatedness to others. Haller feels alienated and alone in the bourgeois world. His relationships to its members are unauthentic; they can be characterized in Martin Buber's terms as "I-it" rather than "I-thou." He does achieve an authentic relationship with Hermine, however, and, through her, with her anti-bourgeois friends (39–42). Lange sees Pablo as a symbol of nature, which is what Haller, who represents *Geist*, has denied and suppressed in himself. In killing Hermine, he reveals his "inability as yet to harmonize and affirm *all* aspects of his sensuous self, and to reject *all* bourgeois inhibitions and judgements" (50; author's italics). But despite this failure, Haller, unlike the bourgeois, has learned "to take existential responsibility for his own self, and his choices" (56).

Harry resembles other existentialist figures in his metaphysical alienation, his estrangement from the universe and from meaning, that is, in his experience of what Heidegger calls *Geworfenheit*. He has experienced nothingness and absurdity and does so again after the murder of Hermine. Yet Haller and Hesse possess a faith and optimism that is uncharacteristic of other existentialists. To borrow a term from the existentialist psychologist A. H. Maslow, the "peak experiences" Haller has on occasion, those moments in which he is aware of the "golden trace" of transcendence, give repeated nourishment to his hope and faith and sustain him with the intuition of transcendence and cosmic harmony as represented by the Immortals and as expressed through humor and laughter (60–69). Furthermore, he has overcome his "divided self," as defined by existentialist psychologist R. D.

Laing, and has achieved "a position of *authentic Selfhood*. In the latter state, Haller's self-knowledge has expanded sufficiently for him to accept and experience all his multiple, subjective Selves" (74; author's italics). In his isolation he achieves communication, relatedness, and even love in the world of Hermine and her friends. He has learned to behave more spontaneously and to move from a position of inaction and passivity to a more abundant life of action. "Perhaps the only direction in which Haller does not develop," Lange writes, "is in his relationship to his culture and society." He remains an outsider (80–81).

The development from a state of unauthenticity to Selfhood is seen by Edward Alfred Farrer, in a 1975 dissertation comparing Hesse and D. H. Lawrence, to be characteristic of the romantic hero, who continues to preoccupy both writers in an era of literary anti-heroes. At a time when old systems of symbols no longer give meaning to life, such a hero's quest to find his identity and thereby to establish his place in a system of absolute values becomes more difficult than ever before. With reference to Joseph Campbell's *The Hero with a Thousand Faces*, Farrer identifies four stages in the hero's life, the first when he renounces his present situation and sets off in search of something better, the second when he finds a guide or mentor who provides an intellectual framework for his quest, the third when he achieves heroic status through an experience of being itself, an experience of enlightenment analogous to the mystic's moment of truth, and the fourth when he recognizes the implications of his experience for his integration into the world (6–12).

As he contemplates suicide, Haller is clearly dissatisfied with himself and his relations to the world. The unauthenticity of his dualistic view of himself is revealed by the Treatise, which challenges him to begin his quest for a more authentic identity. He gains further insight and assistance from the mentor figures Hermine, Maria, and Pablo. After he learns from Hermine what is required to transform his life, he must free himself from her, as he does through the symbolic murder, and continue the quest on his own: further submission to her would be a hindrance and deterrent to his quest. Haller is still bound by the shackles of his bourgeois life and cannot let himself go. He gains the insight that it is not his fate to be happy; it is more important that his life be fruitful and productive (70–71, 121–23). To that end he must externalize the internal world and its images, which he has experienced through his mentors and especially in the Magic Theater. The inner world, which is the goal of the hero's quest, represents a centering and establishes a meaning which were missing in Haller's life at the beginning of the narrative (137–38, 163–65).

Among the investigations of a particular problematic throughout Hesse's works is Christian Immo Schneider's *Das Todesproblem bei Her-*

mann Hesse, (Hermann Hesse and the Problem of Death, 1973). With proper acknowledgment, Schneider looks at many of the same symbols Gontrum listed in his 1958 dissertation, but in each case he makes the connection to death or to the formless state of unity from which life arises and to which it returns. Both fire and water, for example, have deep religious and mythological roots in rites and beliefs associated with birth and death, and both are symbolic expressions for Hesse of the mystical unity of opposites and of purification. They come together in mythical thinking about erotic love, but each has its particular area of symbolic meaning and its special feeling tone (99–103).

With respect to Haller, Schneider notes that Hesse's "metaphysical theory of death" agrees with Jung's concept of individuation. Suicides or potential suicides are sufferers from the feelings of guilt caused by individuation (162). Anxiety, love, and death can be considered stages through which people must pass on the path to the Self (170). Haller passes through these stages, the latter represented by the Magic Theater, another symbol or manifestation of totality and the integration of opposites, and he is able to expand his overly intellectual self and to emerge or be reborn "as a healed, transformed, and totally individualized person," who now knows himself and the world (164).

Schneider also discusses Hesse's and Haller's pessimistic view of culture in this context. They see the decline of culture in the deterioration of language and literature and in the introduction of primitive influences in art and music. Yet, as Hesse makes clear in his essays on Dostoevsky, this development is part of a natural cycle: Western man must return again to the chaos and lack of differentiation Hesse sees manifest in Dostoevsky's "Russian man," that is, to the mother, to Asia, to the sources, to the Faustian Mothers. One must die, as it were, to be reborn and to begin anew (245–57).

In "Who Wrote the 'Tractat vom Steppenwolf?'" (1973) Lynn Dhority addresses a question to which some critics have given answers but which none has discussed in detail. Dhority identifies three positions critics have taken: (1) the author of the Treatise remains unidentifiable; (2) the author is one of the Immortals; (3) the Treatise is a product of Haller's own imagination. Boulby, Rose, and others have taken the second position. The third, according to Dhority, is the only one that has been argued at any length, namely, by Ziolkowski, albeit with insufficient evidence. If the Treatise is the product of Haller's fantasy, that is, an hallucination, as Ziolkowski claims, then so likewise is the whole narrative, according to Dhority, but this position is refuted by the editor's preface, which speaks for the reality of the narrated events — a reality Ziolkowski accepts in his postulate of two levels. Ziolkowski's argument is also undermined by the difference in style and tone between the cool, objective irony and omniscient perspective of the Treatise and the confessional outpouring of Haller's narrative: they cannot have been written by the same person, Dhority concludes (60–61).

According to Dhority, Beda Allemann took the first position in an article published in 1961, but this simplification does not do justice to Allemann's argument. Allemann points out that the author of the Treatise knows both more and less about Haller than Harry does himself. He appears to be above the matter, objectively holding out a mirror in which Harry can see himself (Allemann 318). His superiority does not lie in his possession of absolute knowledge, however, but in his impartiality and reasoned approach to the danger which Haller only dimly perceives and intuits.

> The voice of a doctor speaks from the Treatise, a doctor who dares to apply the scalpel, although he knows that the procedure is painful and life-threatening. In some passages one can even identify this doctor with a psychoanalyst from the school of C. G. Jung. Indebted to depth psychology is above all the thought that a curative effect can already be achieved by making half-repressed contents conscious and by integrating the wolf elements into the personality. (Allemann 322)

In this view, the Magic Theater is intimately connected to the Treatise, at the conclusion of which it is mentioned and anticipated, in that it provides the opportunity to bring repressed contents into consciousness and to achieve the attitude of humor, which the Treatise advocates (322).

In Dhority's view, on the other hand, Haller entirely misses the point of the Treatise, which is to educate him, and with him the reader, about the problem of the outsider and about a possible solution to that problem. As indicated by his comparison of a poem he wrote with the Treatise, Haller is "remarkably insensitive to the complexity of the picture of himself" revealed in the latter (Dhority 61). Furthermore, by concluding that the Steppenwolf must die, Haller demonstrates that he has failed to understand the Treatise's message with regard to the significance of humor and self-distance. Nor does he change through his experience in the Magic Theater, which

> culminates not in self-transcendence but in self-destruction, for Haller's final act, the murder of Hermine, his alter ego and mirror-image, may be understood as a vicarious suicide. In finally succumbing symbolically to his long-harbored death wish, Haller is more true to character than in his last lines. His actions speak louder than his words of hope. (64)

Dhority sees an unresolved tension in the novel between Hesse's longing for a social reality into which Haller can be integrated — an elite brotherhood on the order of the Society of the Tower in Goethe's *Wilhelm Meister*, as Egon Schwarz has pointed out — and the reality of Haller's situation as a modern man (63). Hesse's ambiguity on this is reflected in the discrepancy between the "comprehensible, meaningful frame of reference" postulated in the Treatise and the questionable end of the hero. It is also revealed in the lack of clarity as to who wrote and is responsible for the Treatise.

> Neither the world of the Treatise nor that of Harry Haller dominates at the end of the novel, and it is this mood of irresolution which gives both the Treatise and the work as a whole a certain contrariety, which is in part responsible for the novel's uneasy place among Hesse's works. (64–65)

Readers who do not have that sense of uneasiness and who can accept Hesse's statement on the optimistic content of the novel may incline more to Allemann's explanation of the Treatise's authorship.

Volker Knüfermann agrees with Dhority that Hesse faces and does not resolve the problem of attempting to describe modern reality with language and concepts from a different time and a different social, historical context. Knüfermann refers to the comparison made by Schwarz and Dhority of the Magic Theater with the Society of the Tower in *Wilhelm Meister* and of Haller with Faust, and he concurs with Dhority's conclusion that

> Hesse's problem in wanting to set the drama of his hero against a background of comprehensibility and meaning, much as Goethe had done for his seeker in the 'Prologue in Heaven' in *Faust*, is that he is writing one hundred years after Goethe and can no longer rely even metaphysically on such universals as Heaven, God, and the Devil. Hesse betrays his modernity in his inability to provide such a framework unambiguously. (Knüfermann 1979, 279)

In Knüfermann's view, Hesse uses language and terminology which derive from the "area of pietistic-bourgeois education [Bildung]" and, like Faust's metaphysical universals and Wilhelm Meister's humane social organization, no longer have validity or relevance for Haller. In fact, Haller's neurosis, and the neurosis of the transitional period in which he lives, is at least in part a result of the discrepancy between language and content. Haller and Hesse face the dilemma of presenting linguistic and conceptual coherence without believing in the validity of the concepts they use and without being able to produce their own context in this language. "Herein lies both the linguistic and the thematic aporia of the novel" (278–79).

Lack of clarity in the novel with regard to spirit and intellectuality (*Geist* and *Geistigkeit*) is a case in point: "what we learn about it eludes exact comprehension because of circular or tautological argumentation" (280). The novel's editor repeatedly refers to Haller as an intellectual, but he gives no clear idea as to what he means by that term: it is supposedly visible in Haller's appearance and manifest in the fact that he has thought more than

other people, that he exhibits the attributes of "calm objectivity" and
"certainty of thought and knowledge, such as only really intellectual men
have," that his look "pierced our whole epoch . . . the whole superficial play
of a shallow, opinionated intellectuality" and "went right to the heart of all
humanity," so that he recognized "what monkeys we are!" what "monkey
tricks" our "intelligence, all the attainments of the spirit, all progress towards the sublime" (St 9–10). With every crisis of his life, Harry notes in his
records, he has gained "in freedom, in intellect, in depth," but these qualities are not defined. These terms are bound to a formally closed system that
operates with opposites such as surface and depth, thinking and not thinking; they reveal little about the content of that thought as it corresponds to
Haller's new experiences and modern perspective (280).

Knüfermann finds a similar lack of clarity and specificity in Haller's observations on music and culture. Compared to the true and authentic music
represented by Mozart, jazz is "eine Schweinerei" (a dirty mess) and
"Scheinkultur" (mock culture). A similar relationship between contemporary products and works of the past obtain for literature. But Haller never
defines his criterion for determining what is authentic and real, and what
unauthentic and illusory. "Intellectuality, authenticity, reality are determined here by a philosophic-religious perspective," a perspective which is
no longer natural for Haller, but which he applies nevertheless to criticize
modern music and culture. Haller's vocabulary suggests the continuity of a
reliable system of language and thought, but since the context has changed,
his words and concepts become purely relational and no longer allow for
definite orientation. Harry uses these positive terms in an attempt to avoid
confronting his lack of orientation in a world that has lost its meaning
(281).

Again and again the gulf between the Christian, philosophic connota-
tions of terms relating to "spirit" conflict with Haller's skeptical experiences.
Hermine sees him and herself as "children of the devil," because they possess spirit and have "fallen out of nature and hang suspended in space." She
intends to free him from his "ascetic intellectuality" and illusions and lead
him back to nature, yet she also compliments him on his being versed in the
"the deepest and most beautiful" things, namely, "spirit, art, and thought"
(St 144). Likewise, the goal defined for him by the Immortals is to join
them in the cosmic realm of truth and spirit. Haller comes to accept Pablo
and his jazz music, but he never changes his mind about the superiority of
the true cultural figures who represent, albeit in diverse and undefined ways,
higher forms of spirit.

Because Haller does not develop a new language, Knüfermann concludes, his attempt to free himself from the content of Christian, bourgeois
culture cannot entirely succeed. The contradictory meanings of concepts are

disorienting and cause Haller to vacillate between the optimistic hope of understanding the Immortals and thoughts of suicide awakened by his despairing recognition of the futility of all intellectual endeavor. Rather than achieve a breakthrough to the laughter of the Immortals, which is based on their identity with themselves and their language, he remains neurotically bound to repetitive cycles of behavior determined by the conventions of the bourgeois society he despises (283).

In a contribution to the history of the reception of Hesse's works, Andrew Hollis deals with the problems caused by the ambiguity or ambivalence in Hesse's *political* statements, an ambiguity he relates to the aesthetic ambiguity of the double perspective described by Ziolkowski. He begins by wondering why Hesse, an avowed pacifist and anti-nationalist, was tolerated by the National Socialists; in particular, what is it in *Steppenwolf* that could have encouraged readers allied with Hitler and fascism to continue celebrating Hesse. Hollis notes that romantic, existentialist, and *völkisch* thought have some elements in common which are also characteristic of Haller's thinking, such as his "catastrophe-mindedness," which is manifest in his condemnation of jazz as music of decline (*Untergangsmusik*), in his apparent agreement with Gustav's claim that "this world must be destroyed," in his Romantic, retrograde rejection of capitalism and technology, and in his belief that his era lacks *Geist* (1978a, 112).

More significant from a political point of view are his "anti-bourgeois affections and the 'philosophy' he builds up around them" (110–12). The author of the Treatise scorns the laws and political system of the bourgeoisie and even suggests that some people are expendable. Whether or not so intended by Hesse, Hollis concludes, reactionaries may see their beliefs affirmed by these and other ambiguous and open-ended pronouncements (113).

The same may be said of Hesse's use of the *dritte Reich* (usually translated as "Third Kingdom" in Hesse's works to avoid association with Nazi Germany), a term used by Möller van den Bruck in his 1923 book of that title to describe a higher, harmonious synthesis of the conflicting forces besetting Germany, conflicts arising from differences of confession, region, and class. In Hesse's use of humor Hollis sees a synthesizing function on the individual level that is analogous to the collective synthesis van den Bruck envisions for his Third Reich (117). Humor is politically ambivalent because it affirms everything, implies the overcoming of opposites, and requires no action, no attempt to change the world. Even Haller's attacks on nationalism and war are equivocal, Hollis maintains: following his confrontation with the professor Haller rebukes himself and thinks the professor may represent the "moral world" and is to be envied (114). Likewise, at the end of the "Marvelous Training of the Steppenwolf" Haller concludes that, although he is a "humanely minded opponent of war," he had been "silly and childish" to have been horrified by pictures of war casualties and to have condemned the generals, since he has the potential in himself to act as they had (115; St 224). Haller desires to become humanized, which demands, as Pablo says with regard to making music, the attainment of maximum intensity as well as "total dedication to personal truth, to authenticity, no matter where it may lead." According to Hollis, Hitler would have agreed with this view (117–18).

To compare Hesse with Hitler or Hesse's thought with the ideology of the Third Reich is certainly unjust. A discussion of this subject would have to be based on detailed analysis of documentary evidence rather than on the mere observation of what appears on the surface to be congruence between elements of Nazi ideology and isolated thoughts and opinions of Hesse's characters. The desire for a state of harmony and wholeness, for example, is as old as religion; it is the essence of all mysticism, and it underlies religious and mythical postulates of an original paradisiacal state and of chiliasm. If one's only criterion for comparison is the desire for wholeness, then the Third Reich of Möller van den Bruck and the National Socialists, the Communist utopia, the Christian millennium, and Plato's Republic may all be considered "parallel" to each other as well as to Hesse's use of humor or his realm of the Immortals. Each set of ideas must be seen and interpreted in its complete context.

Furthermore, the fact that Hesse was still read in the Third Reich is no indication that his works conform to Nazi ideology or even that they were accepted by the Nazis. To address these questions one would have to determine which Germans were reading Hesse and why: was it the audience Hesse thought he could reach and encourage, or was it dedicated Nazis? One cannot discuss this subject without citing the hate mail Hesse received from party stalwarts and the vicious polemical condemnation of him in the fascist press, including claims that this defender of Jewish writers and husband of a Jew was himself half Jewish (see Michels 1972, 224–28; 1976, 94–99; 1992, 87–105), a threatening identification at the time. Likewise, Hollis's conclusion that Haller's attacks on nationalism and war are equivocal is based on his particular interpretation, which requires further scrutiny. Is blaming himself for his bad behavior at the professor's house really enough evidence to imply a refutation of Haller's anti-nationalist and pacifist views, which he published at the risk of the kind of censure the professor unknowingly subjects him to? And does the discovery in himself of the potential to behave like the generals he had condemned exonerate those generals, or is it not meant rather to subvert his attempt to absolve himself from blame and to affirm his belief in the unity of life, just as Hesse discovered through his psychoanalysis that he shared in the collective guilt for the First World War and had no right to blame others (GS 4:481)?

In one of his several contributions to the study of Hesse's reception, Egon Schwarz writes of the then predominant scholarly approach to literature that it "overlaps with the phenomenological act of evaluation, and of course, presupposes it, to such a degree that it has been confused with it. But its more discriminating practitioners know better" (1970, 980). Literary scholarship, he continues,

> is replete with unreflected values and engages in indirect evaluation all the time. But when a scholarly discipline engages in evaluation as a matter of practice, in spite of all protestations to the contrary, it should do so consciously and systematically. Thus we need a theory of literary evaluation in order to cleanse our other scholarly acts of prejudice and evaluative preconceptions, but above all in order to come to grips with the important dimension of literature that constitutes its temporal side, its participation in the process of history. (981)

Schwarz argues that literary scholars should attempt to become conscious of the unreflected value judgments or prejudices which influence their evaluations of literary works, and they should recognize that their perceptions are part of what the literary work means to them and that their perceptions will not be the same as the author's, since both are conditioned by time, place, and circumstances (985). Without knowledge of their own conditioning circumstances, readers' interpretations will be inadequate. Likewise inadequate is literary scholarship that ignores the conditions of life which produced the literary work and to which it is addressed, scholarship that fails to relate to the milieu from which the work is perceived and into which it is absorbed (986).

By taking the author's and the readers' perceptions and circumstances into consideration, Schwarz is able to explain what attracts American youth to the author their German counterparts reject. Young American readers have much in common with Hesse: a yearning for spiritual values, mysticism, free love, drugs, interest in psychoanalysis, reaction against all authority except the spiritual, and rejection of the manifestations of modern industrialism such as capitalism, nationalism, institutionalized religion, militarism, and war (981–82). What Hesse's American admirers do not understand and share is his reverence for history and tradition, his profound ambivalence toward the bourgeois world, and the whole dimension of his language. Schwarz characterizes Hesse succinctly as "a left-wing, indeed as an anarchistic Romantic, for that is what one becomes when insisting on an extreme individualism and a rejection of the national state, all at the same time" (984). Young Americans are able to exploit the anarchistic tendencies in Hesse without being troubled by his inwardness, his metaphysical orientation, and his romanticism, which can in fact be mobilized against the materialism and other-directedness they resist. The German dissidents, on the other hand, are struggling to "free themselves of their Romantic heritage, of which National Socialism was the last and ultimate perversion. They see Hesse as fully representing that tradition, as an apostle of inwardness, mysticism, nature worship, and antirationalism," when their goal is to recapture the rationalism of the eighteenth-century Enlightenment, which has been lacking in German history for more than a century (984). For them, Hesse's anarchism and individualism is tainted by his roots in Romanticism.

Awareness of these same cultural differences underlies Jeffrey L. Sammons's attempts in "Notes on the Germanization of American Youth" (1970) and "Hermann Hesse and the Over-Thirty Germanist" (1973) to dampen the naive enthusiasm of American youth for the works of Hesse and other writers representing a tradition so different from, and incongruous with the "pragmatism, liberalism, tolerance, and democracy" of their own heritage. The German tradition is rooted in German Idealist philosophy and in Romanticism, and it arose in political and social circumstances that denied the individual the rights that Americans take for granted.

Sammons does not suggest in the 1970 article that the German perspective is bound to any particular ideology; it is found on the political right, but it also infuses the work of Marx and prevails in the writings of Herbert Marcuse, the other author, along with Hesse, whose influence Sammons wants to undermine. Sammons has high regard for Hesse as a person: he considers him to be "the nearest thing to a saint that modern German literature has produced," a man whose "life and personality are characterized by an extraordinary degree of kindness, generosity, tolerance, and fine moral judgment" (348). Though he never denounced Nazi Germany publicly, which has been held against him, he is untainted by any sympathy for the movement or its leaders. But Hesse is "one of the most spectacular prisoners of the German tradition in modern letters" (349). In his opposition to modern technology and the degeneracy of the modern world, he immersed himself in a literary past consisting primarily of Goethe and the German Romantics with an admixture of Rousseau. He is a talented writer, who is skilled in composition and in maintaining a narrative flow, and who has a highly developed, workmanlike control of style, but he is lacking in intellect and is simply unable to deal adequately with the issues that concerned him throughout his career. Even *Steppenwolf*, "his best, or least silly, book," in which he attempts to "escape from the constipation of *Bildung* into a phantasmagoria of anarchy and polymorphous perversity" is full of anti-modern and Romantic-mystical elements (349).

Sammons develops and sharpens his arguments in his 1973 essay. He admits to being vexed by the continuing enthusiasm for Hesse, since he and others consider Hesse to be a mediocre stylist rather than a writer of first rank. To further undermine his influence, Sammons attempts in this article to associate Hesse's intellectual position with the political right, in part by identifying Romanticism as a common source for his thought and for Nazi ideology. Sammons does not claim that Hesse was a fascist, but by citing a letter written by the eighteen-year-old Hesse in which he expresses hatred for Socialism and refers to his shift to the right, he has prepared his readers to conclude from the few similarities he points out that Hesse is or may be tainted by certain fascist ideas and inclinations (117). What he fails to add is that the mature Hesse, who had changed his mind by the end of the First World War, repeatedly stated his preference for Communism, though not without some strong reservations, and was one of the first German writers to publicly attack Hitler and National Socialism. In July 1922, a year after Hitler became the head of the National Socialist Party, Hesse wrote in an essay entitled "Verrat am Deutschtum" (Betrayal of the German Ideal) that it was now time "to say something about one of the most despicable and most ridiculous forms of young-German nationalism, about the idiotic, pathological hatred of Jews (Judenfresserei) on the part of these swastika-bards and their numerous, especially student supporters" (Michels, 1992, 87). A year earlier he had already distanced himself from this "German pseudo-*Geist*," this "one-sided, idealistic-ideological Germanity," which was responsible for the war and which had made true Germans into internationalists and pacifists (Michels, 1992, 88) These and many other statements that could be cited indicate that Hesse rejected and attacked vehemently some of the same diseased outgrowths of German Romanticism and Idealism that Sammons warns against. In order to avoid the unwarranted suggestion of guilt by association, it is necessary to look at Hesse's use of the elements from the German tradition in their own right, not as they may relate to the very different and distorted use made of them by others, though the latter may serve to point out weaknesses and potential dangers of various elements in that tradition.

Sammons identifies two themes that run throughout Hesse's works: the inner way and the search for wholeness. As Peter Gay demonstrates in *Weimar Culture: The Outsider as Insider* (1968), a desire for wholeness was prevalent during the Weimar period. In general this longing was connected with an antipathy to political involvement, one of the negative manifestations of the German tradition, and took a variety of forms in religious, social, and political contexts, the latter not only on the right in the concept of the Third Reich, but also on the left in the communist utopia. Most, but not all its forms involved a strong element of the irrational. Sammons has little regard for this hunger, which "generated among German and Austrian intellectuals a quantity of irrationalism, mystagogy, mythopoesis, assaults on science, democracy, and civilization, and sheer crackpot lunacy that strains belief, although today it seems that we are condemned to recapitulate some of it" (1973, 125). At the time he was writing, the recapitulation was taking place among the hippies, who were seeking wholeness in communes, love-ins, drugs, Eastern religions, and Hesse's novels.

Whereas the unified utopian state envisioned by Hesse was anti-modern and rooted in the past, the progressive utopias being pursued by the restless youth of the sixties had no such foundations. Without knowledge of Hesse's intellectual and cultural background, these readers were unable, in Sammons's view, to gain a proper understanding of the works. As is evident in *Steppenwolf*, salvation and truth lie for Hesse and for Haller in the heritage of high culture represented by Mozart, Goethe, and the other Immortals. The German ideal of humanity, which was developed in the period of high culture, was a valiant effort to find a cultural and moral substance that would hold society together, but in the circumstances in which it originated, this ideal had little contact with reality. "Thus the German tradition became, in one of its main currents, antimodern and antidemocratic. The solutions to the dilemmas of the modern world were found in the status quo or in a historical, premodern situation." Because the higher culture of the mind was divorced from the actual developments of society, the bourgeoisie could claim "to draw its inspiration from *Humanität* and Romantic inwardness while at the same time tolerating and from time to time encouraging the increasing barbarousness of German society and politics" (119). According to Sammons, Hesse continued to accept and propagate these inadequate and impotent ideals.

Sammons's objections to what Knüfermann identifies as Hesse's essentially philosophic-religious faith are motivated in part by the negative consequences it has on the individual's behavior and regard for others in Hesse's works. Figures following the path inward and searching for mystical wholeness are unlikely to be engaged in the kind of political activity that could result in the improvement of social conditions. Sammons claims that Hesse had a simplistic view of politics and only one political opinion: his opposition to war. This view has since been clearly refuted by the publication in 1977 of Hesse's political writings in two volumes. Hesse was not a political activist, but he did occupy himself a great deal with politics and had keen insights on many political issues.

Sammons is especially concerned about the recurrence of two "clichés" in Hesse's works, one of which is the *Führer* principle and the related existence of an elite group. This theme sometimes occurs in association with a seeming lack of regard for the lives of those who do not belong to the elite. In *Demian*, for example, Sinclair benefits from the leadership of Demian, identified at the end as *Führer*, and joins the elite of those who bear the mark of Cain. The Treatise in *Steppenwolf* states that the men "running around on the streets by the millions" are to be no more regarded than "sand in the sea or drops of the surf: a couple millions more or less do not matter, they are material, nothing more" (Sammons's translation; St 74). Contrasting with the tendency of Hesse's figures to rebel against authority is the continuous pattern of subordination to superior, wiser authority (130), which culminates in the emphasis placed on service by Josef Knecht in *Glasperlenspiel*.

The second complex Sammons identifies has to do with "the apocalypse of the bourgeois society." Although Hesse did not have a "thirst for holocaust, a loud insistence that only a cleansing bloodbath could clean the trash out of bourgeois society and restore heroism and purity," such a tone is sounded in some of his writing. Referring to the vision of collective destruction near the end of *Demian*, Sammons confesses to having difficulty "distinguishing this rhetoric from the early years of the S.S. into which the spirit of apocalyptic, elitist heroism eventually flowed" (132).

Sammons states at the beginning of his essay that he is unable or unwilling to read Jung, but Jung's psychology provides the context for properly understanding some of the images and symbols he objects to. Demian, for example, is more than the *Führer* Sammons considers him to be: he represents Sinclair's Self, which Jung defines as the fate guiding one's development. The achievement of self-sufficiency is indicated at the end by the fact that Sinclair internalizes his guide; Demian can die because he has now become an integral part of Sinclair. As misleading as they can be, Hesse's apocalyptic visions, when seen as fantasy or projections of inner reality, may be meant to suggest the symbolic death that precedes the individual and collective rebirth he hoped for, just as Demian's death accompanies Sinclair's rebirth. To be sure, the use of such ambiguous metaphors and symbols at the time in which Hesse was writing was indeed problematic and subject to unfavorable interpretation.

Whereas Hollis and Sammons point out certain apparent congruities between Hesse's thinking and *völkisch* and even Nazi ideology, congruities that stem from their common roots in German Romanticism, Klaus von Seckendorff engages in an unreasoned and unbalanced polemic against Hesse's philosophical view of man and society and is intent on portraying him as a fascist *(Hermann Hesses Propagandistische Prosa: selbstzerstörerische Entfaltung als Botschaft in seinen Romanen von "Demian" bis zum "Steppenwolf.")* [Hermann Hesse's Propagandist Prose: Self-destructive Development as a Message in His Novels from *Demian* to *Steppenwolf*], 1982. Von Seckendorff completely ignores the all-important religious and psychological content of Hesse's novels and claims that they have nothing to offer beyond Hesse's ideology (8), which, as can be seen from the following examples, he attempts to identify with fascism. According to von Seckendorff, the vocabulary Hesse uses in *Steppenwolf* to describe the disease of the times is fascist in its [Nietschean] references to weak and strong individuals (72). Against the evidence of his own experience, Hesse feels compelled to attribute meaning to the world which it obviously does not have. In this he resembles Hitler (145). His cynical disregard for life is shared otherwise only by fascists (147). His view of suffering is fascistic, as is his enjoyment of the suffering of the wounded (157, 165). In recognizing the necessity of war he is a fascist (161). Hesse advocates self-subordination as in the Third Reich. Furthermore, since Hesse does not tolerate positions other than his own to be represented in his novels, they are devoid of conflict and tension. As mere projections, his figures are unbelievable constructs (119–20).

Statements such as these from someone claiming to be a scholar are completely misleading and indefensible. They demonstrate to what extremes some writers are willing to go to attack and defame a writer whose world view they do not accept and cannot tolerate. They are no less excessive, misguided, and irrational than the attacks on Hesse by Nazi critics and journalists in the early years of the Third Reich. Without any reflection on perspective and circumstances as advocated by Egon Schwarz, and unlike Jeffrey Sammons, who acknowledges Hesse's positive qualities and opposition to fascism, von Seckendorff is completely biased and paints only in black.

Whether or not one agrees with the irrational, mystical, Romantic elements in Hesse's works, they deserve to be understood on their own terms. And because of the powerful impact his novels have had and still have on young readers, it behooves teachers especially to discover and appreciate the reasons for their appeal. As Hesse's phenomenal popularity has demonstrated, the power of the irrational is still very much in evidence and needs to be understood and taken into account even by avowed rationalists. Hesse's "message" in *Steppenwolf* is not propaganda for fascism or any other ideology or form of irrationalism, but rather a warning of what can befall an intellectual and rationalist who fails to acknowledge and come to terms with the "dark" side of himself.

From these observations on reception we return to *Steppenwolf* and a reevaluation of its structure by Lynn Dhority, who disagrees with Ziolkowski's widely accepted analysis of the novel's musical structure. Since Hesse used several different musical analogies in referring to the novel's form, Dhority maintains, it is likely that they "are not intended to carry any literal or theoretical exactness, but are used as general examples of structural coherence where themes are contrasted and balanced" (1974, 150). Ziolkowski, we recall, equates the editor's introduction with the "exposition," the first part of Haller's notebooks with the "development," and the Treatise with the "recapitulation" sections of the sonata form. According to Ziolk-owski, the two main themes, the Steppenwolf and the Bürger, are stated in the exposition and receive their fullest "development" in the first section of Harry's notebooks. Dhority claims, on the contrary, that those same themes are more fully developed throughout the rest of the novel. Furthermore, the Treatise, which must be the recapitulation according to the sonata scheme, is "far from being the repetition of the themes 'as they occurred in the exposition.'" In fact, the Treatise further develops the original thematic material and is "the apex of the thematic development in *Steppenwolf*" (151). Rather than the ABA structure of the sonata, Dhority identifies a progressive and expanding development of the same themes throughout the novel. Finally, Ziolkowski's observations on the musical key relation-ships would be valid only if the Treatise were written from the Steppen-wolf's point of view rather than *sub specie aeternitatis* as Ziolkowski himself interprets it (151).

Dhority agrees with Unseld that the novel's structural coherence lies "in a rhythmic triadic patterning of thematic material on a variety of levels" (152). This "patterning motif" is consistent with Hesse's view of human development from innocence to lost innocence, and from knowledge, con-flict, and despair to a newly achieved wholeness and transcendence of con-flict. In *Music and Literature: A Comparison of the Arts*, a book also cited by Ziolkowski, Calvin S. Brown remarks that "musical development is circular, but literary development is linear" (Dhority, 152). As a structure consistent with the expanding elaboration of basic themes, which is "circular in the sense that there is a return to basic themes . . . and somewhat linear in the sense of a progressive transcendence away from limited previous perspec-tives," Dhority suggests a spiral, which, in keeping with the ever-widening scope of the progression in the first part of the novel, might be character-ized "in graphic terms as cone-like" (152–53). Thus the narrative begins with the editor's rather one-dimensional attitude, progresses to Haller's multidimensional conflict, and then to the ironical, sovereign, complex point of view of the Treatise and its anticipation of liberation from conflict on a higher level of integration. The remainder of the novel "manifests the triadic pattern both in the macro- and microstructure": each of the three main sections of the remaining thematic material has a triadic structure (153).

The first of the three major divisions extends from the crisis that befalls Haller after he reads the Treatise to his first meeting with Hermine. The second includes Harry's period of growth and development under Her-mine's tutelage, and the third begins with the carnival ball. The first of these sections is subdivided into a period of despair following the reading of the Treatise; a period of even deeper despair in the outsider's clash with the social world as represented by the funeral and his evening with the professor; and the meeting with Hermine, which parallels the Treatise as the climax of the novel's first triad. Hermine may be understood as an "abridged, simplified personification of the treatise in terms Harry can understand." This triad essentially translates the pattern of the first into episodic narrative terms (153–54). The middle section manifests a triadic progression which is symbolized by the characters Maria, Hermine, and Pablo. Maria prepares Harry for the culmination of his relationship with Hermine, and Hermine prepares him for Pablo and the Magic Theater. The three figures represent the three stages in Hesse's system of human development, from Maria's undifferentiated simplicity through Hermine's multi-faceted complexity to Pablo's complete liberation and his identification with the Immortals of the Third Kingdom (154–55).

The final triad begins with the ball and Harry's dancing with Maria and Hermine, and it progresses to his acceptance of Pablo's guidance. The events of the Magic Theater are not organized according to the same triadic substructure as the preceding stages. "Within its climactic section . . . the triadic rhythm is distinctly broken," but since the Magic Theater is itself a substructure of the final triad, it should not be expected to display a triadic rhythm. It should be considered analogous to the Treatise at the end of the first major triad and the meeting with Hermine at the end of the second, neither of which was analyzed in terms of further subdivisions. On the other hand, since the breakdown of the pattern in the Magic Theater has interesting consequences for an interpretation, the first section of the ball might better be considered an intermezzo or transition to the final triad of the Magic Theater. As Dhority sees it, a triad of sorts is begun as "Haller begins his journey through the Magic Theater of the self in naive curiosity" and on a rather simple, one dimensional level. His encounters then increase in complexity, Dhority claims,[2] until

> the momentum of Haller's development is suddenly arrested. The characteristic structural rhythm of expansion is broken, creating a cold-shower effect. Haller fails; at the crucial juncture where he must finally deal with Hermine and his relationship to her, he falls back into his suicidal attitude and into the old hostile, polar categories, thereby destroying his bridge to transcendence before having fully crossed it. (155–56)

The novel thus ends both structurally and thematically with Haller's collapse. Dhority maintains that this conclusion, "however effective as an abrupt return to 'so-called reality,' is not very consistent with the preceding

[2] If the development were consistently toward more complexity, one might object, the chess scene with its multiple personalities would have to follow the "Taming of the Steppenwolf," with its presentation of duality and the simple conflict between opposites.

structural patterns as I have outlined them. Nor is it consistent with Hesse's own later interpretation of the novel" (156). The reference here is to Hesse's letter calling attention to the healing that supposedly takes place. One might argue that Hesse's interpretation may not be supported by his text, that the breakdown of the structural pattern is indeed consistent with Haller's failure, and that the form therefore does reflect the content. Or, perhaps more appropriately, the healing Hesse refers to, and that he seemed to experience in writing the novel, may be anticipated by Haller's insight into the existence of the transcendent realm and by the hope that he may some day be able to enter it, a hope that presumably overcomes his desire for death. His collapse will be followed by renewal as he tries again to reach his newly discovered goal.

Ziolkowski's analysis of the novel's musical structure also comes under attack by Marko Pavlyshyn, who claims that Ziolkowski applies the concept of theme in a literary rather than a musical sense to denote a topic frequently referred to in the novel rather than a sequence of tones presented in a particular order, which is then modulated and otherwise transformed. The two major themes identified by Ziolkowski, the dual elements of Haller's personality as seen by Haller himself, are not presented consecutively and independently of each other as they must be in the sonata form, but simultaneously. And whereas the development section of the first movement of a sonata "explores the potentialities of the two themes by means of modulation, may introduce new thematic material, and is characterized by a dynamism arising from the creation and transformation of tensions through key change," the segment of Haller's notes which Ziolkowski identifies as the development section, is "essentially static and constitutes a descriptive definition of Haller's psychological condition" (1979, 40, n.5).

Pavlyshyn's investigation reveals "two recurrent sequences of associations, the first of which appears three times and contains the following elements in the given order: public house, 'Bürgertum,' music, and foreshadowing of the magic theater" (40). As Pavlyshyn demonstrates, this sequence occurs in the beginning of Haller's report and extends to his glimpse of the sign announcing the Magic Theater. It is then immediately repeated, ending this time with the placard carrier's reference to the Magic Theater. The final restatement of this sequence takes place in the events leading up to his entrance into the Magic Theater. It differs from the previous two in that Haller does not reflect on music but instead experiences it directly at the ball, which is followed by the direct experience of the Magic Theater (40–41).

The recurrent elements in the second sequence identified by Pavlyshyn include images as well as idea complexes. This sequence may be summarized in the following series of terms:

the "Welt" [world] image, the "Spiegel" [mirror] symbol, the dismissal of Harry's over-simplified self-image as man and wolf, the dissolution of individuality, the multi-faceted ego, the laughter motif. These elements are first stated as possibilities in the final section of the "Tractat" and are later transformed into experience in the magic theater episode. (40)

Original in Pavlyshyn's restatement of these images and idea complexes is the observation that Haller attempts to carry out in the "Globussäle" (globe rooms) of the hotel the Treatise's recommendation that he must attempt a "leap into the cosmos (*Weltall*)" in order to attain the higher wisdom that comes through humor (40).

According to Pavlyshyn, the two sequences he describes occupy some 91 of the novel's 230 pages in the WA edition, and in a significant portion of the remaining text various elements from the sequences occur in altered form and out of sequence. For example, the first sequence, occurs in altered order just prior to Haller's first meeting with Hermine, and most of its elements recur in his conversations with her. Pavlyshyn detects in this structural organization "certain similarities to the standard first movement of a classical sonata. The identified sequences are comparable to sonata themes in that they form regular patterns which recognizably recur, although in modified form" (42).

Whereas Ziolkowski identifies the first part of the novel up to the end of the Treatise with the first movement of a sonata, Pavlyshyn considers this segment to be equivalent only to the exposition of the sonata's first movement. The development follows in the "'thematically' variegated middle section, in which the potentialities of the two 'themes' are explored by modification and rearrangement," with the introduction of Hermine as a new element (42–43). The recapitulation extends from the point of Harry's departure for the ball to the end. In contrast to Ziolkowski, then, Pavlyshyn sees the whole novel as a single movement, whose form is loosely analogous to that of a sonata.

> The point of comparison where the analogy is of significance to an interpretation of *Der Steppenwolf* is the correspondence of the recurrences. A movement in sonata form possesses a dynamism that is dialectical in nature: it ends with the same two themes that began it, except that between their first and last statements everything that was originally inherent in the themes is made explicit. The whole movement proceeds towards a restatement of the original position and a return to the tonic key. There is an essential optimism and affirmativeness in such a movement towards resolution.
>
> This cyclic development is analogous to the progress of Harry Haller: at the end, after failing the test of the Immortals, he returns to his initial position, that of the bourgeois intellectual. (42–43)

As a dominant form of the harmonic mode of music which Nietzsche recognizes as characteristic of the Dionysian, the sonata is

a musical form which conceptually unites the two seemingly contradictory aspirations of Haller's ego: on the one hand the striving towards (and even temporary achievement of) the level of the Immortals, and on the other, the return to the starting-point, which for him is the individual personality. (43)

Initially, Haller has a very bourgeois appreciation of the intellectual aspects of Mozart's music and a negative judgment of all subsequent music, for which jazz stands as an extreme form. He must learn that there is a common ground between jazz and Mozart, that both "are expressions of the Dionysian spirit of the dissolution of individuality, Mozart through his mastery over the Dionysian power of harmony, jazz through its sensual arousal of the instincts to a Dionysian 'Rausch'" (44).

Learning to dance introduces Haller to the Dionysian element of music and prepares him for the Magic Theater. Once he learns to appreciate what jazz and the classical style have in common, he can see Pablo and Mozart as one and the same person. Common to Pablo's Magic Theater and harmonic music, according to Pavlyshyn, is the Dionysian dissolution of individuality and the harmonious blending of parts and potentialities in a higher unity, which underlies the laughter and humor of the Immortals. When "put to a test to discover whether he can follow Mozart into the sphere of the Immortals," Haller fails and confirms his unworthiness by killing Hermine, which, "although it occurs only on the level of imagination, is performed with a seriousness which demonstrates how little humor he has acquired" (46). Hesse's desire to leave readers with an optimistic message based on the existence of the realm of the Immortals fails, according to Pavlyshyn's surprising interpretation, because he excludes Beethoven and his successors. While Beethoven may lack Mozart's optimism, the relevance of his view of the world cannot be denied (47).

Given the nature of Haller's problem, his failure as recognized by Dhority and Pavlyshyn is inevitable, for, as Hans Jürg Lüthi concludes in his thorough study of this conflict, the fundamental antinomy between nature and intellect, which threatens in its many forms to tear man apart, appears to be incurable (1970, 81). As Goethe suggests in Harry's dream, and as Harry's occasional experiences of the "golden trace" exemplify, it may be possible in special moments to bring the poles together in harmony, but polarity can only be permanently transcended by the Immortals, that is, in death. Through his experiencing of the Dionysian expansion and *unio mystica* of the ball, Harry learns another way to escape from the *principium individuationis*, another way to apprehend the golden trace from the realm of the Immortals. But in killing Hermine, he destroys that part in himself that leads to nature, to Eros, and to love, and he restores the predominance of his cold intellect. Though Harry has not successfully bridged the gap between nature and intellect, he, or at least his creator, does appear to have restored his belief in the meaning of life and the world. With *Steppenwolf* Hesse completes his journey through chaos and overcomes his crisis at its high point. He experiences a catharsis and with it the cure he mentions in the letter referred to above (87–89).

Noteworthy not for any new light they shed on Hesse's works but as the first major studies of Hesse in the German Democratic Republic are Fritz Böttger's *Hermann Hesse: Leben, Werk, Zeit* (Hermann Hesse: Life, Work, Times, 1974) and Eike Middell's *Hermann Hesse: Die Bilderwelt seines Lebens* (Hermann Hesse: The Image-World of his Life, 1975). In an essay by Hans-Joachim Bernhard, which is appended to Böttger's book, we are told: "Only socialistic culture is in a position to receive the actual message of authors such as Hesse and to recognize and preserve the human greatness in the often petty narrow-mindedness" (Erst die sozialistische Kultur, und nur sie ist in der Lage, das eigentliche Anliegen solcher Autoren wie Hesse aufzunehmen und in der oft kleinlichen Begrenztheit die menschliche Grösse zu erkennen und zu bewahren": 472). The major purpose of Böttger's study is to investigate "whether and to what extent Hesse's works can become productively effective in a socialistic national culture" (7).

While Hesse, unlike Heinrich Mann, "does not belong to the bourgeois pioneers, who themselves made the transition to socialistic humanism," members of the socialistic literary society may nevertheless see him as a "partner from the bourgeois world, a messenger from the 'threshold,' who spoke his 'no' to the old order, who considered change to be imperative, and who strove to develop building components for the culture in a new era" (14). Indeed, Böttger sees similarities between Hesse's secularized chiliasm and socialist consciousness. The humanistic goal of *Steppenwolf*, for example, is to lead the outsider and "desperado" Harry Haller out of the barren desert of his loneliness and isolation and to save him from his sick relations to human life. The novel's editor is wrong to claim in his preface that Harry's sickness is characteristic of the times, for in fact he represents only a small group of "late bourgeois intellectuals," about whose problems the petit bourgeois and the enterprising bourgeois, let alone the workers, know nothing (326). (Of course Hesse's lack of class consciousness and appreciation for the rising power of the proletariat is a major weakness in the eyes of Marxist critics.)

According to Böttger, Haller is to be saved through three therapeutic processes: "overcoming loneliness through resocialization; confrontation with the Steppenwolf-trauma; and the application of humanistic traditions as a corrective to decadence" (329). His socialization is accomplished through Hermine, Maria, and Pablo, with whose help he is able to build bridges to the other and the group (the *Du* and the *Wir*). But in the end, the help of such marginal figures of the capitalistic entertainment industry ("Randexistenzen der kapitalistischen Vergnügungsindustrie") proves to be deceptive (339–40). The Magic Theater gives him the opportunity to see into his unconscious and to discover what resources, reserves, and values he has to draw on. Böttger deals at some length with the episode "Great Hunt in Automobiles" and briefly with "Guidance in Building the Personality." The former confirms Hesse's critical view of the existing capitalistic social order without indicating what should replace it. In this episode Haller learns what potential destructiveness and agression lies within him, and, by equating Bolsheviks with American capitalists, he demonstrates that he despises reason and, as a journalist no less, is ignorant about recent profound social changes in Russia, which Böttger then dutifully lists (334–36).

The purpose of the scene "Building Personality" is to reveal the error of Haller's assumed split into wolf and man, according to Böttger, who does not mention that the alternative is not unity of the personality but a split into multiple parts as described in the Treatise. In keeping with his lack of interest in the subjective, psychological, existential elements of the narrative, Böttger has nothing to say about the Treatise beyond the fact that its message is contradicted by the Immortals at the novel's end. The judgment of Mozart, who stands for the "great humanistic tradition of world culture," is absolute: despite the contradiction between the humanistic ideal and the capitalist reality, Harry should compromise with existing conditions and integrate himself into bourgeois society. This does not eliminate the contradiction between the humanistic ideal and the capitalist reality: "that would be reactionary liberalism" (336–37).

> The ideal striving of the "Immortals" remains correct in its demand vis-à-vis the existing social conditions but receives a tragic accent, because it is not able to overcome the opposition and limits that prevent its realization; it must be prepared to make concessions to the status quo. Neither Mozart nor Pablo reconcile themselves with chauvinism, war, expansionist politics, and colonialism. But they see no way out of the commercialization of all art; in their view, one must accept this process.
>
> In its willingness to compromise, *Steppenwolf* proves to be a characteristic work of the second post-war period [that is, the "golden twenties"] with its relative stability of the imperialist system. It is assumed that the bourgeois social and cultural order and way of life will remain unchanged for a long time. Compromise with this order is recommended. (338–39)

Whether and to what extent Harry will follow the path of compromise remains open. When he awakens from his drug-induced dreams, he is cured of his suicide complex, but he is not a changed person. The author was not able to find a solution to the Steppenwolf problem. Indeed, there can be no flight from the bourgeoisie for "esoteric protest-intellectuals." Hesse's path inward proves to be a blind alley (339–41).

Eike Middell's study has the advantage over Böttger's of being less dogmatic and shorter. It appeared in a series of "Biographies and Documents" published by the Leipzig branch of the popular Verlag Philipp Reclam and was meant to contribute to the reintroduction of Hesse to East German readers. As is typical for the biographical approach, the literary works are only briefly discussed in the context of the artist's life. Middell finds much to appreciate in Hesse, but he also criticizes him for his elitism and his emphasis on the individual rather than the collective as the potential source of solutions to the problems of the age.

Middell sees in *Steppenwolf* "the retraction and the rectification of Hesse's mythically heroicizing affirmation of the war at the end of *Demian*" (186). He characterizes Haller as "an oppositional, homeless leftist without approach to the proletariat" (187). Like Hesse, who sympathized with the German revolution of 1918 and with its Marxist leaders, he is an anarchist who lacks insight into the historical process. And like the figures in the street films of the twenties, his solution to his discontent with bourgeois life is to flee into the world of disreputable taverns and girls of dubious repute. Hesse has nothing to put in the place of the bourgeoisie he rejects. Haller's emphasis on his unique individualism is refuted by the Treatise, and the Magic Theater demonstrates that he is very much a part of the bourgeois world he criticizes. Although Haller, like Hesse, opposes modern mass media and technologized art, for example, his "Great Hunt in Automobiles" is influenced by film, especially the slapstick of Charlie Chaplin, whom Hesse admired (188–89).

While Middell might be expected to argue on the side of the novel's realism or to criticize its departure from realism, he in fact recognizes as a formal peculiarity and artistic advantage "the exactness with which Hesse's book is crafted, the mixture of the real and the unreal, the almost imperceptible transition from the one sphere to the other, and at the same time the very conscious and intentional relativization of reality by the imagination" (188). Middell joins those who consider Hermine to be the product of Harry's imagination. He finds support for this view in the editor's preface, in which no mention is made of Hermine's visits to Harry's room or of the dance lessons held there, events not likely to have escaped the careful attention and close observations of the landlady's nephew (188).

Hans Mayer, another Marxist and sometime resident of the GDR, has published several appreciative but not uncritical essays on Hesse, including one in 1964 on *Steppenwolf*, which was anthologized in *Zur Deutschen Lit-*

eratur der Zeit (On Contemporary German Literature, 1967) and again in Volker Michels's *Materialien zu Hermann Hesses 'Der Steppenwolf'"* (Material on Hermann Hesse's *Steppenwolf,* 1972). Mayer was one of the very few German critics in the sixties to take Hesse seriously. Despite their historical significance, I have not discussed these essays here, because they contribute little new information or interpretive insight. His 1977 essay, "Hermann Hesse und das magische Theater," however, is more specific and does address a problem of interpretation.

Mayer recognizes the importance of Jungian psychology in the presentation of the Steppenwolf as Haller's "persona," that is, as a mask representing a "compromise between the individual and society concerning that 'which one appears to be'" (529). The Magic Theater does not represent a counterpart to, or alternative for, that society; on the contrary, it serves as an instrument for its continuation and for its integration into the life of the Steppenwolf. Haller appears in the Magic Theater not as a humanistic Bürger but in the persona of the wolf. Rather than affirm the Steppenwolf's identity, the Magic Theater is meant to expose it through irony as a mask. But for the moment it fails.

> Hence *Steppenwolf* becomes a book of warning and the Magic Theater a social danger, not because of alcohol and drugs, but because of the Bürgers' frivolous play at being anti-bourgeois. Precisely this most important aspect of *Steppenwolf,* however — that the bourgeois world can continue to function thanks to Steppenwolves — has until now been least understood. (529)

The novel is a warning against illusory solutions to social problems, a warning against Steppenwolves.

Andrew Hollis takes a similarly negative view of Harry Haller in his analysis of humor as "the philosophical center of the entire novel" (1978b, 22). Throughout the narrative Haller is portrayed in a "comic/ironic light whenever the Steppenwolf's seriousness or self-pity get the better of him": Hermine treats him with sympathetic scorn at their first meeting; Goethe and Mozart both deride him for his inability to appreciate their buffoonery; and he eventually becomes the butt of the irony he directs at Pablo (17). His bitter, cynical satire of the funeral and his ambiguous satire of the professor reveal more about his outsiderdom and estrangement from society than about the people and events he would satirize. True satire, according to Hollis, presupposes feelings of security and the ability to love one's self, both of which Haller lacks. He seems to realize as much when he questions indirectly his own right to satirize the professor and "eventually despises himself for not being able to stand the company of those he holds in contempt." As his later, more successful satire of the film about Moses reveals,

Hermine has helped Harry get the distance from himself that satire requires (19–20).

The Treatise, Goethe, Mozart, Pablo, and Hermine all agree that Haller must learn to have humor, Hollis continues, but they do not all agree on what humor is. While Mozart and Hermine appear to postulate a view of humor

> which distinguishes between different kinds of reality — those which are worth taking seriously and those which are not — the tractate puts forward 'Humor' as a means of regarding *all* forms of reality, both trivial and sublime, as belonging to an essential unity. (23; author's emphasis)

By advocating the affirmation of all existence, the Treatise presupposes the suspension of normal moral judgment. "Here it is possible not only to extol the saint and the profligate in one breath and to make the poles meet, but to include the bourgeois, too, in the same affirmation" (St 62–63).

According to Hollis, Harry can learn to have or exercise the kind of humor advocated in the Treatise, which always retains something bourgeois and is therefore a compromise. This kind of humor requires distance from the objects being described, which in Harry's case is society and himself; by gaining detachment Harry can overcome his narrowly moralistic view and will take himself less seriously (24). As seen above in connection with satire, he makes some progress. The higher form of humor, however, involves a flight from reality to the transcendent realm of the Immortals, which is outside time and space and beyond life. Because it is ultimately unobtainable, Hollis concludes, the world of humor "suggested as a means of solving Harry Haller's existential problems, is criticized implicitly in the novel from an existentialist point of view" (27). One might conclude, however, that affirmation of the striving toward that world is indeed an appropriate existentialist solution: as is indicated by Harry's determination "to begin the game afresh," it gives meaning and purpose to his life.

Among the contributions to the 1977 centenary celebration of Hesse's birth were major biographies by Joseph Mileck (*Hermann Hesse: His Life and Art*) and Ralph Freedman (*Hermann Hesse: Pilgrim of Crisis*). In keeping with his positive reevaluation of the novel, Mileck expands his earlier study to include more analysis of style and structure. The approach remains primarily biographical, however, with about half of the twenty-three pages on *Steppenwolf* given to identifying the parallels between Harry Haller and Hermann Hesse. Mileck also responds to the debate on double perception by attempting to determine what part of the novel reflects reality and what part is symbolic.

Where Mileck had previously considered *Steppenwolf* to be a "fascinating confusion of symbol and irony, fantasy and realism," an untenable criticism of Western Civilization in the machine age, and an overly frank revelation of Hesse's inner state at a time of maximum disturbance (1958, 22, 30–31, 39), he now comments on the novel's modernity, careful craftsmanship, and unity of style and content and considers it the high point of Hesse's narrative technique (1978, 196–97). Noting Thomas Mann's observation that *Steppenwolf* is no less daring as an experimental novel than Joyce's *Ulysses* (1922) and André Gide's *Les Faux-Monnayeurs* (1926), Mileck adds that the experimental element in each case is less in substance than in form. New for Hesse is the multimethod of his portraiture and the resultant tetra-partite structure of the tale (195). As did Unseld, Mileck distinguishes three different perspectives and three distinct modes of expression: the editor's prosaic language and unadorned literality in the preface; the "facetious tone and the casual ironic manner" of the Immortals in the Treatise; and Haller's appropriately literary depiction of his thoughts and feelings.

Mileck's application of a new critical or *werkimmanente* approach to the novel's form and content effectively reveals Hesse's careful craftsmanship on all levels. Haller's tedium, for example, is expressed "in the lagging flow and monotonous rhythm of inordinately protracted sentences with their drag-ging repetitions and their long and dangling chain of interlinked clauses and phrases" (196). The opening paragraphs of Haller's manuscript provide a good example of the congruity of form and content, which Mileck describes as follows:

> moments of bleak despair or of exciting elation find their accentuating ex-
> pression in a rapidly flowing and frantically pulsating torrent of clauses and
> phrases, irregular in their brevity, in an emphatic rush of verbs and a hectic
> heaping of words, in restless rhetorical questions, frantic exclamations, and
> staccato repetitions, and in a liberal use of anaphora and parataxis. This
> restive verbal deluge is used to its best advantage in Haller's recounting of
> the climactic moments of the ball. The dance crests in a mad vortex, Haller
> glows feverishly, and the prose reflects and accentuates outer situations and
> inner state. Verb follows rapidly upon verb, repetition crowds repetition,
> and phrases and clauses whirl by. The verbal tempo becomes as frantic as
> the dance tempo and Haller's inner agitation. The dance ends, the fever
> abates, and language begins again to flow slowly and evenly. (196–97)

Here the critic emulates the poet.

Mileck recognizes that *Demian* is a "mythic account," an "externalization of psychic integration, an illumination of the inner and an adumbration of the outer world, more symbol than actuality," which is not to be taken literally (187), but he agrees with Ziolkowski in his resistance to reading *Steppenwolf* in the same way. In contrast to *Demian*, he considers *Steppenwolf* to be a fanciful but very *real depiction of a surrealistic experiencing of life,* an account of a psychological crisis both personal and typical, a tale that is both appearance and implication, and that for full comprehension must be approached both actually and symbolically. (188; emphasis added)

From the fact that his defense of realism often runs counter to his own arguments and interpretation — for example, would not a real depiction of surrealistic experiencing appear to be surrealistic? — it seems that Mileck may think that the novel's stature and survival depend upon its being anchored in reality. He feels, for example, that Haller's "surprising anticipation and calm acceptance" of Hermine's order to kill her when he falls in love with her "appear to mar the realness of the narrative, to add a mystification reminiscent of the many obfuscations of *Demian.* But in fact these questionable remarks detract only from literality and not from actuality" (189).

After reviewing the real or literal aspects of Haller's relationship to Hermine, Mileck concludes:

Like the Sinclair-Demian relationship, Haller's encounter with Hermine is clearly symbolic: unlike the former, however, it is also and most immediately, excitingly actual. Though this interlude in Haller's life may not always quite accord with plausibility, its basic realness remains intact. (189)

But Mileck's argument for the novel's basic realness is undermined by his review of its implausibilites: "The literality of the Haller-Hermine affair, but for the hyperbolic death command and its anticipation, is arguable but certainly not essential for the novel's significance or for a better understanding of it." Hyperbole now becomes the operative word, and it is related to the surrealistic. In view of the occurrences that are "literally beyond likelihood, literality becomes less attractive and extended hyperbole very persuasive. It is not only Hermine's death command but Haller's entire crisis that is hyperbolic: actuality surrealistically experienced and fancifully narrated" (190).

But the hyperbolic is really the symbolic and mythic in disguise, and we are back to the resisted analogy with *Demian.* The Treatise, for example, "was not written by *an* Immortal, but is thought out by *the* Immortal in Harry Haller."

Haller's immortal self resorts to the editorial we, affects a learned objectivity, identifies with the community of Immortals, and proceeds to comment on Haller's mortal self. The mortal self is helped by and must become the immortal self, *just as Sinclair is guided by and ultimately becomes Demian.* (190–91; emphasis added)

Furthermore, Mileck continues, the uniqueness of Hermine, Maria, and Pablo is better explained by hyperbole than by literality, and the close interlinkage of Haller, Hermine, and Hermann, while perfectly plausible on the level of reality, can best be explained on the plane of symbolism as the author's self-projections. Hermine functions as "Haller's *daimon*, his guiding and admonishing better self." After noting several similarities between Hermine and Demian, Mileck concludes: "Demian's voice seems at times to be Sinclair's own, and Haller's own soul appears to peer at him through Hermine's eyes. As such, *Hermine and Demian are similar externalizations, and Haller's and Sinclair's conversations with them are self-dialogue*" (191; emphasis added).

Mileck's detection of a major technical difference between these projections of the self is at this point an unconvincing attempt to defend literality: "Demian is simply Sinclair's *daimon* palely actualized, while Hermine is Haller's *daimon* identified with an actual person. Hermine became a vibrant blending of the actual and the symbolic, while Demian remained ghostly, pure symbol" (191).[3] If Hermine is Haller's *daimon* and a projection of his self, as Mileck admits, she may be a more effectively realized symbol than Demian, but there is no technical difference between them: the reality of both is psychological and symbolic. Mileck concedes that literality in the affair between Haller and Hermine is not quite credible, but he claims that what transpires between them

> need not be considered consistently actual nor entirely symbolic. Haller's socializing with Hermine and her intimacy with Pablo are best accounted for actually; their exegetic dialogues are more readily accountable symbolically. The most perplexing of their relationship's many enigmas, Hermine's death, or rather, her imagined death, is as manifestly symbolic as it is actual. Her death order is clearly hyperbole both on the level of actuality and that of symbolism. (192)

Unlike her death order, Hermine's death itself is imaginary on both planes. Considered actually, Mileck writes, it marks the termination of a real relationship between two people and Haller's return to his accustomed life after "having absorbed all that Hermine the prostitute represents, and again reasonably in control of his sexual impulses" (192). If this were the case, however, Haller should not have to begin the game afresh and traverse again the hell of his inner self, which presumably also includes his sexuality. On the

[3]Mileck's repeated reference to Hermine as the "prostitute" seems to suggest that her profession has something to do with his unwillingness to accept her entirely as a symbol, as Haller's *daimon*, as a projection of Haller's inner self. Considering Hesse's knowledge of Gnosticism and the importance it played in his analysis with Dr. Lang, it bears mentioning that Simon Magus, a convert to Christianity and early proponent of Gnosticism, was supposedly accompanied by a reincarnation of Helen of Troy, whom he had rescued from a brothel. Jung writes of the anima that one's first encounter with her "usually leads one to infer anything rather than wisdom. This aspect appears only to the person who gets to grips with her seriously" (CW 9i:31).

symbolic plane, Mileck's argument continues, the imagined murder marks the termination of Haller's imaginary relationship with Hermine as the representation of his *daimon*, which he has now absorbed or internalized. "His better self, temporarily an outer guide, has again become a prevailing inner guide" (192). Thus Hermine's death is exactly equivalent to Demian's. On both levels it represents the withdrawal of Haller's projection on, or, in Mileck's terms, his absorption of her.

Referring to the distinction made by Dorrit Cohn between the "narrating self" and the "experiencing self" in Haller's retrospective account, Russell Neuswanger proposes that the

> distinction between Haller and Harry is more than one of viewpoint, 'experiencing' and 'narrating,' more also than the distinction between narrator and hero. Haller is real (within the world of the young fellow-lodger [who publishes his account]) but Harry is a character Haller has created — Harry is poetry. His experience and reactions are those Haller invents for him. (1980, 233–34)

For Haller, then, Harry is an imagined figure through which he learns to laugh at himself. With the irony admired by Thomas Mann and André Gide, Haller draws a distorted, clownish self-portrait, a caricature, through which he exposes and mocks his deficiencies and undesirable attributes.

Admittedly, "the normal reader . . . is easily left bewildered and unaided in the face of impossibilities which the narrator has invented for his own benefit" (236), that is, the occurrences Ziolkowski and others have attempted to explain through the postulate of a double perspective.

> Haller is not only free in what and how he chooses to narrate; he is free to invent instead of recount, free not only to expound but to create his own events, places, and characters, indeed to create a world, all for his own benefit and not an audience's. He does with Harry (adding Pablo, Hermine, Magic Theater, and so on) just what Hesse does with him (adding landlady, nephew, and boarding house). (237)

However obscure the process may be for the reader, it works for Haller, for he has overcome his initial desire to take his life, has learned the importance of humor, and is determined to go on (236). It is not clear to me from Neuswanger's clever argument what is gained by postulating an additional layer of reality and a further distancing of Harry from Hesse, especially since the technique is admittedly obscure and bewildering to the "normal reader." As Harry is to Haller in Neuswanger's interpretation, all the figures of the novel are to Hesse, and it is Hesse, not the fictive Haller seen as real, who benefits from the construction, manipulation, and mirroring of various parts of himself.

In a study of the beginnings of Hesse's novels, Georgian Germanist Reso Karalaschwili reaches conclusions similar to Neuswanger's with respect to the reality of Haller's record. The fictive editor can vouch for the reality of Haller and the authenticity of his record, but, with a few exceptions, not for the events described. He "has no doubt that they are for the most part fictitious, not, however, in the sense of arbitrary invention. They are rather the deeply lived spiritual events which he has attempted to express by giving them the form of tangible experiences." At the same time, even the fantastic events he describes "have some basis in real occurrence" (St 22). These comments by the editor establish the perspective readers should take: they should direct their attention to the deeper level of "magical reality" (1981, 469). In keeping with Hesse's other novels, the fundamental movement here is in the "gradual liberation of the plot from the social, empirical continuum and in the transition to the metaphysical sphere of the reality of the soul . . . . The processes of the soul are projected outward and take on the form of visible events" (473).

Karalaschwili compares the preface to a bridge that leads the reader from the "outside of reality" to the "inside of the fiction." In works of fiction the preface may be external to the fictive reality or it may be a part of it. Where the author of the preface is presented as a real person, the preface is generally not a part of the artistic work itself and the conversation between editor and reader appears to take place on a real level.

> In those cases, however, when the authorship of the foreword is attributed to a fictive author and when this author becomes personalized in the reader's imagination, then the preface is not a part of real reality (even if it often presents itself as such) but is integrated into the artistic or fictive reality [*Kunstwirklichkeit*],

though it is always closer to external reality than the work it introduces (466–67). Parallel to the shift in his attitude from antipathy to sympathy, the editor of Haller's manuscript appears to move some distance across the bridge during the writing of his preface: near its end he reveals greater intellectual possibilities and artistic ability than one expects from an average Bürger; some of his insights even anticipate part of the Treatise (470).

Based on a comparison of *Steppenwolf* with Kierkegaard's scheme of existential development and his concept of humor, Peter Jansen agrees with those who conclude that Haller and Hesse successfully reach a higher level at the end of the novel. Like Hesse, Kierkegaard was concerned primarily with the individual and identified three existential stages an individual must pass through in the course of becoming himself: the aesthetic, the ethical, and the religious. These stages are roughly analogous to Hesse's three kingdoms. A person in the aesthetic stage is like a child; his state is determined by his birth and environment, and he is directly determined by chance, good fortune, and misfortune. On the ethical level a person has recognized his responsibility for self-determination and has decided to undertake the interminable process of becoming himself. A person in the religious stage has recognized the transitoriness of this world, but without despair and without giving up the task of individuation. At the boundary between the first two stages is irony and between the second and third, humor. For Kierkegaard, irony and humor are determinants of existence, not occasional manifestations. Humor is not the ability to speak humorously; it is the ability "to live life in a meaningful way despite all contradictions" (1978, 211).

According to Jansen, Haller is still in the first stage because he lacks self-irony and humor. This is a weak point in Jansen's comparison, since Haller is clearly on the second level both in Hesse's system, and, because he can scarcely be compared to a child who is determined entirely by forces outside himself, in Kierkegaard's too. The comparison is nevertheless illuminating. According to Jansen, Haller has recognized the existential responsibility of individuation but has not yet fully and finally decided to accept it. The source of his despair lies in his inner division and lack of direction and in his weakness and inability to commit himself (212). He needs to gain the

> insight that he must not destroy the oppositions in himself but must mediate them, that he must accept himself with his contradictions, that he must decide absolutely for himself, but also, that he cannot travel the path to his own personality with self-destructive anger and repression; he must acquire self-irony and humor. (214)

Through the latter he can replace his despair and melancholy with sobriety and serenity (*Heiterkeit*), which are attributes of ethical existence. Whereas Haller's irony is hostile, aggressive, and self-destructive and drives him further and further into isolation and despair, self-irony and humor would enable him to accept and endure with equanimity the inevitable setbacks in the developmental process (214).

What distinguishes a person in the ethical stage of existence, Jansen explains, is not the distance he displays toward the bourgeois world but his absolute decision to the self and its humanization or individuation. A person in this stage has no need to insist on his uniqueness, as Haller does. Haller is torn by the conflict between his critical rejection of the bourgeoisie and the fact that he and his actions are determined by the bourgeoisie. Through his acquaintance with Hermine he learns that his suffering is not unique, that it does not come from the world with its incongruities but from himself and his inability to accept his own internal contradictions. He must accept his suffering, which is a fundamental part of existence, and overcome his despair, and he must develop self-irony and commit himself to self-development. Once he has gained these insights and made this progress, Hermine leads him to the Magic Theater, a "school of humor" that can serve as a bridge to Kierkegaard's religious stage (215–16).

Passage through the Magic Theater is extremely difficult because it involves confrontation with the self and its possibilities, dangers, polarities, and limitations, and it requires making the decision for self-development. Although Haller demonstrates by killing Hermine that he has not yet learned what is to be taken seriously and what to laugh at (St 243), he has nevertheless been purged in the process:

> he has left his despair and melancholy behind and recognized self-irony and humor as existential exigencies for self-development . . . . With this absolute decision for becoming himself Harry Haller has opened the ethical realm. This decision is supported by an ethical seriousness that excludes all despair; it has been made with knowledge of his own transitoriness and suffering; but this knowledge no longer leads to despair but to humor. (218)

In a close reading of Haller's dream about Goethe-, Reso Karalaschwili discovers an illuminating triad of interrelated or "identical" symbols: the leg, the scorpion, and Molly. By drawing on religion, mythology, folklore, and psychoanalysis, Karalaschwili amplifies, sometimes overamplifies, these symbols. Goethe himself is seen as the personification of the totality of psychic events, conscious and unconscious, hence as the Self and the goal of individuation. Haller is described as a thinking type whose feeling function is unconscious and undifferentiated. (Although Karalaschwili's method of amplifying symbols, his viewing of Goethe as the Self, his remarks on the hero's typology, and the fact that the dream anticipates the hero's subsequent development are all based on Jung's psychology, his only mention of Jung's name is in a book title cited in a footnote.)

According to Karalaschwili, the scorpion is a Zoroastrian and Mithraic symbol for sensuality, passion, and sexual desire. In the literature on dreams it is considered to be a symbol for illness or impending death. This relates to Haller's preoccupation with suicide and to the transformation foretold in the Treatise. In astrology the scorpion stands for woman and also for water and therefore the unconscious. The sexual meaning of the symbol is enhanced by the fact that Haller's meeting with Goethe takes place in a room, which Freud identifies as a dream symbol for woman, and the scorpion climbs up Haller's leg, which, according to Karalaschwili, is a well-known phallic symbol that often expresses repressed erotic content in dreams (1980, 228). To this list G. W. Field adds the superstitious belief that the pain from a scorpion's sting can be cured homeopathically by the application of oil derived from a scorpion, which suggests that Haller can overcome his fear of sex by engaging in it (1970, 96).

As noted above, Molly, the sister of August Bürger's wife, became Bürger's lover and de facto second wife. Haller confuses Bürger with Matthison, who wrote "bloodless, boring classicistic poems," which are quite the opposite of Bürger's passionate and sensual poetry. Karalaschwili relates the contrast between these poets to the opposition represented by Schiller and Goethe: Schiller admired the moral and passionless poetry of Matthison, while Goethe preferred Bürger. What Bürger and Goethe represent, Haller needs to develop in himself. The connection is reinforced by the mention of Vulpius, Goethe's common law wife for many years, whose name means fox in Latin: the fox has the same symbolic meaning as the wolf. Both animals have recourse to diabolical forces, and the fox has the magical ability to transform itself into other figures. In a similar vein, Goethe is compared to a raven, a soul-bird which accompanied gods and heroes in mythology but which, like the wolf and the fox, came to be linked with the devil. Psychologically they represent the unconscious elements Haller needs to integrate into his consciousness (229–32).

Goethe demonstrates his skill in the Dionysian art of dancing, a skill Haller will subsequently spend some time learning. Karalaschwili associates dancing with legs, which he then connects to the attractive effigy of a female leg Goethe shows to Haller. When Harry reaches for the leg, it seems to be transformed into a scorpion. In folklore the leg is believed to have magical power. Karalaschwili sees the occurrence of this symbol as a typical manifestation of dreams, where the object of desire, the positive symbol, is displaced by an opposing symbol. He fails to mention that Haller had been prepared for this incident: when he sees the scorpion at the beginning of the dream, he thinks it "might be a kind of messenger from her [that is, Molly] — or an heraldic beast, dangerously and beautifully emblematic of woman and sin" (St 107). But when the opportunity presents itself, his desire is offset by dread, and he lacks the courage to touch the leg, whereupon Goethe laughs at him. This anticipates his similar failure at the end of the Magic Theater (232–33).

In *Hermann Hesse's Fictions of the Self: Autobiography and the Confessional Imagination* (1988), Eugene L. Stelzig reverts to a biographical approach to the author, but biography seen from a post-modernist perspective. Stelzig cites Hesse's praise of Ball's biography for capturing the *legend* of his life, which is truer even than the facts and biographical data. "I see only now how well you have written, not the banal history, but the legend of this life," Hesse writes to Ball, "how you have found the magic formulas. Even there, where you are actually in error, that is, where you assume false dates, you are still right and hit the nail on the head." Hesse also describes a dream he had in connection with the biography: he sees himself sitting "not in the mirror, but really myself as a second living figure, more living than myself," but an inner restraint prevents him from looking at himself directly, for "that would have been sinful" (203; GB 2:178). Stelzig attempts to demonstrate how Hesse's autobiographical, confessional writing, whether factually true or not, "creates his biography, for the process of writing himself is his most satisfying and complete mode of being." In a way he "*de*-realizes his ordinary self so as to re-realize and textualize it in and through his work." Art triumphs over life (34).

Stelzig sees the "visionary and self-refracting hermeneutic of *Steppenwolf*'s Magic Theater" not as something new in Hesse's works but as the "culmination of Hesse's contrapuntal self-multiplication through mirror images and double perspectives in his writing of the 1920s" (198). On the one hand, *Steppenwolf* is Hesse's most autobiographical fiction, as Mileck has stated, but it is also his most fantastic and, because of its ironic perspectives and experimental style, his "most spectacular fiction of the self" (202). Its perspective ranges "from the intensely subjective and uncritical to the extremely ironic and detached — that calls into question, revises, and extends the author's self-understanding" (208). Hesse's irony helps to undermine and subvert Haller's "sentimental self-presentation as the lonely outsider, doing all good, yet suffering all ill" (209).

In his discussion of the three major perspectives, Stelzig notes how Hesse uses the editor and the Treatise to get outside himself and see himself as others see him and thus to obtain results and insight beyond the reach of the autobiographer. Haller, on the other hand, strives in his record for a more subjective self-reflection that ultimately coincides with the other two. The aim of Hesse's multiperspectival self-mirroring is "not to refract and fragment the self out of existence, but rather to explode the fiction of an identity simplex, or simply unified, in order to work toward a more representative and inclusive sense of personal identity as a complex unity-in-multeity," a multeity which also includes the unconscious, and which is expressed metaphorically in the chess game of the Magic Theater (210).

While the editor's account is pervaded by bourgeois attitudes and assumptions, which Haller hates but also shares, and Haller's records are subjective and uncritical, the Treatise presents an objective, scientific account that could have been written by the Immortals, as Ziolkowski, Mileck, and others have suggested, or "by a panel of (unusually literate) social scientists." In that it provides a psychological profile of Haller and presents the major ideas around which the plot is structured, it may be seen as the novel's thematic center (213–14). It also criticizes and demystifies some of Haller's beliefs (for example, the belief that his personality is a duality and that he can regress to animal or child), informs him that suicide is not a viable solution to his problems, and points the way to the Magic Theater and the knowledge and insight he will gain there.

Stelzig describes the Magic Theater as "a modernist fun house in which the three major narrative viewpoints . . . are confounded in an internalized *theatrum mundi* of mirror images upon mirror images," where Haller discovers the repressed or undeveloped areas of his emotional life (219). Hesse ironically spoofs himself and his hero through the various episodes of the Magic Theater. Haller's imaginary stabbing of Hermine brings a hidden complex of erotic and aggressive desires into consciousness and expresses "a homicidal fantasy that may be the symbolic equivalent of both Hesse's guilt and resentment at the failure of his two marriages" (222).

This is but one possible interpretation of an occurrence which Stelzig considers to be symbolically overdetermined. As we have seen, some interpreters consider Haller's murder of Hermine to be beneficial to or indicative of a positive development, while others see it as detrimental. Stelzig concludes from this that Hesse, in what is at once an autobiographical self-exposure and a confessional fantasy, "reveals that a fundamental psychic conflict — instinct versus intellect, *eros* versus *logos* — is far from resolved for him" (222–23). He has not yet succeeded in harmonizing this basic polarity of his life and his art. In Stelzig's view, Haller has experienced a setback in his quest for unity but not a definite defeat or downfall: Mozart's ironic lecture to Harry about classical music heard on the radio is a "way of keeping the door open to continuing growth, whose precondition is not succumbing to despair," and his sentence makes light of Haller's most recent failure. Furthermore, Pablo's shrinking of Hermine and putting her figure into his pocket is a reminder

> of the artificiality of art, of the fact that [Hesse's] book is *only* a fictional construct. The writer's self is always more than the fiction of the self, which is here wryly deconstructed with the notion that both life and art are, like music, an unending game with infinite combinations, to be played again and yet again. (223)

In the only extended Freudian analysis of the novel published to date, Renate Delphendahl considers the doubles in *Steppenwolf* to be personifications and projections of Haller's narcissistic self-love, which is the result of his lack of object cathexis: since "he is unable to find suitable objects to cathect his projections," they "fall back on him in terms of counter-cathexes, which cause severe psychic disturbances" (1988, 151). Haller's desire for destruction and for an erotic relationship with Hermine, his female double, are manifestations of Freud's dual drive theory of love and aggression, which are linked to his narcissism. According to Delphendahl, Hermine represents the ego-ideal Haller is seeking; the desire to possess her is equivalent to the desire for oneness between ego and ego-ideal.[7] But Delphendahl also sees her as the "manifest double of Harry's dissociated mind" and, along with the wolf in the Magic Theater, as an allegorical death figure, both of which roles seem to contradict her function as his ego ideal. Still another role is identified in connection with Lacan's view of the mirror phase of narcissistic development, according to which Harry's encounter with Hermine, his mirror image, should effect a progression from love of self to love of the other (147), that is, to the object of cathexis he lacks.

Delphendahl interprets Harry's murder of Hermine as a symbolic suicide and as a panic reaction in response to Pablo's taking possession of his beloved, which is a symbolic castration (212). Psychologically, she adds in apparent contradiction, the slaying of a double "symbolizes arrested narcissistic ego-development" and is "analogous to the splitting of a troublesome ego" (213), hence to its multiplication rather than suicidal destruction. Also, this murder comes near the end of Haller's journey through the Magic Theater, which she claims depicts the conflict and reconciliation between his two sides, or at least the acceptance of dualism, which again runs counter to its interpretation as a symbolic suicide. Furthermore, the refractions of the Magic Theater are seen to "function as a parody of a unitary self shattered into many pieces, comparable to Lacan's notion of *le corp morcele*, the fragmented body, which precedes the unification of the whole body in the mirror state" (214). But in anticipating such a unification, Delphendahl ignores and thus discounts the Treatise's insistence on the multiplicity of parts which constitute the personality, a message that is confirmed in the Magic Theater by the chess episode, the mirror imagery, and the many potential roles Haller is able to choose from.[8]

[7]In an illuminating psychoanalytical study of Hesse, Johannes Cremerius identifies Hesse's ego-ideal with his overdeveloped superego, which was determined by his rigid and demanding father. Hesse had an extremely sensitive sense of evil and consciousness of guilt. His abnormally powerful superego weakened and reduced the functions of his ego and his ability to enjoy life and sensual pleasure. Furthermore, a profound disturbance in his relationship to his mother had a negative effect on his relationships with women, who appear in his works as the "products of pubescent male fantasies" (Ausgeburten pubertärer Knabenphantasien) (1983, 185). What Hesse sought in psychoanalysis was the "sympathetic understanding, loving guidance, and supportive companionship" that was lacking in his childhood (186). He considers the goal of analysis to be self-understanding, which is similar to the awakening or conversion experienced by Pietists. Hesse's analysis failed, Cremerius maintains, because the superego structure was not dissolved (198).

[8]In a psychoanalytic study of *The Double in Literature*, Robert Rogers recognizes that Hesse's view of the divided or multiple self is opposed to Freud's balance of power theory and the psychoanalytic goal of achieving ego integrity and a "kind of harmony or balance among various components of the self." "On the other hand," he adds, "Hesse's emphasis on the radical multiplication of the self holds true insofar

Implicitly Freudian in the importance it gives to individual and collective repression is Marc A. Weiner's illuminating analysis of the psychological and sociological significance of music in various works that reflect the unstable collective and individual psyches of imperial Germany and Austria. Weiner considers a number of historical and fictive figures who may be seen, as Haller is by the editor of his papers, as representative of "the sickness of the times themselves, the neurosis of that generation" to which they belong.

> Because the makeup of the personality depicted in these works operates as a mirror of the forces under which it is formed, the breakdown or trans-formation of the psyche has social significance; an alternative psychological constitution not based on the denial and repression characteristic of the Wilhelminian personality suggests an alternative, less repressive order. Music is the art that transforms the psyche and points to an elusive, alternative community. (1993, 105)

Weiner identifies a number of similarities and some differences between Harry Haller and Gustav Aschenbach in Thomas Mann's *Death in Venice*. The personalities of both were formed by an oppressive and repressive up-bringing and by the conservative values of Wilhelminian Germany. In both works, a hierarchy of the arts reflects different degrees of repression and so-cial stratification, with "high-epic" writing and the classics on top and las-civious music on the bottom, and both figures recognize that the higher forms of art are achieved through denial, repression, and general compliance with social norms and conventions. Unlike Aschenbach, however, whose repression is stronger, Haller is aware of the dilemma which results from the conflict in him between his cultural, conservative, and elitist tastes and his more liberal political and social proclivity. By questioning and reevaluating cultural works and figures, especially Goethe and Mozart, Haller combats the oppression of the psyche and the rigid stratification of society and is eventually able to accept the forces Aschenbach continues to deny, includ-ing the Dionysian power of music, to which Aschenbach ultimately suc-cumbs in a fatal breakdown.

By pointing out to Haller that his own image of Goethe is no less cul-turally determined and biased than the bourgeois representation admired by the professor and his wife, Hermine initiates the developmental process that includes reevaluation of high and low culture. Haller's unconscious imme-diately responds to her rebuke with a dream in which his view of the exalted and repressed classical hero is refuted by Goethe's childlike playfulness and

as it applies to fantasy life in general, notably that of writers and actors" (1970, 98). Delphendahl cites Rogers but, to the detriment of her argument, apparently does not accept his conclusions.

spontaneity and by his irony, mirth, and humor. A similar revision takes place in his image of Mozart, who is transformed in his mind from an "imperial icon of a repressive elitism" to a "playful representative of an alternative social order" (118).

According to Weiner, Haller's cultural elitism is also manifest in his view of jazz as music of decline, sensuality, and instinct, which is as "hot and raw as the steam of raw flesh," a "miserable affair" when compared to the "real music" of Bach and Mozart (St 43). It is the music of an egalitarian, unrestrained, and international society, which is antithetical to German tradition. To Haller, as to the popular imagination at the time of the Weimar Republic, "jazz functioned as an acoustical sign of national, social, racial, and sexual difference" (121). For his German contemporaries Hesse's incorporation of jazz in his narrative "could automatically refer through a musical sign to a host of volatile issues in the polarized society and culture of the Weimar period." Like the Dionysian music in *Death in Venice*, it represents a threatening alternative to European society and culture.

> Haller's changing relationship to jazz is paradigmatic of the psychosocial change he undergoes in the course of the novel from an introverted, masochistic, and obsessive intellectual alienated from the world around him to a man accepting of contradictions and open to new impressions, be they social, racial, aesthetic, or sexual. (124)

Weiner considers Haller's ambivalent reaction to jazz to be a reflection of his ambivalence toward his own culture and society. As he comes to accept jazz and popular dance music with their social and cultural implications, he undergoes a transformation of social consciousness which is reflected not only in his revised view of Goethe and Mozart but also in his changed attitude toward Pablo and in the sense of community he feels with others at the masked ball. Jazz thus becomes a "catalyst that effects a gradual transformation of the psyche molded by the repressive values of the late Wilhelminian and Weimar age." Through the "dismantling of psychic repression achieved through jazz comes an emancipatory, revolutionary view of the powerful political and social forces of the German-speaking empires." The anarchical influence of this supposedly primitive and chaotic music prepares Haller for the "Anarchist Evening Entertainment" he experiences in the Magic Theater (141).

Works Cited

Allemann, Beda. "Tractat vom Steppenwolf." Afterword to Hesse's "Treatise on the Steppenwolf." Frankfurt am Main: Suhrkamp, 1961. Rpt. in *Materialien zu Hermann Hesses "Der Steppenwolf,"* ed. Volker Michels, 317–24. Frankfurt am Main: Suhrkamp, 1972.

Böttger, Fritz. *Hermann Hesse: Leben, Werk, Zeit.* Berlin: Verlag der Nation, 1974.

Brown, Calvin S. *Music and Literature: A Comparison of the Arts.* Athens, U of Georgia P, 1948.

Cremerius, Johannes. "Schuld und Sühne ohne Ende: Hermann Hesse's psychotherapeutische Erfahrungen." In *Literaturpsychologische Studien und Analysen,* Amsterdamer Beiträge zur neueren Germanistik, ed. Walter Schönau, 169–204. Amsterdam: Rodopi, 1983.

Delphendahl, Renate. "Narcissism and the Double in Hermann Hesse's *Steppenwolf.*" *Journal of Evolutionary Psychology* 9 (1988): 141–53, 208–17.

Dhority, Lynn. "Toward a Revaluation of Structure and Style in Hesse's *Steppenwolf.*" In *Theorie und Kritik: Zur vergleichenden und neueren deutschen Literatur: Festschrift fur Gerhard Loose zum 65. Geburtstag.* ed. Stefan Grunwald and B. A. Beatie, 149–58. Bern: Francke, 1974.

Dhority, Lynn. "Who wrote the *Tractat vom Steppenwolf?*" *German Life and* Letters 27 (1973): 59–66.

Farrer, Edward A. "The Quest for Being: D. H. Lawrence and Hermann Hesse." Ph.D. diss., Purdue University, 1975.

Gay, Peter. *Weimar Culture: The Outsider as Insider.* New York: Harper and Row, 1968.

Hollis, A. "Political Ambivalence in Hesse's *Steppenwolf.*" *Modern Language Review* 73 (1978): 110–118.

———. "*Steppenwolf:* The Laughter in the Music." *New German Studies* 6 (1978): 15–30.

Jansen, Peter. "Personalität und Humor: Hesses *Steppenwolf* and Kierkegaard's Humorkonzeption." *Sprache im technischen Zeitalter* 67 (1978): 209–20.

Jung, C. G. *The Archetypes and the Collective Unconscious.* Translated by F. C. Hull. Vol. 9i, *The Collected Works of C. G. Jung.* Princeton: Princeton U P, 1969.

Karalaschwili, Reso. "Harry Hallers Goethe-Traum: Vorläufiges zu einer Szene aus dem *Steppenwolf* von Hermann Hesse." *Goethe-Jahrbuch* 97 (1980): 224–34.

———. "Der Romananfang bei Hermann Hesse: Die Funktion des Titels, des Vorworts und des Romaneinsatzes in seinem Schaffen." *Jahrbuch der deutschen Schillergesellschaft* 25 (1981): 446–473.

Lange, Marga. *"Daseinsproblematik" in Hermann Hesse's "Steppenwolf": An Existential Interpretation.* Queensland Studies in German Language and Literature. Brisbane, Australia: U of Queensland, 1970.

Knüfermann, Volker. "Sprache und Neurose: Zu Hermann Hesses *Steppenwolf.*" *Études Germanique* 34 (1979): 276–83.

Lüthi, Hans Jürg. *Hermann Hesse: Natur und Geist.* Sprache und Literatur, 69. Stuttgart: Kohlhammer, 1970.

Mayer, Hans. "Hermann Hesse und das Magische Theater. Ein Vortrag." *Jahrbuch der deutschen Schillergesellschaft* 21 (1977): 517–32.

Michels, Volker, ed. *Materialien zu Hermann Hesses "Der Steppenwolf."* Frankfurt am Main: Suhrkamp, 1972.

Michels, Volker, ed. *Über Hermann Hesse.* Vol. 1. Frankfurt am Main: Suhrkamp, 1976.

Michels, Volker. "Zwischen Duldung und Sabotage. Hermann Hesse und der Nationalsozialismus." In *Hermann Hesse und die Politik*, 7th International Hermann-Hesse Colloquium in Calw, ed. Martin Pfeifer, 87–105. Bad Liebenzell: Verlag Bernhard Gengenbach, 1992.

Middell, Eike. *Hermann Hesse: Die Bilderwelt seines Lebens.* Leipzig: Reclam; Frankfurt am Main: Röderberg, 1975.

Mileck, Joseph. *Hermann Hesse and His Critics: The Criticism and Bibliography of Half a Century.* Chapel Hill: U of North Carolina P, 1958.

Mileck, Joseph. *Hermann Hesse: Life and Art.* Berkeley: U of California P, 1978.

Neuswanger, R. Russell. "The Autonomy of the Narrator and the Function of Humor in *Der Steppenwolf.*" In *Hermann Hesse heute*, ed. Adrian Hsia, 233–41. Bonn: Bouvier, 1980.

Pavlyshyn, Marko. "Music in Hermann Hesse's *Der Steppenwolf* and *Das Glasperlenspiel.*" *Seminar* 15 (1979): 39–55.

Rogers, Robert. *A Psychoanalytic Study of the Double in Literature.* Detroit: Wayne State U P, 1970.

Sammons, Jeffrey L. "Notes on the Germanization of American Youth." *The Yale Review* 59 (1970): 342–56.

Sammons, Jeffrey L. "Hermann Hesse and the Over-Thirty Germanist." In *Hesse: A Collection of Critical Essays,* ed. Theodore Ziolkowski, 112–33. Englewood Cliffs, N.J.: Prentice Hall, 1973.

Schneider, Christian Immo. *Das Todesproblem bei Hermann Hesse.* Marburg: Elwert, 1973.

Schwarz, Egon. "Hermann Hesse, the American Youth Movement, and Problems of Literary Evaluation." *PMLA* 85 (1970): 977–87.

Seckendorff, Klaus von. *Hermann Hesses propagandistische Prosa: Selbstzerstörerische Entfaltung als Botschaft in seinen Romanen von "Demian" bis zum "Steppenwolf."* Bonn: Bouvier, 1982.

Stelzig, Eugen L. *Hermann Hesse's Fictions of the Self: Autobiography and the Confessional Imagination.* Princeton: Princeton U P, 1988.

Weiner, Marc A. *Undertones of Insurrection: Music, Politics, and the Social Sphere in the Modern German Narrative.* Lincoln, Nebraska: U of Nebraska P, 1993.

5: Metaphors, Symbols, and Archetypes

Simultaneous with the American discovery of Hesse during the sixties and seventies and part of the same phenomenon was the counterculture's fascination with the writings of C. G. Jung. The emphasis both authors gave to inwardness and the individual's striving for wholeness and for the full development of his or her innate personality gave support to the hippies and other youth in their questioning of conventions and their rejection of the personas being imposed on them by the authority of school, state, and religion. Also appealing to this generation and compatible with their own goals was the recognition of both authors of the compensatory relevance for Western man of the attitudes and moral precepts of Chinese and Indian religion and philosophy, including the belief in the unity and interconnectedness of all life and the corollary demand for greater love and respect for others and for nature and the environment. Hesse's *Siddhartha*, whose popularity preceded that of *Steppenwolf*, provided a model for these readers.

Again the students were ahead of their teachers. As Jeffrey Sammons noted in 1973, his undergraduate students knew more about Jung than he did; consequently, he was not able to appreciate the validity of their Jungian interpretations of Hesse's works. The most serious and articulate of the Hesse enthusiasts among his undergraduate students were almost always disciples of Jung, he reports: "For such an audience a critique of Hesse involves a larger confrontation with Jungian principles, for which I am unequipped due to my inability to concentrate on the subject" (1973, 112, n.1). This inability, which is by no means unusual among critics, reveals itself in his disagreement with his students over the interpretation of Kromer in *Demian*: where he sees a manifestation of Germans' incapacity to deal with class conflict, the more knowledgeable students realize that Kromer is not an independent character but rather a manifestation of the Jungian "Shadow," an "aspect of Sinclair's self that needs to be internalized" (124, n.36). As this example demonstrates, some knowledge of Jung's theories is an unavoidable prerequisite for interpreting texts which owe as much to Jung's psychology as *Demian* and *Steppenwolf* do.

In the introduction to the collection of criticism which includes the essay by Sammons discussed above, Theodore Ziolkowski writes that he was discovering "the fascinating parallels and relationships between Hesse and Jung, which are only now beginning to come to light" (1973, 10). As awareness of these parallels and relationships increased, application of Jung's archetypal psychology to the interpretation and analysis of the texts from the period of Hesse's analysis became more and more common and has now become the predominant approach. Because of the number and importance of these studies, and in order to present a cohesive summary of their findings and arguments, I will review them together in this final chapter.

Although Hesse's Jungian analysis and the influence of Jung's psychology on his works has often been noted, few critics prior to the seventies subjected this relationship to critical analysis or attempted archetypal interpretations of Hesse's works. Those who did attempt to apply Jung's theories generally did so only superficially, perhaps because of their lack of sufficient knowledge of Jung's psychology and their unwillingness to undertake a thorough study of his difficult, sometimes obscure, works. The early, rather preliminary attempts by Boulby, Rose, and others were cited in previous chapters. Preceding and influencing their discussions are three works, a dissertation, an article, and a book, which helped to initiate this approach.[1]

The first detailed study of Jung and Hesse is Emanuel Maier's 1953 dissertation entitled "The Psychology of C. G. Jung in the Works of Hermann Hesse." Maier reproduces letters written by Hesse and Jung in response to his requests for information that might connect them. Jung indicates in his reply that he was the source of much of the information on Gnosticism which Dr. J. B. Lang transmitted to Hesse and which was the basis of *Demian*. He also claims to have had a more indirect influence on *Siddhartha* and *Steppenwolf*, but since this took place in his relationship as Hesse's analyst, he is not at liberty to provide details:

> The origin of *Siddhartha* and the *Steppenwolf* is of a more hidden nature. They are — to a certain extent — the direct or indirect results of certain talks I had with Hesse. I'm unfortunately unable to say how much he was cons[c]ious of the hints and implications which I let him have. Unfortunately I'm not in a position to give you full information, since my knowledge is strictly professional. (Maier, preceding p. 5; original in English.)

---

[1]Another dissertation, Elizabeth Leinfellner's 1962 study, "Polarität und Einheit im Werke Hermann Hesses" (Polarity and Unity in Hermann Hesse's Works), contains frequent references to similarities between Hesse and Jung, some of which connect both authors to Indian and Chinese philosophy. An example of the latter is both authors' equation of Tao, Atman, the Self, God, and the eternal I, all of which represent a unity of opposites which may be considered the ultimate goal of man's striving. Both authors also see the mother in her archetypal form as another symbol of unity. Furthermore, Hesse accepts Jung's view that art originates in the collective unconscious, and Hesse's description of Faust in *Steppenwolf* agrees with what Jung had written six years earlier in *Psychological Types*. (See CW 6:187–88, 206–7.)

Maier sent a copy of Jung's letter to Hesse for his comment, but Hesse, being a "friend of discretion," returned Jung's letter unopened. He briefly notes that he was analyzed by Lang, that he had read and was impressed by Jung's *Symbols of Transformation* and some other works, and that he was also analyzed by Jung. In general he respects and has a good impression of Jung, he states, but he claims that Freud's works made a stronger impression on him and that he lost interest in psychoanalysis around 1922, because he began to realize at that time that "an authentic relationship to art is unobtainable by analysts; they all lack the proper understanding for it" ("daß für die Analytiker ein echtes Verhältnis zur Kunst unerreichbar ist, es fehlt allen dafür das Organ"; Maier, following p. 4).

In his competent analysis of several relevant texts, Maier does not give *Steppenwolf* the space and attention that Jung's claimed influence would seem to warrant. He does identify Hermine as an anima figure and compares her to Beatrice in *Demian*, the novel he treats in greatest detail, and to Teresina in *Klein und Wagner*. He interprets her death as a sign that Haller has withdrawn his projection from her, an indication that the old Haller has died and a new one has been reborn. Maier also sees a parallel between Pablo and Teresina's dark dancing partner, whom Klein could never accept. In learning to accept Pablo and what he represents, Haller goes beyond Klein. Unlike Klein, he is able to experience the unconscious unity of opposites and survive (149–52).

Maier observes that the Magic Theater is a "temenos" (Greek) or "stupa" (Sanskrit), a holy area or space "in which the various aspects of the personality are gathered for the purpose of unification." It is thus also a mandala, a symbol of unity and the Self. Referring to Jung's *Psychology and Alchemy*, Maier notes the importance of Haller's movement in the Magic Theater to the left, that is, in the direction of the unconscious and the dissolution of the personality, and of Hermine's to the right, that is, in the direction of consciousness. In Jung's words: "The leftward 'circumambulatio' . . . is one of the paths to the center of the non-Ego. The Rosarium Philosophorum says: 'make a round circle of the man and woman . . . and you will have the Philosophers' Stone,'" which is a symbol of the Self (Maier 152–53).

The symbol of the unification of opposites found at the center is often represented in alchemical literature by the embrace or 'conjunctio' of a naked couple, usually depicted as king and queen and often juxtaposed with symbols of the sun and the moon. It may also be represented by a hermaphroditic being such as Abraxas in *Demian*, a deity who is both male and female as well as good and evil. Likewise, the conjunction of Pablo and Hermine, both of whom have been given hermaphroditic or androgynous characteristics, symbolizes Harry's unified Self. In Maier's view, Harry has achieved unity of the Self: "Having assimilated the Anima projection by killing Hermine, Harry Haller is 'condemned' to continue living. He is advised to find a sense of humor because it will help him to hear beneath the miserable 'radio music' of life the divine creation of Bach or Handel" (154). Such an interpretation is not supported by what follows Haller's killing of Hermine, however, for had he assimilated the anima and achieved the unity represented by the final image of the Magic Theater, Mozart's rebuke would be unjustified.

Malte Dahrendorf's short analysis of Jungian elements in *Demian* (1958) provides an additional demonstration of the relevance of Jung's psychology for the interpretation of that novel. Even those scholars who would diminish the importance for Hesse of Jung's psychology must acknowledge its relevance for *Demian*, which was written in connection with, indeed, as a part of, Hesse's Jungian analysis. (See Richards 1987.) Subsequent Jungian studies identify a number of parallels between *Demian* and *Steppenwolf.*

Noteworthy because of the close connection it established between Hesse and Jung is Miguel Serrano's *El circulo hermético de Hermann Hesse a C. G. Jung*, which appeared in 1965 and was published in English as *C. G. Jung and Hermann Hesse: A Record of Two Friendships* (1966).

At about the same time American scholars were beginning to use concepts from Jung's psychology to interpret the works from Hesse's period of crisis, Ludwig Völker, a Germanist teaching in Belgium, published a similar attempt in *Études Germanique* (1970). Following *Demian*, he notes, Hesse's readers have been prepared to see the figures in these confessional, monologic works more as symbols than as real people. The difference becomes clear if one compares Hermine, for example, with Teresina in *Klein und Wagner*. Both figures have a similar function and meaning, but whereas Teresina is comprehensible without a psychological explanation, Hermine is not. In *Steppenwolf* "the concepts of Jungian psychology have to a much greater degree become component parts of the story." That Hermine is to be considered complementary to Haller's ego or persona, that is, as his anima, is quite clearly demonstrated when she claims to be his mirror and when he sees her as his opposite and his soul (43–44).

Völker finds evidence in Jung's psychology for a deeper and more meaningful interpretation of Hermine's relationship to Harry's childhood friend Hermann than had previous interpreters, who saw it primarily as further evidence for her hermaphroditism. Whereas a man's "soul-image" is usually personified by the unconscious as a woman, "in every case where the *individuality* is unconscious, and therefore associated with the soul," Jung writes, "the soul-image has the character of the same sex" (Völker 46; see Jung CW 6:470; Jung's italics). Völker's understanding of Hermann is based on this theory: at a time when Harry's individuality was still unconscious, Hermann functioned as his soul-image. As Harry's individualism developed and became identified with his persona, his unconscious produced a feminine soul-image, namely, Hermine.

> If this explanation is correct, Hermann and Hermine would be related soul-images of Harry Haller, which are only separate from each other by time and Harry's stage of development. In comparison to Teresina, Hermine has more depth. Her relationship to Harry is closer and takes on magical characteristics. (46)

Harry faces the task of accepting the side of himself he has consistently suppressed, of falling in love with Hermine, the representative or image of his unconscious, and of becoming one with her. This is tantamount to being healed of his neurosis. In the nuptial dance he appears to be close to such a union, which could be symbolized by "murdering" Hermine, that is, by depotentiating the anima. Murdering her out of jealousy, however, represents a return to his former psychological attitude and therefore his failure to achieve integration (49–50).

Völker concludes his discussion by addressing the problem of the double function of Hermine as a real and as a symbolic figure. *Steppenwolf* is self-observation and self-confrontation, he observes. The novel deals only with Haller's confrontation with his own self. And of course Haller stands for Hesse, for whom a new work began to arise in the moment he could envision a figure who could serve for a time as a symbol and carrier of his experience, his thoughts, and his problems. Hesse specifically identifies Haller, among others, as such a figure and *Steppenwolf* as autobiography, in which it is "not a matter of stories, complications, and tensions," but of "monologs, in which a single person . . . is considered in his relation to the world and to his own ego" (GS 7:303). Hesse's artistry manifests itself, according to Völker, in his ability to transpose internal experience into narrated reality. Jung's psychology helped him to combine psychological knowledge and artistic craftsmanship: the more he learned about psychology, the more life and independence his figures gained. "The figure of Hermine . . . is in the middle between *Demian* and *Narziss und Goldmund*: on the one hand, she is no longer just a symbolic figure (like Demian and Frau Eva), on the other hand, she is not yet a complete person like Goldmund or Narcissus" (51–52).

In his 1971 article "Hermine and the Problem of Harry's Failure in Hesse's *Steppenwolf*," Eugene Webb asserts that none of the various attempts to apply Jungian ideas to Hesse's writing have produced a generally satisfactory interpretation. Neither Rose nor Boulby mention the idea, which is important for Jung, "that the development of the individual normally proceeds beyond the stage with which the anima archetype is associ-

ated to a higher stage in which the guiding figure is not a woman but a magician or a wise old man" (117).

The process of individuation described by Jung begins with the
"persona," that is, the personal consciousness, the face or mask through
which a person relates to other people and adapts to the world. Harry's persona is the bourgeois side of his personality. The part of the personality that
must be suppressed in order to develop and maintain the persona is the
"shadow," which is represented in Harry by the wolf. In Harry's case the
suppression has not been entirely successful, and the wolf raging inside him
has become so independent and powerful that Harry has virtually split into
two conflicting parts. But this painful split also constitutes an opportunity:
recognizing and coming to terms with the shadow is the first stage of the
inward journey or process of discovery (118).

The second stage is represented by the "anima," the countersexual representative of the soul or deeper levels of the unconscious. "The anima will
usually take the form of an appealing feminine figure representing the at-
tractiveness of self-knowledge to a person who has begun to outgrow his
initial fear of learning the truth about those aspects of himself of which he
has previously suppressed all awareness" (118). As most interpreters agree,
Hermine is that guiding figure. Webb suggests that her role deviates from
the Jungian pattern in that she wants Harry to fall in love with her, and she
also attempts to lure him towards death. Jung considers "succumbing to
the fascinating influence of the archetypes" to be the chief danger of psychological exploration. Contrary to Völker, Webb considers falling in love
with the anima, rather than killing her, to be an indication that Harry has
become too fascinated with the archetype and has not mastered it; he has
not sufficiently assimilated those elements of the total self that were symbolized by it (119).

That being the case, Harry is not yet prepared for the next stage of development, which is under the influence of the archetypal wise old man,
who is represented by Pablo, but also by Goethe, Mozart, and the chess
player in the Magic Theater: Webb notes that the chess player is dressed like
Pablo and has the same eyes; and Mozart becomes Pablo and also
"resembles like a twin brother" the man who taught Harry to play chess.

> In Jungian psychology the archetype of the wise old man or magician is as-
> sociated with a stage of experience in which the individual can begin to
> grow out of the passive role that one adopts in the relation with the anima
> and can begin to play a more active part in ordering his own life. (120–21)

But Harry is not yet ready to learn what Pablo and Mozart attempt to teach
him. He remains on the level of the anima. The only episode in the Magic
Theater to which he responds well, for example, is "All Girls are Yours," for·

which he has been prepared by Hermine. "Hermine represents to him at this point the one image of himself that he can accept, and falling into a jealous passion for her, he succumbs to the temptation of falling totally in love with himself. Psychologically, the attempted murder [of Hermine] is a kind of symbolic suicide," as the prosecutor points out. At the end, however, Haller is optimistic that his psychological growth will continue (123–24).

In an article published the same year as Webb's, Peter Hertz gives yet another interpretation of the murder. Harry does not kill Hermine as she is, but as he has created her, and this death is the absolute prerequisite for loving her as what she is and on her own terms. He must also kill his own attitude to himself, which he does in the Magic Theater. It is this, according to Hertz, which explains the novel's appeal to students, especially those who have been pushed to college but would rather experience life: like Harry, they must kill the past in themselves and the image they have been taught to have of themselves before they can step back into the world of society as authentic individuals (1971, 445–46).

In an interpretation amply supported by quotations from a number of Jung's works, Susanne Meinicke recognizes that Hermine's influence on Harry declines as he finds more and more of his own attributes in her. The more unconscious the anima is, the greater is its power. As Harry learns from Hermine and incorporates her function as a projection of the anima into himself, she loses her power of attraction. To fall in love with her would mean fully integrating her into himself, that is, withdrawing his projection, at which time she would cease to exist for him as an external entity. She would then be dead for him, which is how Hermine understands the last command that she will give him, namely, to kill her. In killing her too soon, Harry also kills something in himself and terminates the process before it is complete (1972, 36–39). Meinicke's interpretation of the relationship between Harry and Hermine differs somewhat from Völker's and Webb's, but she is in agreement with them on the meaning of her death.

Meinicke first identifies Pablo as a part of Harry's ego, as his "shadow," which, according to Jung, personifies what the subject does not recognize in himself, in this case his childlike or primitive attributes. Yet she recognizes that his meaning also goes beyond that of the shadow and even of the anima: in the Magic Theater he is the master over Harry's soul images and a powerful, transpersonal guide into his unconscious. He dissolves Harry's personality into numerous parts, thereby demonstrating the truth of the Treatise. In the guise of the chess player, he tells him how he can vary the constellation of the parts of his personality at will, and as Mozart he instructs him about the Immortals and humor. Though she does not identify him as such, Pablo, as Meinicke describes him, actually fits Jung's definition of the archetype of the wise old man rather than the shadow.

Noting Pablo's godlike role, Meinicke compares him, as did Weibel in 1952, to Hermes, whom Jung considers to be a personification of the unconscious:

> Hermes is the one who brings up the "life of the underworld"; Pablo guides Harry's unconscious into the light of consciousness.
>
> Just like Pablo, Hermes is the director of dreams and skilled in magic.
>
> Both are connected by a close relationship with music; Hermes is said to have invented the lyre and improvised song; Pablo is an enthusiastic jazz musician.
>
> Hermes is considered to be the inventor of language; Pablo supposedly speaks all languages of the world.
>
> As Eros-figures both are without shame . . . .
>
> Hermes accompanies souls to Hades; Harry is lured to "hell."
>
> Finally, Hermes is the guide of the "tiny people," i.e., the shades of the dead, who, after drinking from the river Lethe, forget everything, that is, fall back into unconsciousness. Pablo is the director of the chess figures, which symbolize the unconscious possibilities dwelling in Harry. (46–47)

Meinicke thus considers Pablo and Hermes to be representatives of the same archetype, which she does not name. Its function, however, is to diminish the deadly opposition in Harry's personality by guiding him into the chaos of his soul and enabling him to sense the meaning of life.[2]

In the end Harry achieves a position similar to one later described by Hesse in a letter:

> I believe that, despite its apparent absurdity, life nevertheless has meaning; I accept not being able to comprehend with reason this ultimate meaning, but I am prepared to serve it, even if I have to sacrifice myself in the process. I hear the voice of this meaning in myself, in the moments when I am real and completely alive and awake. (GS 7:499)

Harry has learned that all the parts of his personality are necessary constituents of the whole; if he can but learn to adopt an attitude of humor, he can

---

[2]Because he considers Hermine rather than Pablo to be representative of the psychopomp, Peter Huber disagrees with comparisons of Pablo with Hermes. If the wordplay on names is to have any meaning, he claims, it is in connection with Hermes Trismegistus. "The hermetic literature . . . favors the treatise, is related to the ancient mystery cults (Orphic, Dionysian), and deals with rebirth and ecstasy as well as the mystical unity with god (*unio mystica*)" (1994, 97). Since Pablo and Hermine function together and may be seen as parts of a greater whole, however, they both serve as psychopomps. Pablo clearly has that role in the Magic Theater. Furthermore, Hermes Trismegistus and the hermetic, alchemical tradition are themselves related to Hermes and may be considered a further enrichment of Hesse's multiple references. (See Jung, CW 13:178 and below.)

laugh at the apparent conflicts and contradictions in himself with the assurance that they are an inescapable and ultimately meaningful part of the human condition.

Reaching this insight was cathartic for Hesse, Meinicke writes, but it did not remove his suffering and gloom. Because of his belief that the deeper layers of all individuals' souls at a particular historical moment are identical, because they are part of the collective unconscious, he felt justified in drawing negative conclusions for the development of history from the chaos and sickness in his own soul. As demonstrated in his "Great Hunt in Automobiles," even the pacifist Harry is capable of destruction and violence in protest against an existing order and in the hope of a better one to follow. Hesse shares the hopes of many in the expressionist generation that a new man and a new order will grow out of the destruction of the old (95–99).

According to Ted Spivey, it is this affirmation of life in the midst of chaos and tragedy that makes Hesse appealing to young readers. Like Joyce and other symbolist writers, Hesse sought and found the image of the cosmic man, namely, the hero as a quester on a mythic journey which leads from despair through fragmentation to visions of reintegration and the renewal of hope. With mythopoeic power Joyce and Hesse create figures originating in the archetype out of which the mythical heroes arose. They set out in search of the hero's image and power, which is awaiting discovery and activation in every individual. It is presumed that activating this power will bring about the reintegration of man. Unlike Siddhartha, Haller does not find spiritual unity, but he does learn "the meaning of the quest, and in a visionary moment he glimpses the archetype of the cosmic man" (1970, 50–52, 55).

David Artiss identifies four key symbols in *Steppenwolf*, which constitute a "rich fund of archetypal imagery, consciously worked and relatively unexplored, a tribute to Carl Gustav Jung, the *éminence grise* behind this work" (1971, 86). In order for their full significance to become apparent, these four symbolic motifs — the wolf, the mirror, flowers, and laughter — must be considered against the background of the predominant theme of schizophrenia. Following up on a statement of his theory of neurosis in *Kurgast*, Hesse sets out to demonstrate through Harry Haller that neurosis is not a disease but a highly positive, albeit painful process of sublimation: positive in that integration may ultimately result from it (87).

Because of Hesse's knowledge of Western and Eastern mythology, it can be assumed, Artiss writes, that he was aware of the implications of the wolf as an archetypal image associated with the devil and evil demons. From the beginning the wolf had a split personality, as is indicated by the old saying: "Weil der Teufel ihn schuf, und im Namen Gottes belebte, weiß der Wolf heute noch nicht, ob er für Gott oder den Teufel Partei nehmen soll"

(Because he was created by the devil and brought to life in the name of God, the wolf still doesn't know today whether he should side with God or the devil). Hesse consistently develops lupine imagery to describe the bestial side of Harry, which is a necessary part of his humanization. Artiss agrees with Kenneth Hughes that the development from bestiality to humanity is a "conscious, studied echo of the ancient Babylonian allegory of *Gilgamesh*" (87–88).

Like Ralph Freedman, Artiss considers the novel's central symbol to be the mirror, "an archetypal image of very ancient significance . . . . The mirror-image, like the shadow, was considered an extension of oneself and interpreted animistically as a 'soul' or *Doppelgänger*" (88–89). The mirror has traditionally possessed magic powers which may be dangerous. When it occurs in psychoanalysis, it is usually with ominous undertones.

> The mirror can symbolize the power of the unconscious to "mirror" the individual objectively, thus giving him a view of himself that he may never have had before. This is exactly the function of the mirror in the Magic Theatre and it reflects Hesse's familiarity with Jungian methods of psychoanalysis. Jung maintained that only through the unconscious can such an objective self-encounter be obtained — a self-encounter that often shocks and upsets the conscious mind. (89)

According to Artiss, Haller is prepared for his descent into the underworld of his unconscious by three "'mirror' characters — Hermine, Pablo, and Maria, each representative of repressed aspects of his own personality" (90). Artiss is probably correct in identifying Pablo as the key player in this triad, but his claim that Pablo represents both a repressed aspect of Harry and the guru-figure and model of perfection represented by the synthesis of body and soul in transcendental form (91) requires some qualification, since his model role does not become fully apparent until his dissolution or transformation into Mozart at the end of the novel. It seems likely that he first represents the ideal form of the repressed "body," which Hermine helps Harry to discover. His transformation into, or, perhaps more accurately, integration into Mozart reveals that he is split off from Mozart, as Hermine is split off from him. As with the pieces in the chess game, the roles and constellations change, but ultimately all are part of a central unity and totality. Haller must first discover the repressed in himself and the multiplicity of the parts of his personality before he is ready to encounter a model of integration and synthesis.

In disagreement with Freedman's suggestion that the mirror exhibits a double nature, Artiss maintains that its nature is multiple, "for, like some surrealistic conceit, the mirror is a symbol of the fragmentation of Harry Haller" (92). That is the message of the Treatise, which is itself a mirror, and of the Magic Theater, where it is symbolized by the shattering of a hand mirror into many pieces. Dissolution of the personality is a prerequisite of synthesis and unity.

Beginning with Middleton (1954), Hesse's use of flowers has been mentioned by a number of critics without much elaboration. As one of his four central symbolic motifs, Artiss gives flowers the attention he claims they deserve. Most frequently noted has been the connection of the araucaria and the azalea with the middle class respectability Haller both condemns and longs for. Artiss sees irony in the use of these exotic plants — the araucaria comes originally from Chile, the azalea from Asia — as a mirror for Haller's dichotomy: he is attracted both by their "bourgeois 'aspidistra' cleanliness and well-tended air" and their superb and evocative fragrance (93). Also exotic and symbolically dichotomous are the orchids Harry presents to Hermine. Orchids are traditionally the flower of courtesans, but they also have a close connection with religious practices and are "venerated to the point of deification" in various parts of the world. The orchids presented to Hermine thus subtly mirror the synthesis of nature and *Geist* she represents. They are also linked to her revelation that she will eventually ask Harry to kill her, "for as she gives the command, she bends over the orchid and stares at it: . . . The killing will thus be a symbolically religious act. The orchid therefore combines for Harry his subconscious spiritual as well as fleshly aspirations" (94).

Similarly exotic and symbolic is the lotus, which first appears in Harry's vision of paradise at the masked ball. The lotus is of particular importance in Hindu mythology and religion, Artiss writes, where it is also connected with Eros: Hindu gods and goddesses are frequently depicted in intimate embraces on a lotus blossom, and the cross-legged "lotus posture" is the traditional position for meditation. The blue lotus serves as a symbol for the creative force in nature and may have provided the prototype for Novalis's *blaue Blume* (blue flower). In that respect, and as associated with Hermine, the lotus may be seen as a symbol of unity and hence of androgyny. (One might add that the lotus is also the center where Brahma dwells; it is often represented in connection with the mandala, which also symbolizes totality.) By associating Hermine with the lotus and through it with the blue flower of German Romanticism, "Hesse subtly underscores Harry's longing for ultimate unity and final transcendence" (94–95).

Other flowers mentioned by Hesse are the camellia, "an exotic flower with similar function to the orchid, and the violet, a traditional Romantic symbol of love . . . . Hesse's flowers are, with few exceptions, the flowers of life, creative symbols of transcendence" (95).

Artiss considers laughter, the fourth key symbolic motif, to be a "major synthesizing factor," which combines in itself the characteristics of the other motifs, and he identifies a surprising range of humor used or "explored" by Hesse in *Steppenwolf*:

> Here we find comic situation and character, burlesque and farce or scene of high comedy, ironic character, theme and gesture. *Galgenhumor* vies with *jeux d'esprit*, lustful grin with beatific smile, buffoonery with divine, choral laughter; cynical aside gives way to macabre parody, *badinage* to black humour. In one striking aspect of humour Hesse shows himself to be the complete master, namely, in self-irony.... Hesse presents his theme with delightful irony and characteristic paradox as a Nietzschean attack on seriousness. (95–96)

Artiss attributes Hesse's use of humor and laughter to his Swabian roots, the importance of which has entirely escaped the notice of Hesse critics, and to his clever use of mythology. The Swabians, Artiss claims, are virtually alone among the Germans in their capacity for self-irony, a quality Hesse possessed to a high degree. Their character is supposedly marked by the conflict of polarities that subjects them to the dangers of disintegration and makes them appear schizophrenic. (Artiss relates an anecdote about a North German psychiatrist who had worked at a hospital in Tübingen and who kept returning "[um] einmal wieder diese herrlichen schwäbishen Schizo-phrenen zu sehen" (to once again see these superb Swabian schizophrenics [96].)

According to Artiss, the Greeks and Egyptians considered laughter to be a "creative attribute of the gods." As an expression of joy in living, laughter traditionally can "break the power of death and animate Life. Through laughter man becomes human and laughter is a symbolic sign for the entry of the soul into man, his actions, and his perceptions. Laughter is widely considered to be the polar opposite of death" (97).

Artiss identifies Nietzsche as a third source of Hesse's use of laughter. Hesse shares Nietzsche's distinction between two kinds of laughter, the base laughter of the multitude or bourgeois and the *Gelächter der Höhe* (laughter of the heights) or *Gelächter des Jenseits* (laughter of the beyond). The goal of philosophy, according to Nietzsche, is to be able to laugh well and live well, which is precisely the standpoint of Pablo and Mozart. The initially humorless Harry Haller is given the opportunity in the Magic Theater to confront the chaos of his Self and to gain the insight and dis-tance of humor and laughter, which would enable him to bridge the gap between polar opposites and to bring the disparate elements of his person-ality into a healthy and creative balance, to take possession and control of his Self (97–99).

In his *Underground Man* (1973), which has not attracted the attention of Hesse scholars it deserves, Edward F. Abood considers the central figures of *Steppenwolf* and of novels by Kafka, Sartre, Camus, Genet, Malraux, and

Koestler as representatives of the type of modern man Dostoevsky describes in *Notes from the Underground.*[3] Underground man is generally a rebel against the prevailing norms of the society and the various institutional powers that perpetuate them. "His indictment may include not only society but also Nature, Being or God. His antipathy may take the form of active revolt, or it may turn inward and be expressed in despair and a longing for death" (1973, 1–2). The rebel rejects and condemns the values and codes of conduct by which the majority of his contemporaries live, and he reacts against the forces of the past century which have destroyed spirituality and faith and have resulted in

> the climax and denouement of imperialism in a series of global wars; the emergence of modern Leviathans — the Fascist, the Communist, the Welfare states; the violent acceleration of industrialization, with its virtual obliteration of rural life, its transformation of the cities into overcrowded infernos and the countryside into monotonous suburbia, its dreary cycles of prosperity and bust; the triumph of organization, the dilution of culture, the refinement of the Establishment, the anaesthetization of mass man, the dehumanization of art, the despiritualization of religion, and so on. (2)

Lacking commitment to an absolute that justifies life and gives it meaning, underground man is malcontent, anxious, tense, and in need of rediscovering God or finding some equivalent for Him. As opposed to Kafka, whose quest for an inaccessible God always ends in frustration, Hesse conceives of a God who inheres in the world as a cosmic order which can be apprehended through "maximum knowledge and experience of this world," and he postulates a practical way to God, a "unique synthesis of Zen-Taoism, on the one hand, and Jungian psychotherapy on the other" (7). Because he catches a glimpse of that goal and of the method for achieving it, Harry Haller is one of the more successful underground men.

Like the other representatives of this type, Haller is torn by conflict with society and within himself, and he is also discontent with the human condition. He longs to escape these conflicts and to gain access to what he envisions as a transcendent world, the timeless realm of the Immortals. In the depths of his despair he receives as if by magic a Treatise which analyzes him and his problems and describes the difficult way out of the underground. It attempts to motivate him to undertake the journey by attacking his simplistic belief in the duality of his Steppenwolf being; by criticizing and exposing the ignorance and hypocrisy in his thinking about society, that is, the bourgeoisie, and his relationship to it; and, finally, by challenging his view of sui-

---

[3]Abood's chapter on Hesse is a revised version of his article, "Jung's Concept of Individuation in Hesse's *Steppenwolf*," which was published in 1968. In the book he discusses Hesse and Kafka in a section headed "Underground Man and God."

cide and the comfort he proclaims to take in it, when in fact he knows that it is reprehensible and a sign of defeat (55–59).

In its argument against suicide and against the desire to regress to either the wolf or the child, the Treatise expresses what is, in effect, "Hesse's personal reinterpretation of Hinduism and Buddhism," the postulate, namely, of a "single, timeless essence (Brahma, the Buddha-nature), of which the visible world, including human life, is only a passing manifestation." Since Hesse rejects the Hindu's and the Buddhist's rigid morality and denigration of the world, however, he is more inclined to their indirect offshoot, Zen Buddhism, and to Chinese Taoism. In common with these philosophies, Hesse sees all the opposites as relative; one must accept all things, including the dark nature represented by the wolf in Harry, as manifestations of a single divine whole. And one must accept and be involved in the world. The goal is not the Hindu nirvana but *satori*, "the flash of total, exhilarating awareness which the enlightened devotee can experience in the here and now" (59–61), as Harry does on the occasions when the Immortals reveal themselves to him.

To be able to live in the society he scorns, Harry must develop the fundamental Zen attitude of humor, the ability to be in the world but also, by avoiding attachment, to be "beyond" it. Humor "presupposes incongruity and imbalance"; and to "grasp incongruity we must have a notion of its total structure from which the absurd part has deviated: it is the simultaneous intuition of the two that evokes our laughter" (62).

Abood notes the correlation of basic concepts of Jung's psychology with Taoist philosophy and Zen Buddhism. "The substance of the Treatise is at the core of Jung's thinking," Abood writes, but "it is chiefly his analytic method, roughly as it was practiced in his clinic in Zurich, that Hesse took over in *Steppenwolf*. Jung offers the means of realizing in practice the lofty mandates of the Treatise" (65). The Treatise is addressed to Harry's intellect, but its message must also reach his heart. To escape the underground he must remake himself, and to that end he needs the guidance of Hermine, Pablo, and Maria, who, as Hermine says of herself, are mirrors for him in which he can see and discover his Self.

As the embodiment of Jung's anima, Hermine represents Harry's unconscious and the means for him to recognize what is "welling in the depths of his mind," knowledge he needs in order to achieve self-realization and to continue along the path of individuation. "Only on meeting Hermine, that is, facing the anima objectified as an autonomous personality, does he begin to accept the teachings of the Treatise with emotional conviction." The activation of Harry's unconscious by his meeting with Hermine immediately produces his dream about Goethe. "The dream functions like the Treatise by revealing to Harry his deficiencies: he lacks a sense of humor, he has ignored his body, he has an ambivalent attitude toward sex. But the dream, unlike the Treatise, is a direct revelation of the unconscious" (67–68). In submitting to Hermine's guidance, he recognizes and attempts to rectify his deficiencies in the area of sensuality and the "little arts of living." When it is time for him to learn or re-learn the art of loving, Hermine selects and sends Maria to him, "since it is always the anima that determines what woman a man gravitates toward" (68). He learns through Maria that Eros is no stranger to him but had only been suppressed following unpleasant experiences. This insight enables him to accept the women in his past life as precious parts of himself. Realizing that his experiences with them were as "indestructible and abiding as the stars" marks his "union with the total Woman, or anima," which is celebrated in the nuptial dance with Hermine at the masked ball (68–69).

Like Hermine, Pablo, too, "functions as both an objective character and as a personification of psychic elements in Harry." According to Abood, he has arrived where Harry should be: he is in harmony with his environment and at peace with himself (70). He replaces Hermine as Harry's guide into deeper layers of his soul or unconscious. Unfortunately, Abood does not pursue his analysis of Pablo's relationship to Hermine and his psychological meaning as an archetype; instead, he shifts his perspective and compares Pablo to an Eastern guru and Zen master, specifically the Buddhist Hui-neng, the Zen Master of the Great Mirrors (70–71).

The purpose of Harry's experiences in both contexts, however, is similar. Before he can plunge into the "picture gallery" of his soul, the entrance to which is "For Madmen only," he must sacrifice his excessively rational and intellectual mind. This symbolic suicide is accomplished through drugs and represented by the shattering of the mirror in which he sees his conscious perception of himself. The various experiences in the Magic Theater resemble each other in their recapitulation of relationships involving some kind of imbalance: "Harry's relationship to society, to women, to the other 'Harrys' within him, and to the Immortals" (72). They enable him to recognize the inconsistencies and contradictions of some of his attitudes and positions.

To interpret the murder of Hermine, Abood returns to Jung. He recognizes that this event must have a symbolic meaning in addition to the realistic ones that may be conjectured such as "simple jealousy, coupled with a regression to his old bourgeois sense of honor" or the fulfillment of his promise to kill her upon her command, which she supposedly expresses by deliberately allowing herself to be caught with Pablo. In Jungian therapy, Abood writes, the patient "strives to free himself from subjection to the unconscious as expressed by the anima. Until he confronts her, she exerts a mysterious power, or *mana*, over him" (75). In the beginning of Harry's (the ego's) dialogue with Hermine, he mainly listens and follows. As their relationship progresses, however, she adopts more and more of his attitudes until it becomes clear that they are opposite poles of the same unity and that she speaks his unconscious thoughts and reflects his soul. As he grows in self confidence, "he attempts to appropriate the mana from Hermine, that is, dominate the anima" (75). In Abood's view, Harry "becomes what is for Jung the *mana-personality*," a dominant of the collective unconscious and an archetype of the "mighty man in the form of hero, chief, magician, medicine man, saint, the ruler of man and spirits, the friend of God" (75; Jung quotation from CW 7:228). I will return to this argument below.

Experiencing a new sense of power, which has been enhanced by some of his experiences in the Magic Theater, Harry

> symbolically asserts his mastery over Hermine by stabbing her. But he fails to realize that the naked Pablo is really his own masculine self, which Hermine has helped him to fashion, and that Hermine is his feminine self. The beautiful picture formed by Pablo and Hermine . . . is an image of the ideal Harry, whose feminine and masculine counterparts have merged into perfect union. Or, stating the premise in reverse, we can say that this picture cancels out sexual differentiation — another of Harry's dichotomies — and depicts the sexless condition of the Immortals. (76)

According to Jung, the anima may be "killed" or depotentiated if the ego has come to terms with the unconscious and established a balance of power between the two worlds, which in this case would be equivalent to creating the "bridge between nature and spirit" which is mentioned in the Treatise, but Harry has not progressed that far: his impulsive act is an attempt to master what cannot be mastered. By destroying the unity represented by the embrace of Pablo and Hermine, Harry demonstrates his continuing lack of humor and his failure to reconcile the opposites in his psyche. Since first reading the Treatise, he has gone well beyond underground man, but he still has a long way to go (76–77).

Lewis W. Tusken identifies two reasons for the skeptical attitude of Abood, Boulby, Ziolkowski, and other critics toward Hesse's claim that *Steppenwolf* is the book of a believer and depicts a "higher, eternal world" rising above Haller's problematic life: The first is a misunderstanding of Hermine's 'death,' the second, the failure to recognize the magnitude of Harry's transformation. In every critical study he examined, Tusken claims to have found confusion on one or both of these points, the proper understanding of which is necessary to establish a balance between the subjective and the objective levels of the novel. Tusken intends to correct this by "a close look at the Jungian-inspired subjective level — an approach begun by Edward Abood but one which he failed to carry to its logical conclusion" (1974, 159–60).

Tusken also takes exception to Ziolkowski's attempt to account for subjective events on the objective or "real" level. "It matters little," he asserts, "whether Hermine and company actually exist, and the role of the tract makes it quite apparent that the entire psychic change which Harry undergoes is simply transformed into objective terms for the sake of expression." Rather than a "metaphysically translated" (Ziolkowski) reading of a banal booklet with an entirely different content — Ziolkowski suggests as a possible title "How can I Become Twenty Years Younger in One Week" — the Treatise is "an *a posteriori* analysis written by Harry himself to express his experience" (161).

Tusken, whose only bibliographical reference to Jung is *The Integration of the Personality*, claims that the professor represents Haller's "shadow," through whom "Harry faces his present self eye to eye," which brings him to the depths of despair. Hesse's introduction of Hermine at this point is done "with the Jungian concept of anima in mind" and represents a further extension into the subjective level (162–63). And Pablo is supposedly Harry's "'collective unconscious' and/or the 'male archetype,'" whose function in the novel is to objectify the more primitive basic urges, and, through the Magic Theater, to enable Harry to come to terms with the remainder of his emotional problems (164). Tusken claims to go beyond previous critics in his clarification of why Hermine appears as a boy and why her "death" is not a more tangible concept. He explains that "Hermine is wearing masculine garb to indicate that she is a part of Harry himself," that a "symbolic union with the anima has been accomplished," and that "individuation is nearly complete." Pablo's embrace of Hermine indicates that the collective unconscious has joined with the anima and the ego. "By killing Hermine, Harry destroys only the *personified* anima, the crutch he needed for the objective narrative, thereby asserting his independence which is the concomitant result of the process of individuation" (165; author's italics). Tusken compares the "marriage" of Harry and Hermine/Pablo with the unity on the subjective level of Pablo's music and Mozart's, neither of which can take place on the objective level (165).

The proof that individuation has been accomplished is in Harry's trial. "For killing Hermine, Harry would normally be sentenced to death; instead he is sentenced to eternal life which is, in fact, immortal life. In other words, he can now distinguish life's eternal values and coexist with what remains." Objective and subjective levels meet when he is forced to kill Hermine on the subjective level, whom he loves on the objective level, in order "to come to the realization that what one must laugh at is, in fact, not a laughing matter" (165). In assuming that Haller completes his Jungian individuation, Tusken argues against the evidence of the novel and Harry's own final remarks. He also oversimplifies the complexity of the process as defined by Jung and presented by Hesse.

In his detailed discussion of opposites and polarity in Hesse's works, Dieter Hensing concludes that "the unity of the world is ultimately not a harmonizing and synthesizing of opposites in reality and in this life but an otherworldly *unio mystica*" (1976, 809). As seen by Hesse in his Dostoevsky essays and elsewhere, overcoming or transcending the opposites is not compatible with rational, logical, scientific thinking but is a characteristic of magical thinking, which presupposes the unity of the internal and external worlds. One may experience the transcendent unity in special mystical, magical moments and in dreams, but its sustained occurrence in life would result in chaos. This state, Hesse's "Third Kingdom," is seen *sub specie aeternitatis* and "signifies as a magical experience a kind of revelation or pre-experience of the unity of the beyond" (818). It cannot be reached through continuing individuation but through the "delimitation and dissolution of the ego in the unity of eternity"; it presupposes the recognition and acceptance of opposites as equally valid components in a polar relationship, the whole of which is a unity. Since transcendence is realized through immanence, the path remains inward. In his experiencing of the *unio mystica* in rare moments, Haller makes occasional contact with this higher world (818–20).

The psychological dimension of this problematic, which is missing in Hensing's discussion, is the subject of a 1978 dissertation by Kenneth L. Golden, in which the problem of opposites in several modern novels is analyzed from the perspective of Jungian psychology and comparative mythology. In contrast to Freud, who views the opposites dualistically as diametrically separated and opposed, and who believes that one pole can exist without the other and that it is therefore possible and desirable to eliminate unconscious content by making it conscious, Jung considers the opposites as complementary, compensatory, interdependent, and ultimately unified. The unconscious and conscious form a dynamic unity in which both poles are valuable and necessary (3–4).

Comparative mythology enters into Golden's study in his identification of consciousness and the *principium individuationis* with Apollo and the Apollonian principle as described by Nietzsche. This principle is what Jung terms the ego or ego-persona. Opposed to ego consciousness is the Dionysian principle, which is represented psychologically by the Jungian "shadow" personality or what has been repressed by the ego. On a deeper level, the instincts, sexuality, and the complex of all opposites constitute the Dionysian content of the unconscious. Thus, although it represents but one side of a polarity, the Dionysian principle also contains opposites within itself: it is an embodiment of feminine psychological values, which, according to Joseph Campbell, are related to the principle of the identity of opposites. The Dionysian and the feminine principles affirm and deify all elements of life, good and evil (98–107).

Haller's life has been too Apollonian, Golden continues, too much under the dominance of the masculine intellect. As indicated in the Treatise, there are two paths to the cosmic: the "tragic," serious, masculine Apollonian path, and the Dionysian path through the sovereign world of humor and the acceptance of polarity (113). Through the guidance of the "Dionysian whore" Hermine and through the Dionysian arts of music and dance, Haller begins to correct and complement that imbalance. The "Immortal" representatives of the Self also attempt to lead him from the narrowly tragic path through the Dionysian realm of humor and the earthy goddess to the icy world of the Immortals, which is the realm of the mythical father. "Atonement with the father is the final step in the mythic hero's journey, a corroboration of the process of individuation" (118). Haller experiences Dionysian unity in the ecstasy of the ball and continues through the experiences of the Magic Theater along the path to the Immortals, but when he sees Pablo and Hermine together, the old Apollonian moral principles triumph over life, and he reverts to his earlier state of self-pity, guilt, and willingness to accept death.

The first book-length study to deal with Hesse and his works exclusively from a Jungian perspective, *Spinning on a Dream Thread: Hermann Hesse: his life and work, and his contact with C. G. Jung* (1977) was written by Rix Weaver, a Jungian analyst, for the Analytical Psychology Club of Perth, Australia. Although somewhat general and selective, this study contains valuable insights, especially into Hesse's use of the technique of active imagination, which is an important component of Jungian therapy. As opposed to "passive fantasying," the ego or conscious mind initiates the fantasy in active imagination in order to bring up material from the unconscious, which may then be analyzed in the same way the content of dreams is. The sequence of images produced by Sinclair in *Demian* is a good example of the functioning of this technique: these images reflect Sinclair's condition and bring unconscious contents into consciousness where they can be "amplified" and ultimately understood and integrated into consciousness. In Sinclair's case the amplification and analysis take place through the production of images and his discussion of them with Pistorius and Demian.

Steppenwolf differs from *Demian*, according to Weaver, in that the author's ego is not embodied in the protagonist, as it was in Sinclair, but in the editor: thus the report he publishes is the result of his own process of self-discovery. In Haller the ego is combined with the bestial shadow, and both parts are juxtaposed in the Treatise. When he was writing *Steppenwolf,*

Hesse was again suffering from his unsolved "anima problem," which caused him to choose the wrong women for his first two marriages. In this case it was Ruth Wenger, from whom he fled after a mere two months together. "For Hesse the feminine was, as *Demian* showed, the Great Mother, the archetypal figure who draws all men into her embrace" (136). It might be said that the archetype of the Great Mother is a form of the anima archetype which comes from a deeper layer of consciousness and is closer to the collective representations of mythology and religion. On both levels the archetype involves the complex union of opposites: the Great Mother is Eve and Sophia, sin and wisdom, love and death. It is therefore not surprising that Harry's anima appears as a prostitute, but also as a mother figure and sister figure and with a high degree of spirituality. The scorpion of the Goethe dream may indicate both desire for and fear of sex, but it also contains a warning that the anima can be dangerous. "The dangerous aspect of the anima is a result of her being stifled in the function of her role as man's relating ability, his understanding and his Eros" (152). Through Hermine and Maria, a split-off part of Hermine as it were, Haller confronts his anima problem.

Weaver sees the murder of Hermine with the knife that is composed of part of Harry — the chess figure he put in his pocket — as a "healing message," apparently because he learns from it "that he can destroy what he loves *out of his own nature*" (159; author's emphasis). Weaver probably means healing for Hesse, for, as her own argument indicates, Harry is not healed. Mozart hopes that Harry committed the act from jealousy, at least, which would indicate the functioning of emotion that Harry seems to be lacking, but that is little benefit to derive from the destruction of the figure who represents and attempts to guide him to the part of himself that is least developed, yet necessary for his well-being.

From his analysis of Hesse's relations to Freudian and Jungian psychology, René Breugelmans supports the conclusion that Hesse's views, despite his assertions to the contrary, are much closer to Jung's than to Freud's. The polarization described in the "mock-psychoanalytic Tract," for example, "could be seen in Freudian terms as the basic conflict between the natural, instinctual *Id* and the sublimating, repressing *Ego*. But the Tract condemns a similar explanation by Haller as simplistic." Its proposal that Haller's life consists of thousands of polar pairs is in keeping with "the Jungian principles of mutually complementary polarity, of enantiodromia, and of the myriad possible configurations of archetypal elements in the unconscious. Thus the Tract seems to reject a Freudian tenet in favor of a Jungian one" (1981, 39–40). Breugelmans also suggests, however, that the mocking element of the tract with its "pedantic, professorial" tone, might be a "veiled criticism of Jung and a recalcitrancy against the father-archetype," which "appears as an ironical transformation of Hesse's intellectual contact with depth psychology, whether Freudian or Jungian" (40). It can be compared with Sinclair's rejection of Pistorius and his book-learning.

Be that as it may, the *figurae* in the novel, Hermine, Maria, and Pablo, serve as analyst-healers and represent Jungian archetypes. Hermine, the "very Jungian mother or sister figure . . . as 'anima' . . . i.e., as Haller's soul [is] an archetypal guide to the exploration of the unconscious in him. She brings about his 'remothering' in Jungian progression, not in infantile regression." Among her multiple functions she is also "the female counterpart of the Wise Magician (Pablo)." As the wise magician or 'puer senex,' Pablo is "the archetype of masculinity to Haller (rather than the father figure in the Freudian sense) and an aspect of his Shadow" (41). Breugelmans does not do justice to the meaning of this archetype, but he is correct in noting its ability to absorb the anima, as when Pablo puts the shrunken figure of Hermine into his pocket.

In keeping with the postulate of two levels of reality, Breugelmans interprets Haller's murder of Hermine on the realistic level as the manifestation of a fit of jealous rage and on the symbolic level as

> the logical, indeed expected, outcome of total erotic possession, the fascination of the death-aspect of the unconscious, the *Liebestod*, the absolute mystical union of *hieros gamos* of the conscious mind with the 'anima.' . . . Haller's overconscious cynical mind is being remothered into a new non-ego centered spirituality or 'Geist,' modelled on the Spirit Mother, i.e., a Self which eventually might attain the numinous experience of the Realm of the Immortals, the God-archetype of the unconscious. (41–42)

Hesse now understands the "old triadic mythologem" described in "Ein Stückchen Theologie" in psychological terms as individuation. He identifies the

> perennial 'Geist-Natur' dichotomy with Jung's typological distinction between the extroverted, paternal-male ego-consciousness, the rational mind, and the introverted maternal unconscious, the pious mind . . . . Like Jung he foresaw their eventual union in the Self, i.e., the Third Kingdom in theological terms. (42)

In a series of investigations of Hesse's novels, Reso Karalaschwili, whose articles on Haller's Goethe dream and on the beginning of *Steppenwolf* were discussed in the previous chapter, has placed ever greater emphasis on the fundamental similarity between Hesse's understanding of the individual's development through three stages and Jung's process of individuation. Jung's psychology differs from Freud's in its teleological, progressive orientation: whereas Freud generally related images and symbols produced by the unconscious to past experiences, especially childhood traumas, Jung recognized that they may be attempts by the psyche to guide the individual's development into the future (1986, 60–64). Not only in *Demian* and *Steppenwolf*, but in all Hesse's novels, according to Karalaschwili, the heroes are involved in a developmental process similar to the one described by Jung. Following the departure from the unity of the childhood world and the development of the persona, the individual is torn between the extremes of various polarities and experiences the despair of Hesse's Second Kingdom. Then, through a process involving the guidance of the archetypal images from the unconscious and perhaps also therapeutic assistance from outside, the individual strives to overcome the conflicting opposites and to achieve a state of harmony and balance, which is equivalent to the attainment of the Third Kingdom in Hesse's scheme or the achievement of the Self in Jung's. While not actually attainable in this life, the desired goal does serve as a model and an ideal to direct the individual's development through a progressive series of cycles (11–15, 191–95).

For Hesse, the conclusion of *Steppenwolf* was like the end of every life, "a door into the eternal" which is wide open (106). Like Kafka's figures, Hesse's heroes do not live in the real world, according to Karalaschwili, but are symbols, whose meaning goes beyond the immediately comprehensible. Their external attributes, habits, and expressions are metaphorical. Likewise, the secondary figures represent split-off aspects of the hero or projections of archetypes from his unconscious; they too are symbols. In Hesse's view, fiction "only lives and is effective where it is true fiction, that is, where it creates symbols" (175). All fictional figures are symbolic to a degree, but whereas formerly "the character and the typicality of the figure were emphasized, Hesse does not so much accentuate the representational as rather the creatively formative and generative side of the epic figure." Like Musil's *Der Mann ohne Eigenschaften* (Man without Qualities), who is characteristic of the modern hero in general, Hesse's figures, too, have few physical or behavioral characteristics that identify them as individuals (176).

Thus all the figures in Hesse's novels are "complements, correlates, and variations of the central figure" (184). Karalaschwili points out that Novalis recognized the internal unity of all the figures in Goethe's *Wilhelm Meister* and consciously worked out a justification of this procedure in his own work. To this insight of one of his favorite poets Hesse brings the confirming perspective of Jung's psychoanalysis: the figures of *Wilhelm Meister* as seen by Novalis and the figures in Hesse's novels stand in the same relationship to each other, Karalaschwili maintains, as do the archetypes described by Jung, and they are symbols for different aspects of the poet's soul. Jung's concept of the structure of the soul "served Hesse as the model upon which he based the representation of the figures in his works" (188–91, 200). In

Jung's psychology as in Hesse's novels, symbols, as represented by archetypal images or figures, mediate between the unconscious and the conscious and are therefore the means through which a union of opposites can take place. Hence they are critical to the process of individuation (61, 104).

In agreement with Peter Jansen, Karalaschwili relates Hesse's three kingdoms to Kierkegaard's tripartite development through aesthetic, ethical, and religious phases, but he substitutes "magical" for "religious" as the designation for the final stage. In Hesse's works the aesthetic stage often has the form of a fairy tale, the ethical is realistic, and the magical is symbolic (51–52). Corresponding to Haller's development from the second stage to the third, the plot of *Steppenwolf* begins realistically and moves into the timeless, spaceless world of symbolism and magic, which is to say the mirror-world of the unconscious, elements of which, according to the Jungian process of individuation, Haller needs to bring into and integrate with his consciousness (102–4).

This progression from one realm into another constitutes an alternative to the "futile" attempt by Ziolkowski and others to distinguish between real and imaginary events occurring simultaneously, which is implausible in the latter part of all the novels and especially in the latter part of *Steppenwolf*. Such an endeavor, Karalaschwili maintains, "not only contradicts the concept of the Magic Theater but also leaves the particularity of Hesse's plot construction out of consideration, which . . . consists in the progressive disappearance of chronological sequence and its concentration in the symbolic essence" with which the novel concludes (102–3).[4]

Given the number of Jungian studies discussed in this chapter, one has to wonder at Günther Baumann's claim that no "comprehensive and systematic analysis of Hesse's works from a Jungian perspective" preceded his own published dissertation from 1989 (6). To be sure, his study does treat more works in greater detail than any previous Jungian analysis, but it also duplicates work done by others without proper attribution, either in the text or in the bibliography. To have done so would have meant giving up the claim to originality for his interpretation of *Demian* and diminishing his contribution to the interpretation of some other works. Despite these unfortunate shortcomings, enough originality remains to make this a valuable treatment of the subject.

Baumann considers *Steppenwolf* to be the account of an exemplary cure of a neurosis according to Jungian methods and concepts. It cannot be properly understood and evaluated, he claims, "without an exact knowledge

[4]Karalaschwili agrees with and goes beyond Ziolkowski in considering the sonata form to be applicable not only to *Steppenwolf* but to all of Hesse's novels, corresponding as it does to the developmental model of Hesse's three kingdoms and Jung's process of individuation.

of the individual structural elements" which shape the content (27). Like Ziolkowski, Baumann takes Hesse at his word with regard to the work's sonata form, but he thinks that the form applies to the whole, not just to the first three segments. He agrees that those segments follow the sonata pattern, with the editor's preface serving as the exposition of Haller's neurotic conflict. The first part of Haller's record constitutes the developmental presentation and expansion of the conflict from Haller's perspective and introduces a first anticipation of the means for its resolution. Finally, the Treatise recapitulates all the previous motifs and makes a first attempt to clarify them and to offer "a comprehensive overview combining subjective and objective aspects of the psychological problematic which combines subjective and objective aspects" (194).

According to Baumann, however, the Treatise not only constitutes the recapitulation of the sonata form but is itself in the form of a sonata consisting of three thematic parts: the first has to do with the basic problem of Haller's split into wolf and man; the second attempts to integrate Haller's neurosis into a general anthropology and typology. The typology constitutes a Jungian quaternity consisting of two categories of complementary pairs: the saint and the sinner, and the Bürger and the outsider. The saint and the sinner both overcome the *principium individuationis*. The saint develops his spiritual self, and his path leads to God and eternity and is the path of the "Immortals"; the sinner develops his basic instincts and Dionysian self, and his path leads to decay and death. Both these types are tragic in their isolation and radical development of the Self. The Bürger takes a compromise position between all extremes and attempts to preserve the ego rather than to develop the Self. The outsider, which includes Haller, occupies a position "between all fronts" (194–98). In his position between Bürger and saint and between Bürger and sinner he is torn between ego and Self. Where Jung sees this tense position as natural and necessary, Hesse sees it as a tragic dilemma involving the irreconcilability of ego and Self. "A solution of Haller's psychological problematic seems possible only if he can fight his way to the pure egocentricity of the Bürger or to the complete conquest of his ego according to the model of the Immortals" (200).

The third part of the Treatise presents and discusses possible solutions for Harry's inner division. It, too, is divided into three subparts. In the first part, Haller's dualistic, Freudian view of his personality is refuted in favor of a view based on Jung's postulate of a collective unconscious consisting of thousands or "uncountable" pairs of opposites, hence a multiplicity of personality fragments and potentials. One possible solution for Harry is to "accept his empirical internal multiplicity, break through the '*principium individuationis*,' and follow Buddha" and all great men who have taken this path, which requires overcoming of the personal ego and which leads to the Immortals, to the suprapersonal, collective, and eternal Self. Those who have attained that state, for example, Jesus, Buddha, Mozart, and Goethe, are symbols of the Self. Baumann also includes Pablo in this category. The second solution proposed in the Treatise is humor. This is an easier, more comfortable solution than realizing the Self, but also an inferior, mediocre, bourgeois solution, in which the ego is not overcome and transcended but reconciled with the other parts of the personality in a compromise position comparable to Romantic irony (201–3).

In that it serves both as the recapitulation section of the first sonata movement and as the exposition of the main sonata movement that follows, the Treatise also functions as an intermezzo, just as Hesse claims. Before the main movement with its contrapuntally developed themes of humor and self-realization can begin, Harry has to gain knowledge of himself and his condition, which he does in three stages: (1) on the basis of the insight he has gained into his lonely and failed existence, he decides to commit suicide the next time he feels despair and disgust with life; (2) his experience of the bigotry and hypocrisy of a funeral service fills him with disgust; (3) these feelings reach a high point following the catastrophic episode with the professor and his wife, through which Haller manifests and becomes more aware of the neurosis which brings him into conflict with others and with himself. In the depths of despair and on the verge of suicide, that is, in need of and ready for transformation, he is led by his unconscious Self to Hermine, the anima and psychopomp (204–7).

As the archetypal manifestation of the male's feminine soul and as the unconscious compensation to his conscious ego, the anima may appear in any feminine guise and role: Hermine first mothers Haller; later she identifies herself as his sister. As representative of the life principle, which she strives to awaken in him, she can be identified with the archetypal Great Mother, and she may appear as a prostitute. To the degree that the male's consciousness includes feminine components, the compensatory anima may have masculine ones, as is manifest in Hermine's hermaphroditism and bisexuality, attributes Baumann interprets as "symbols for the lost *joie de vivre* and psychic universality of Haller's youth" (210). Baumann also sees Hermine as a person in her own right with an intellectual aspect that can be as keen as Haller's. Like Haller's, hers is a shattered, tragic existence. As he seeks life through her, she seeks *Geist* through him. He is an animus-projection for her, as she is an anima-projection for him (211–12). One need not postulate her real existence, in my opinion, to explain her individuality, since the relationship of opposites is inherent in her compensatory function: she has undeveloped in her the opposite of what he has undeveloped in himself. The reciprocal development of the undeveloped elements would result in the achievement of the unity of the Self. This relationship may be compared to the Taoist symbol for the unity of Yin and Yang, a divided circle in which each component contains a small amount of the opposite in itself.

Because of the transformative influence the experience of Eros has on Haller, Baumann thinks Maria's role has been underestimated by critics. That is only the case, however, if one sees her as a separate entity rather than as a part of Hermine or at least her representative. Baumann considers Maria to be what he calls "an anima-symbol of the first level (Eve-phase)." Since Hermine is part of Haller, she cannot introduce him to sex, Baumann argues, but no matter what level she represents, one might object, as an "anima-symbol" Maria is no less a part of him. In any event, what is important is the change brought about in Haller's attitudes, especially in his aesthetics. He learns to appreciate the artistry of the American songs he had despised, and this helps prepare him for the Magic Theater (213–15).

Baumann claims that previous interpretations of Pablo's archetypal significance have been incorrect and that he has discovered that Pablo represents the Self. But if one compares Pablo with Sinclair's description of Demian, it is apparent that he lacks the complexity and wholeness of that archetype.

> I saw Demian's face and I noticed not only that it was not a boy's face but that it was a man's. I also saw more; I believed I saw, or felt, that it was also not the face of a man, but something else. It was as if there were something of a woman's face in it, and, in fact, this face seemed to me, for a moment, neither masculine nor childlike, neither old nor young, but somehow a thousand years old, somehow timeless, bearing the marks of an entirely different history from what we experience. Animals could look like that, or trees, or stars . . . .I saw only that he was different from us, he was like an animal, or like a spirit, or like a picture. I don't know what he was like, but he was different, unimaginably different from the rest of us. (D 43)

Demian clearly possesses the fascination, numinosity, and complexity of the archetypal Self, which participates in the timeless collective unconscious and has its roots in the animal, the vegetable, and even the inorganic world. Pablo, on the contrary, represents the part of life Haller has suppressed or failed to develop. To begin with, he is compensatory to Haller's persona in much the same way Hermine is. As he later demonstrates in the Magic Theater, however, his power as a psychopomp goes beyond Hermine's; he can actually lead Harry into his unconscious and enable him to experience it directly. Only when he merges with Mozart, one of the Immortals, does he become a symbol of the Self. Baumann points out that in Jungian psychology it is usually the anima that "mediates entry to the Self as the deepest ar-

chetype of the collective unconscious" (216). Hermine does indeed introduce Haller to Pablo, but Pablo then becomes a guide into greater depths
of the psyche rather than the goal of Haller's development. As we have
seen, he resembles Hermes in his role as psychopomp and can legitimately
be compared to the archetype of the wise old man as defined by Jung.

When analyzing the appearance of archetypes in a work of art, it is important to keep in mind that they are symbols, not signs or allegories. They
vary with individuals and circumstances, and they are highly mutable and
capable of transformation. This is apparent from the diverse examples and
definitions that occur in Jung's works. An interpreter must therefore be
flexible in attempting a "Jungian" or "archetypal" interpretation. The figures' functions are more significant than the forms in which they appear.
The archetypal "wise old man," according to Jung, "appears in dreams in
the guise of a magician, doctor, priest, teacher, professor, grandfather, *or
any other person possessing authority*" (CW 9i:216; emphasis added). It is
noteworthy that Jung defines this archetype in terms of *authority* not of
age. As a "magician," who has great insight into Haller's personality and the
power to open up his unconscious to him, Pablo certainly is an authority
figure.

A close relationship with the anima is also characteristic of this figure, as
is the fact that the two together may be considered parts of a single whole.
In his *Alchemical Studies* Jung writes:

> Since the mercurial serpent of the alchemists is not infrequently called
> *virgo* and, even before Paracelsus, was represented in the form of a
> Melusina, the latter's capacity to change her shape and to cure diseases
> is of importance in that these peculiarities were also predicated of
> Mercurius, and with special emphasis. On the other hand, Mercurius
> was also depicted as the grey-bearded Mercurius *senex* or Hermes
> Trismegistus, from which it is evident that two empirically very com-
> mon archetypes, namely the anima and the Wise Old Man, flow to-
> gether in the symbolic phenomenology of Mercurius. (CW 13:178)

Among the various names given to Mercurius, Jung adds, were *muta-
bilis* and Proteus. Pablo's connection to Hermes/Mercurius was discussed above.[5] The transformational function of his Magic Theater is
clearly stated in the inscription on the first of its countless doors:
"Mutabor [=I will be transformed]. Transformation into any animal or
plant you please" (St 217). Hermine may be considered a split-off part
of Pablo: he picks up her shrunken figure and puts it in his pocket just

---

[5]With regard to Pablo's role in the Magic Theater, Baumann, too, notes his similarity
to Hermes as psychopomp. In considering this role to be an "advancement" over
being "merely [!] a symbol of the Self," however, Baumann reverses the importance
of these symbols.

as Haller pockets the pieces representing parts of his personality. In their function as Harry's Mercurial psychopomps, they indeed "flow together" and become united in a symbolic embrace, as do the anima and wise old man archetypes. Pablo is therefore not the Self to which Hermine leads Harry, but a guide to the Self. Like Hermine, Pablo represents what Harry needs in order to become whole, which explains why Haller has difficulty recognizing his value during their initial meetings. Finally, as Maria is essentially part of Hermine, and Hermine is part of Pablo, Pablo is assimilated by, or becomes identical with Mozart, one of the Immortals, who are, as Baumann recognizes, symbols of the Self. Thus the symbol of totality includes all of its parts, which is obvious when so stated but not so obvious in symbolic representation.

Baumann notes the metamorphosis of the motif of the Immortals following their appearance in *Die Nürnberger Reise*, where they were seen as "tragic-problematic artist-geniuses like Hölderlin, Mörike, Hamsun, and Nietzsche" (219). With the choice of Goethe and Mozart in *Steppenwolf*, there is a turn to healthy, synthesizing, classical figures. Haller's Goethe dream is compensatory to his meeting with the professor and to his view of the Immortals as tragic, despairing figures. He learns from Goethe that his own view of the master is no less subjective and prejudiced than the professor's and that his belief in the serious nature of art is self-contradictory. The motifs of humor and immortality come together here for the first time.

Goethe refutes the position presented in the Treatise that "humor always has something bourgeois in it" (St 62). On the contrary, it is not only compatible with the ideal of immortality and with the realization of the Self, it is "the actual mark and criterium of the Immortals" (Baumann 220–22). According to Baumann, Haller learns for the first time in this dream that humor, realization of the Self, and affirmation of life and the Self go together. This opens up new possibilities for him, but, as his ambivalent reaction to the woman's modelled leg reveals, he has much to overcome.

Indeed, Haller fails to achieve either humor or realization of the Self. Thus the execution of the basic themes of the novel ends "as in the classical sonata form with an unreconciled state" (225). His problematic is solved in a ritual way, according to Baumann, by a rite of initiation, which takes place at the masked ball and in the Magic Theater. Baumann's discussion of the ball and the Theater are somewhat confusing in that he presents them both as a unity and as separate units with similar functions. He refers to them together and separately as constituting the recapitulation of the sonata form, in which important persons, themes, and motifs recur. His claim that Haller's process of individuation is also recapitulated is less convincing for the ball section than for the Magic Theater, as is the assertion that he undergoes a rite of initiation (226–29).

With regard to the ball scene, Baumann identifies the room designated as "hell" with Haller's "shadow" and the main room as well as the Magic Theater with his collective unconscious. He claims that the identification of hell with the shadow agrees with Jungian psychology, but hell for Jung is much greater than the individual's shadow in that it includes also the collective shadow, which is manifest in the underworld figures of religion and mythology. When Hesse refers to his journeys through hell, he appears to mean the unconscious as a whole; hence they would be similar to experiencing the Magic Theater.

Baumann's interpretation of the role of Hermine in "hell" as a representative of the shadow contradicts his previous interpretation of her role, and his claim that Haller's entry into the main room is a symbolic opening into his collective unconscious through which he experiences the "the long-desired dissolution [*Aufhebung*] of his ego and the '*principium individuationis*,'" which is equivalent to initiation, is inaccurate (228–9). While rites of initiation do involve a ritual death and rebirth, as Baumann writes, it is death to the world of childhood under the dominance of women and rebirth into the world of the fathers and their world, which is quite the opposite from the process Baumann describes.

A stronger argument can be made for interpreting the events of the Magic Theater as equivalent to an initiation ritual. In this case Haller is being led by a male psychopomp not back toward his childhood, but toward the realization of the goals described in the Treatise, to humor and the Immortals. Here he does confront and has the chance to understand and assimilate different parts of himself as represented in the various episodes he experiences, and he does come into contact with an Immortal, namely Mozart, who is a "compensatory manifestation of Haller's Self" (241). But Haller is not yet mature enough to adopt the distanced and synthesizing attitude required by humor. He demonstrates this in murdering Hermine, from whose union with Pablo the Self could have been reborn. Despite this failure, however, he, and Hesse, have gained insight into the possibility and necessity of reconciling the highest humanity with the demands and pleasures of life (245–47).

Works Cited

Abood, Edward F. *Underground Man.* San Francisco: Chandler & Sharp, 1973. Includes revised version of "Jung's Concept of Individuation in Hesse's *Steppenwolf,*" originally published in *Southern Humanities Review* 3 (1968): 1–13.

Artiss, David. "Key Symbols in Hesses *Steppenwolf.*" *Seminar* 7 (1971): 85–101.

Baumann, Günter. *Hermann Hesses Erzählungen im Lichte der Psychologie C. G. Jungs.* Rhenfelden: Schäuble, 1989.

Breugelmans, René. "Hermann Hesse and Depth Psychology." *Canadian Review of Comparative Literature* 8 (1981): 10–47.

Dahrendorf, Malte. "Hermann Hesse's *Demian* and C. G. Jung." *Germanisch-Romanische Monatsschrift* 8 (1958): 91–97.

Golden, Kenneth Lacoy. "The Problem of Opposites in Five Fictional Narratives: Jungian Psychology and Comparative Mythology in Modern Literature." Ph.D. Diss., University of Southern Mississippi, 1978.

Hensing, Dieter. "Nichts ist aussen, nichts ist innen, denn was aussen ist, ist innen." In *Wissen auf Erfahrung: Werkbegriff und Interpretation heute: Festschrift für Hermann Meyer zum 65. Geburtstag,* eds. Alexander von Bormann, Karl Robert Mandelkow and Anthonius H. Tauber, 807–28. Tübingen: Max Niemeyer, 1976.

Hertz, Peter D. "*Steppenwolf* as a Bible." *Georgia Review* 25 (1971): 439–49.

Huber, Peter. "*Der Steppenwolf:* Psychische Kur im deutschen Maskenball." In *Hermann Hesse: Romane.* Stuttgart: Reclam, 1994.

Jung, C. G. *Alchemical Studies.* Vol. 13, *The Collected Works of C. G. Jung.* Princeton: Princeton U P, 1967.

———. *Psychological Types.* Vol. 6, *The Collected Works of C. G. Jung.* Princeton: Princeton U P, 1971.

———. *The Archetypes of the Collective Unconscious.* Vol. 9i, *The Collected Works of C. G. Jung.* Princeton: Princeton U P, 1969.

———. *Two Essays on Analytical Psychology.* Vol. 7, *The Collected Works of C. G. Jung.* Princeton: Princeton U P, 1966.

Karalaschwili, Reso. *Hermann Hesses Romanwelt.* Literatur und Leben, n.s., vol. 29. Cologne: Böhlau Verlag, 1986.

Leinfellner, Elizabeth. "Polarität und Einheit im Werke Hermann Hesses." Ph.D. diss., Vienna, 1962.

Maier, Emanuel. "The Psychology of C. G. Jung in the Works of Hermann Hesse." Ph.D. diss., New York University, 1952.

Meinicke, Susanne. "Hermann Hesse: *Der Steppenwolf.*" Ph.D. diss., Zurich, 1972.

Sammons, Jeffrey L. "Hermann Hesse and the Over-Thirty Germanist." In *Hesse: A Collection of Critical Essays*, ed. Theodore Ziolkowski, 112–33. Englewood Cliffs, N.J.: Prentice Hall, 1973.

Serrano, Miguel. *El circulo hermético de Hermann Hesse a C. G. Jung.* Santiago: Zig-Zag, 1965; translated by Frank McShane as *C. G. Jung and Hermann Hesse: A Record of Two Friendships.* New York: Schocken, 1966.

Spivey, Ted R. The Reintegration of Modern Man: An Essay on J. Joyce and H. Hesse." *Studies in the Literary Imagination* 3, no. 2 (1970): 49–64.

Tusken, Lewis W. "The Question of Perspective in Hesse's *Steppenwolf.*" In *Theorie und Kritik: Zur vergleichenden und neueren deutschen Literatur: Festschrift für Gerhard Loose zum 65. Geburtstag.* ed. Stefan Grunwald and B. A. Beatie, 159–66. Bern: Francke, 1974.

Völker, Ludwig. "Die Gestalt der Hermine in Hesses *Steppenwolf.*" *Études Germanique* 25 (1970): 41–52.

Weaver, Rix. *Spinning on a Dream Thread: Hermann Hesse: his life and work, and his contact with C. G. Jung.* Perth, Australia: Wyvern Publications, 1977.

Webb, Eugene. "Hermine and the Problem of Harry's Failure in Hesse's *Steppenwolf.*" *Modern Fiction Studies* 17 (1971): 115–24.

Ziolkowski, Theodore, ed. *Hesse: A Collection of Critical Essays.* Englewood Cliffs, N.J.: Prentice Hall, 1973.

Conclusion

The reception of Hesse's works since the First World War has been closely connected to historical events. Because of the pacifism and internationalism he advocated during the war, he was both reviled and celebrated following Germany's defeat, a cycle which was repeated following the Second World War. During the period of the Third Reich he was attacked from all sides, by the Nazis for his continuing anti-nationalism, pacifism, and forthright rejection of their ideology and leaders, by the emigrants because he did not publicly reject National Socialism, and by the Communists for his refusal to openly support their ideology. Immediately following the war his position as a representative of the humanistic tradition of German thought and his opposition to fascism was recognized from outside Germany by the conferral on him of the Nobel prize and from the inside by the Goethe prize and other awards.

The positivistic, biographical approach to writers and their works that predominated in the first half of the century was well suited to the autobiographical, confessional nature of Hesse's writing. And with the central importance for him of his psychoanalysis and the inward journey, it was inevitable that this approach would be broadened to include psychological and psychoanalytical investigation and interpretation. Indeed, the first major book on Hesse, Hugo Ball's *Hermann Hesse: His Life and Work* (1927), was identified by a contemporary reviewer as a first attempt in the application of psychoanalysis to the writing of biography. A controversy among critics and reviewers over the validity of such an approach was almost immediately answered by Hans Schmid's 1928 study in which he cites Freud, Rank, Adler, and Jung. In fact, a psychological component is not missing from any of the early investigations of *Steppenwolf*.

The first major departure from positivistic biographical studies of the author and his works occurred in the fifties, when representatives of a new generation of young scholars, those who had discovered and turned to Hesse after the war, wrote their doctoral dissertations on such topics as Hesse's magical thinking, his use of polarity, his relationship to Romanticism, and the form and structure of his works. Others from that generation regarded him as a tainted representative of the romantic, irrationalist tradition they associated with their parents' generation and with National Socialism. This tendency was reinforced by attacks on Hesse in the late fifties and by the move of German students in the sixties to the left. This generation of students had little knowledge of Hesse, since he had been dropped from school curricula, and it was considered chic, as one student wrote, to pay no more attention to him (Muschg, 1992, 11). These students did not realize that Hesse, too, had been "driven to the left" by circumstances in Germany in 1931 (GS 7:512). Until he became disillusioned by the cold war, his sympathies and hopes had been on the side of Communism, a fact not well known before the publication of his letters and political writings.

At the same time he was losing his popularity in Germany, Hesse, the "anarchistic Romantic" (Schwarz 1970, 984), rebel against authority, outsider, and advocate of self-development began to appeal to rebellious American students in the sixties and early seventies. Unburdened by the tradition and immediate past that troubled their German counterparts, American students discovered the anarchistic, individualistic tendency in Hesse's works, regarded him as a hero and cult figure, and initiated the unprecedented explosion of readership which made Hesse by far the most read German writer of the century. If they knew about his condescending criticism of America and Americanism, it did not disturb them, because they too were critical of the country's disregard for the spirit in its emphasis on materialism, technology, capitalism, and nationalism. This puzzling and unexpected phenomenon gave rise to numerous attempts by journalists and critics to understand and explain it, and it motivated scholars to analyze and interpret the works in order to discover the source of their fascination.

While the emphasis of scholarship had shifted during the fifties from the life of the author to close scrutiny of the form and content of his works, a biographical component remained a necessary part of the interpretation of Hesse's admittedly confessional novels, in which he strives to understand and come to terms with his own conflicts, problems, and inner development. This is especially true of *Demian*, *Steppenwolf*, and other writings from the critical period between 1916 and 1927 that are products of and reflect Hesse's Jungian analysis and cannot be fully understood without reference to Jung's psychology, a connection which did not escape the student readers of the sixties. Beginning in the mid-sixties, interpretations of the symbolic and archetypal figures, images, and processes portrayed in the novels included some application of Jung's psychology, and in time a Jungian or archetypal approach became predominant. At their best, these investigations constitute an expansion of the biographical approach to include the personal and collective unconscious as manifest in dreams and myth. Hesse agreed with Jung in considering archetypal images and processes to be structural components of the magical, mystical realm that is inherent in, and therefore shared by, all living beings. And since "what is inside is also outside," this inner realm is also at one with the world and the cosmos, and Harry Haller's condition can be considered symptomatic of his time.

Because of the archetypal universality of the development undergone by Hesse's heroes, they have been compared with mythological and literary representatives of archetypal processes such as Gilgamesh, the Prodigal Son, Goethe's Faust, Novalis's Heinrich von Ofterdingen, and figures in novels and stories by E. T. A. Hoffmann, Dostoevsky, D. H. Lawrence, and Max Frisch, to name a few. Furthermore, the developmental pattern based on Hesse's concept of three kingdoms, which some critics have compared to the three stage progression described by the existentialist philosophers Kierkegaard and Heidegger, also reproduces a structure found in mankind's oldest religions and mythologies: the race and each individual have their beginnings in a state of paradisiacal unity; this harmonious state is inevitably followed by a fall into polarity, conflict, and suffering, which give rise to the belief in, or hope for, the ultimate possibility of salvation and rebirth into a higher state of unity, either on earth or in the hereafter. Insofar as Hesse's symbols correspond to and derive their meaning from mythology, religion, folklore, and literature, they, too, have universal or archetypal significance, as the explications of several critics have demonstrated.

The ongoing debate initiated by Theodore Ziolkowski over the two levels of reality that appear to exist in *Steppenwolf* and the double perspective required to follow the plot simultaneously on both levels is related to the position critics take on the psychological and autobiographical content of the novel. The fact that sound arguments have been made for and against the assumption of a double perspective would seem to indicate that neither side has been able to develop an interpretation that clearly accounts for all the events of the plot. The tendency of more recent scholarship, including especially interpretations based on Jung's psychology, is to take seriously Hesse's repeated assertion that all his figures are parts of himself. Thus even seemingly "real" figures and events are carriers of the author's projections and of personal psychological content; they function as metaphors or, on the deeper level, as symbols. The problematic and controversial "murder" of Hermine, for example, can make sense only as a psychological event; otherwise Haller would be a murderer whose sentence would have to be more severe than being "condemned to eternal life," banished from the Magic Theater for twelve hours, and "laughed out of court." Attempting to establish what is real in the novel may be to "insult the majesty of art" as Haller does by confounding the "beautiful picture gallery with so-called reality." The suggestion that the novel begins on a real level and moves into the internal world which gives the impression of being surrealistic may be the best compromise solution, but it, too, is challenged by the early occurrence of unrealistic events which cannot be fully explained as mere hallucination.

Another element of the novel which has been the object of numerous investigations and considerable controversy is its unique structure. Taking his lead from Hesse, Theodore Ziolkowski attempts to demonstrate in the best known and most often cited of these studies that this modernist text is constructed in the form of a sonata. Other writers have disagreed with Ziolkowski's analysis and proposed alternative structures. Whether or not any of the proposed solutions is entirely accurate is less relevant than the fact that each one reveals how carefully crafted the novel is, which is surely what Hesse wanted to imply in comparing his work to a sonata or a fugue: he did not claim that it is constructed *in the form of* a sonata or a fugue but that it is "proportionally constructed" *like* those forms, that is, according to similar principles of repetition, development, and the interweaving and modulation of motifs, a claim which the various scholarly analyses have substantiated. The repetitions that recur between and within the three different narrative units have been considered redundant by some critics, but in Hesse's view they bring his art closer to music, which he considered to be the highest art.

In the past decade or more critics have contributed relatively few new insights or interpretive strategies. Practitioners of the more recently developed scholarly methods have apparently not found Hesse's texts compatible with their approaches. Hesse scholarship now appears to be in a period of consolidation and synthesis, as is indicated by the number of commentaries and books specifically designed for teachers; by studies comparing Hesse to other authors, thereby establishing his context in world literature; by the exploration of particular themes and motifs throughout his works; and by this review of critical literature. Presumably this period of consolidation will be followed by the further development of detailed analyses and interpretations of the individual works in an ongoing hermeneutic process.

Works by Hermann Hesse

1899. *Romantische Lieder.* Dresden and Leipzig: E. Pierson.

1899. *Eine Stunde hinter Mitternacht.* Leipzig: E. Diederichs.

1901. *Hinterlassene Schriften und Gedichte von Hermann Lauscher.* Herausgegeben von Hermann Hesse. Basel: R. Reich Buchhandlung.

1902. *Gedichte.* Berlin: G. Grote.

1904. *Boccaccio.* Berlin and Leipzig: Schuster & Loeffler.

1904. *Franz von Assisi.* Berlin and Leipzig: Schuster & Loeffler.

1904. *Peter Camenzind.* Berlin: S. Fischer.

1906. *Unterm Rad.* Berlin: S. Fischer.

1907. *Diesseits. Erzählungen.* Berlin: S. Fischer.

1908. *Nachbarn. Erzählungen.* Berlin: S. Fischer.

1910. *Gertrud.* Munich: A. Langen.

1911. *Unterwegs. Gedichte.* Munich: Georg Müller.

1912. *Umwege. Erzählungen.* Berlin: S. Fischer.

1913. *Aus Indien. Aufzeichnungen von einer indischen Reise.* Berlin: S. Fischer.

1914. *Anton Schievelbeyn's ohn-freywillige Reisse nacher Ost-Indien.* Munich: H. F. S. Bachmair.

1914. *Der Hausierer.* Stuttgart: Die Lese.

1914. *Der Lateinschüler.* Hamburg-Grossborstel: Deutsche Dichter-Gedächtnis-Stiftung.

1914. *Die Heimkehr. Erzählung.* Wiesbaden: Volksbildungsverein.

1914. *In der alten Sonne.* Berlin: S. Fischer.

1914. *Roßhalde.* Berlin: S. Fischer.

1915. *Am Weg.* Konstanz: Reuss & Itta.

1915. *Knulp. Drei Geschichten aus dem Leben Knulps.* Berlin: S. Fischer.

1915. *Musik des Einsamen. Neue Gedichte.* Heilbronn: E. Salzer.

1915. *Zum Sieg.* Stuttgart: Die Lese.

1916. *Briefe ins Feld.* Munich: K. A. Lang.

1916. *Die Marmorsäge.* Hamburg-Grossborstel: Deutsche Dichter-Gedächtnis-Stiftung.

1916. *Hans Dierlamms Lehrzeit.* Berlin: Künstlerdank-Gesellschaft.

1916. *Schön ist die Jugend. Zwei Erzählungen.* Berlin: S. Fischer.

1918. *Alte Geschichten. Zwei Erzählungen.* Bern: Bücherzentrale für deutsche Kriegsgefangene.

1918. *Zwei Märchen.* Bern: Bücherzentrale für deutsche Kriegsgefangene.

1919. *Demian. Die Geschichte einer Jugend von Emil Sinclair.* Berlin: S. Fischer.

1919. *Kleiner Garten. Erlebnisse und Dichtungen.* Leipzig and Vienna: E. P. Tal & Co.

1919. *Märchen.* Berlin: S. Fischer.

1919. *Zarathustras Wiederkehr. Ein Wort an die deutsche Jugend. Von einem Deutschen.* Bern: Stämpfli & Cie.

1920. *Blick ins Chaos. Drei Aufsätze.* Bern: Verlag Seldwyla.

1920. *Gedichte des Malers. Zehn Gedichte mit farbigen Zeichnungen von Hermann Hesse.* Bern: Verlag Seldwyla.

1920. *Im Pressel'schen Gartenhaus. Novelle.* Dresden: Lehmann.

1920. *Klingsors letzter Sommer. Erzählungen.* Berlin: S. Fischer.

1920. *Wanderung. Aufzeichnungen.* Berlin: S. Fischer.

1921. *Ausgewählte Gedichte.* Berlin: S. Fischer.

1922. *Siddhartha. Eine indische Dichtung.* Berlin: S. Fischer.

1923. *Sinclairs Notizbuch.* Zurich: Rascher & Cie.

1924. *Psychologia Balneria oder Glossen eines Badener Kurgastes.* Montagnola: Private publication. Published as *Kurgast. Aufzeichnungen von einer Badener Kur* by S. Fischer in 1925.

1926. *Bilderbuch. Schilderungen.* Berlin: S. Fischer.

1927. *Der schwere Weg.* Leipzig: C. Wolf.

1927. *Der Steppenwolf.* Berlin: S. Fischer.

1927. *Die Nürnberger Reise.* Berlin: S. Fischer.

1928. *Betrachtungen.* Berlin: S. Fischer.

1928. *Krisis. Ein Stück Tagebuch.* Berlin: S. Fischer.

1929. *Eine Bibliothek der Weltliteratur.* Leipzig: Philipp Reclam.

1929. *Trost der Nacht. Neue Gedichte.* Berlin: S. Fischer.

1930. *Diesseits. Erzählungen.* Berlin: S. Fischer.

1930. *Narziss und Goldmund. Erzählung.* Berlin: S. Fischer.

1931. *Weg nach Innen. Vier Erzählungen.* Berlin: S. Fischer.

1932. *Die Morgenlandfahrt. Eine Erzählung.* Berlin: S. Fischer.

1933. *Kleine Welt. Erzählungen.* Berlin: S. Fischer.

1933. *Schön ist die Jugend.* Darmstadt: Winklers Verlag.

1935. *Fabulierbuch. Erzählungen.* Berlin: S. Fischer.

1936. *Das Haus der Träume. Eine unvollendete Dichtung.* Olten: Vereinigung Oltner Bücherfreunde.

1936. *Stunden im Garten. Eine Idylle.* Vienna: Bermann-Fischer.

1937. *Gedenkblätter.* Berlin: S. Fischer.

1937. *Neue Gedichte.* Berlin: S. Fischer.

1938. *Aus der Kindheit des heiligen Franz von Assisi.* Mainz: Albert Eggebrecht-Presse.

1940. *Der Novalis. Aus den Papieren eines Altmodischen.* Olten: Vereinigung Oltner Bücherfreunde.

1942. *Die Gedichte.* Zurich: Fretz & Wasmuth.

1942. *Kleine Betrachtungen. Sechs Aufsätze.* Zurich: Büchergilde Gutenberg.

1943. *Das Glasperlenspiel. Versuch einer Lebensbeschreibung des Magister Ludi Josef Knecht samt Knechts hinterlassene Schriften.* Zurich: Fretz & Wasmuth.

1945. *Berthold. Ein Romanfragment.* Zurich: Fretz & Wasmuth.

1945. *Der Pfirsichbaum und andere Erzählungen.* Zurich: Büchergilde Gutenberg.

1945. *Traumfährte. Neue Erzählungen und Märchen.* Zurich: Fretz & Wasmuth.

1946. *Dank an Goethe.* Zurich: W. Classen.

1946. *Der Europäer.* Berlin: Suhrkamp.

1946. *Krieg und Frieden. Betrachtungen zu Krieg und Politik seit dem Jahr 1914.* Zurich: Fretz & Wasmuth.

1947. *Heumond. Aus Kinderzeiten. Erzählungen.* Basel: Verein Gute Schriften.

1948. *Berg und See. Zwei Landschaftsstudien.* Zurich: Büchergilde Gutenberg.

1949. *Aus vielen Jahren. Gedichte, Erzählungen und Bilder.* Bern: Stämpfli & Cie.

1951. *Briefe.* Berlin and Frankfurt am Main: Suhrkamp.

1951. *Eine Handvoll Briefe.* Zurich: Büchergilde Gutenberg.

1951. *Späte Prosa.* Berlin: Suhrkamp.

1952. *Gesammelte Dichtungen.* 6 vols. Frankfurt am Main: Suhrkamp.

1954. *Briefe. Hermann Hesse/Romain Rolland.* Zurich: Fretz & Wasmuth.

1954. *Piktors Verwandlungen. Ein Märchen.* Berlin and Frankfurt am Main: Suhrkamp.

1955. *Beschwörungen. Späte Prosa/Neue Folge.* Berlin: Suhrkamp.

1957. *Gesammelte Schriften.* 7 vols. Frankfurt am Main: Suhrkamp. (Addition of vol. 7, *Betrachtungen und Briefe*, to 1952 edition.)

1960. *Bericht an die Freunde. Letzte Gedichte.* Olten: Vereinigung Oltner Bücherfreunde.

1961. *Stufen. Alte und neue Gedichte in Auswahl.* Frankfurt am Main: Suhrkamp.

1963. *Aerzte. Ein paar Erinnerungen.* Olten: Vereinigung Oltner Bücherfreunde.

1964. *Geheimnisse. Letzte Erzählungen.* Frankfurt am Main: Suhrkamp.

1965. *Erwin.* Olten: Vereinigung von Freunden der Oltner Liebhaberdrucke.

1965. *Prosa aus dem Nachlaß.* Ed. Ninon Hesse. Frankfurt am Main: Suhrkamp.

1966. *Kindheit und Jugend vor Neunzehnhundert. Hermann Hesse in Briefen und Lebenszeugnissen 1877–1895.* Selected and edited by Ninon Hesse. Frankfurt am Main: Suhrkamp.

1968. *Briefwechsel. Hermann Hesse - Thomas Mann.* Frankfurt am Main: Suhrkamp.

1969. *Briefwechsel. Peter Suhrkamp - Hermann Hesse.* Frankfurt am Main: Suhrkamp.

1970. *Gesammelte Werke in zwölf Bänden* (Werkausgabe). Frankfurt am Main: Suhrkamp.

1970. *Politische Betrachtungen.* Frankfurt am Main: Suhrkamp.

1971. *Zwei Autorenporträts in Briefen 1897 bis 1900. Hermann Hesse - Helene Voigt-Diederichs.* Düsseldorf-Cologne: Diederichs.

1972. *Eigensinn. Autobiographische Schriften.* Frankfurt am Main: Suhrkamp.

1972. *Schriften zur Literatur.* 2 vols. Frankfurt am Main: Suhrkamp.

1972. *Briefwechsel aus der Nähe. Hermann Hesse - Karl Kerényi.* Munich and Vienna: Langen Müller.

1972. *"Der Steppenwolf" und unbekannte Texte aus dem Umkreis des Steppenwolf.* Ed. Volker Michels. Frankfurt am Main: Büchergilde Gutenberg.

1973. *Gesammelte Briefe.* Vol. 1: 1895–1921; Vol. 2: 1922–1935 (1979); Vol. 3: 1936–1948 (1982); Vol. 4: 1949–1962 (1986). Frankfurt am Main: Suhrkamp.

1973. *Die Kunst des Müßiggangs. Kurze Prosa aus dem Nachlaß.* Ed. Volker Michels. Frankfurt am Main: Suhrkamp.

1975. *Legenden.* Frankfurt am Main: Suhrkamp.

1975. *Die Gedichte.* 2 vols. Frankfurt am Main: Suhrkamp.

1977. *Politik des Gewissens. Die politischen Schriften.* 2 vols. Frankfurt am Main: Suhrkamp.

Works Cited

Ball, Hugo. 1927. *Hermann Hesse: Sein Leben und sein Werk*. Berlin: Fischer. Rpt. Berlin: Suhrkamp, 1963.

Schmid, Hans Rudolf. 1928. *Hermann Hesse*. Frauenfeld and Leipzig: Verlag von Huber & Co.

Dehorn, W. 1932. "Psychoanalyse und neuere Dichtung." *Germanic Review* 7: 245–62, 330–58.

Carlsson, Anni. 1933. "Vom Steppenwolf zur Morgenlandfahrt." In *Hermann Hesse: Sein Leben und sein Werk*, Hugo Ball, 237–58. Revised and expanded ed. Berlin: Fischer.

Matzig, Richard B. 1944. *Der Dichter und die Zeitstimmung: Betrachtungen über Hermann Hesses Steppenwolf*. St. Gallen: Verlag der Fehr'schen Buchhandlung. Revised version in *Hermann Hesse in Montagnola: Studien zu Werk und Innenwelt des Dichters*. Basel: Amerbach, 1947.

Hafner, Gotthilf. 1947. *Hermann Hesse: Werk und Leben: Umrisse eines Dichterbildes*. Reinbeck bei Hamburg, Parus. 2d rev. ed. Nuremberg: Carl, 1954.

Schmid, Max. 1947. *Hermann Hesse: Weg und Wandlung*. With a biographical appendix by Armin Lemp. Zurich: Fretz & Wasmuth.

Böttcher, Margot. 1948. "Aufbau und Form von Hermann Hesses *Steppenwolf, Morgenlandfahrt* und *Glasperlenspiel*." Ph.D. diss., Humboldt University, Berlin.

Brown, Calvin S. 1948. *Music and Literature: A Comparison of the Arts*. Athens, U of Georgia P.

Campbell, Joseph. 1948. *The Hero with a Thousand Faces*. Princeton: Princeton U P, 1948.

Seidlin, Oskar. 1950. "The Exorcism of the Demon." *Symposium* 4: 325–48. Rpts. in Ziolkowski 1973, 51–75 and Liebmann 1977, 7–28.

Baumer, Franz. 1951. "Das magische Denken in der Dichtung Hermann Hesses." Ph.D. diss., Munich.

Liepelt-Unterberg, Maria. 1951. "Das Polaritätsgesetz in der Dichtung. Am Beispiel von Hermann Hesses 'Steppenwolf.'" Ph.D. diss., Bonn.

Unseld, Siegfried. 1951. "Hermann Hesses Anschauung vom Beruf des Dichters." Ph.D. diss., Tübingen.

Gnefkow, Edmund. 1952. *Hermann Hesse: Biographie*. Freiburg i.Br.: Gerhard Kirchhoff Verlag.

Maier, Emanuel. 1952. "The Psychology of C. G. Jung in the Works of Hermann Hesse." Ph.D. diss., New York University.

Wagner, Marianne. 1953. "Zeitmorphologischer Vergleich von Hermann Hesses 'Demian', 'Siddhartha', 'Der Steppenwolf', 'Narziss und Goldmund' zur Aufweisung typischer Gestaltzüge." Ph.D. diss., Bonn.

Heller, Peter. 1954. "The Writer in Conflict with his Age: A Study in the Ideology of Hermann Hesse." *Monatshefte* 46: 137–47. Rpt. in Liebmann 1977.

Middleton, John Christopher. 1954. "Hermann Hesse as Humanist." Ph.D. diss., Merton College.

Weibel, Kurt. 1952. *Hermann Hesse und die deutsche Romantik*. Bern. Winterthur: P. G. Keller, 1954.

Wilson, Colin. 1956. *The Outsider*. Boston: Houghton Mifflin; London: Gollancz.

Deschner, Karlheinz. 1957. *Kitsch, Konvention und Kunst: Eine literarische Streitschrift*. Munich: Paul List Verlag.

Dürr, Werner. 1957. *Hermann Hesse: Vom Wesen der Musik in der Dichtung*. Stuttgart: Silberberg.

Dahrendorf, Malte. 1958. "Hermann Hesse's *Demian* and C. G. Jung." *Germanisch-Romanische Monatsschrift* n.s. 8: 91–97.

Gontrum, Peter Baer. 1958. "Natur- und Dingsymbolik als Ausdruck der inneren Welt Hermann Hesses." Ph.D. diss., Munich.

Mileck, Joseph. 1958. *Hermann Hesse and His Critics: The Criticism and Bibliography of Half a Century*. Chapel Hill: U of North Carolina P.

Ziolkowski, Theodore. 1958. "Hermann Hesse's *Steppenwolf*: A Sonata in Prose." *Modern Language Quarterly* 19: 115–33; Expanded rpt. in Ziolkowski 1965, 178–228. Rpt. in Liebmann 1977, 90–109.

Allemann, Beda. 1961. "Tractat vom Steppenwolf:" Afterword to Hesse's "Treatise on the Steppenwolf." Frankfurt am Main: Suhrkamp. Rpt. in *Materialien zu Hermann Hesses "Der Steppenwolf, ed. Volker* Michels, 317–24. Frankfurt am Main: Suhrkamp, 1972.

Schwarz, Egon. 1961. "Zur Erklärung von Hesses 'Steppenwolf.'" *Monatshefte* 53: 191–98. Translated as "Hermann Hesse: *Steppenwolf* (1927)" in *Reflection and Action: Essays on the Bildungsroman*, ed. James Hardin, 382–414. Columbia: U of South Carolina P, 1991.

Ziolkowski, Theodore. 1961. "Hermann Hesse's Chiliastic Vision." *Monatshefte* 53: 199–210.

Leinfellner, Elizabeth. 1962. "Polarität und Einheit im Werke Hermann Hesses." Ph.D. diss., Vienna.

Freedman, Ralph W. B. 1963. *The Lyrical Novel: Studies in Hermann Hesse, André Gide and Virginia Woolf*. Princeton: Princeton U P.

Leary, Timothy and Ralph Metzner. 1963. "Hermann Hesse: Poet of the Interior Journey." *The Psychedelic Review* 1: 167–82.

Zeller, Bernhard. 1963. *Hermann Hesse in Selbstzeugnissen und Bilddokumenten.* Reinbeck bei Hamburg: Rowohlt; translated as *Portrait of Hesse: An Illustrated Biography.* New York: Herder and Herder, 1971.

Rose, Ernst. 1965. *Faith from the Abyss: Hermann Hesse's Way from Romanticism to Modernity.* New York: New York U P.

Serrano, Miguel. 1965. *El circulo hermético de Hermann Hesse a C. G. Jung.* Santiago: Zig-Zag; translated as *C. G. Jung and Hermann Hesse: A Record of Two Friendships.* New York: Schocken, 1966.

Ziolkowski, Theodore. 1965. *The Novels of Hermann Hesse: A Study in Theme and Structure.* Princeton: Princeton U P.

Jung, C. G. 1966. *Two Essays on Analytical Psychology.* Vol. 7, *The Collected Works of C. G. Jung.* Princeton: Princeton U P.

Boulby, Mark. 1967. *Hermann Hesse: His Mind and Art.* Ithaca: Cornell U P.

Jung, C. G. 1967. *Alchemical Studies.* Vol. 13, *The Collected Works of C. G. Jung.* Princeton: Princeton U P.

Gay, Peter. 1968. *Weimar Culture: The Outsider as Insider.* New York: Harper and Row.

Richards, Donald Ray. 1968. *The German Bestseller in the 20th Century: A Complete Bibliography and Analysis: 1915–1940.* Bern: Herbert Lang.

Cohn, Dorrit. 1969. "Narration of Consciousness in Der Steppenwolf." *Germanic Review* 44: 121–31.

Hatfield, Henry. 1969. "Accepting the Universe: Hermann Hesse's *Steppenwolf*." Chap. in *Crisis and Continuity in Modern German Fiction: Ten Essays,* ed. Henry Hatfield, 63–77. Ithaca: Cornell U P.

Hughes, Kenneth. 1969. "Hesse's Use of *Gilgamesh*-Motifs in the Humanization of Siddhartha and Harry Haller." *Seminar* 5: 129–40.

Jung, C. G. 1969. *The Archetypes of the Collective Unconscious.* Vol. 9i, *The Collected Works of C. G. Jung.* Princeton: Princeton U P.

Timpe, Eugen F. 1969. "Hermann Hesse in the United States." *Symposium* 23: 73–79. Rpt. in Liebmann 1977, 136–42.

Ziolkowski, Theodore. 1969. *Dimensions of the Modern Novel: German Texts and European Contexts.* Princeton: Princeton U P.

Field, G. W. 1970. *Hermann Hesse.* New York: Twayne Publishers; New York: Hippocrene Books, 1972.

Lange, Marga. 1970. *"Daseinsproblematik" in Hermann Hesse's "Steppenwolf": An Existential Interpretation.* Queensland Studies in German Language and Literature. Brisbane, Australia: U of Queensland.

Lüthi, Hans Jürg. 1970. *Hermann Hesse: Natur und Geist.* Sprache und Literatur, 69. Stuttgart: Kohlhammer.

Rogers, Robert. 1970. *A Psychoanalytic Study of The Double in Literature.* Detroit: Wayne State U P.

Sammons, Jeffrey L. 1970. "Notes on the Germanization of American Youth." *The Yale Review* 59: 342–56.

Schwarz, Egon. 1970. "Hermann Hesse, the American Youth Movement, and Problems of Literary Evaluation." *PMLA* 85: 977–87.

Spivey, Ted R. 1970. The Reintegration of Modern Man: An Essay on J. Joyce and H. Hesse." *Studies in the Literary Imagination* 3, no. 2: 49–64.

Völker, Ludwig. 1970. "Die Gestalt der Hermine in Hesses *Steppenwolf.*" *Études Germanique* 25: 41–52.

Artiss, David. 1971. "Key Symbols in Hesses *Steppenwolf.*" *Seminar* 7: 85–101.

Hertz, Peter D. 1971. "*Steppenwolf* as a Bible." *Georgia Review* 25: 439–49.

Jung, C. G. 1971. *Psychological Types.* Vol. 6, *The Collected Works of C. G. Jung.* Princeton: Princeton U P.

Webb, Eugene. 1971. "Hermine and the Problem of Harry's Failure in Hesse's *Steppenwolf.*" *Modern Fiction Studies* 17: 115–24.

Meinicke, Susanne. 1972. "Hermann Hesse. *Der Steppenwolf.*" Ph.D. diss., Zurich.

Michels, Volker, ed. 1972. *Materialien zu Hermann Hesses "Der Steppenwolf."* Frankfurt am Main: Suhrkamp.

Simons, John D. 1972. *Hermann Hesse's Steppenwolf: A Critical Commentary.* New York: Monarch Press.

Abood, Edward F. 1973. *Underground Man.* San Francisco: Chandler & Sharp.

Dhority, Lynn. 1973. "Who wrote the *Tractat vom Steppenwolf?*" *German Life and Letters* 27: 59–66.

Freedman, Ralph. 1973. "*Person* and *Persona*: the Magic Mirrors of *Steppenwolf.*" In *Hesse: A Collection of Critical Essays*, ed. Theodore Ziolkowski, 153–79. Englewood Cliffs, N.J.: Prentice Hall.

Sammons, Jeffrey L. 1973. "Hermann Hesse and the Over-Thirty Germanist." In *Hesse: A Collection of Critical Essays*, ed. Theodore Ziolkowski, 112–33. Englewood Cliffs, N.J.: Prentice Hall.

Schneider, Christian Immo. 1973. *Das Todesproblem bei Hermann Hesse.* Marburg: Elwert.

Ziolkowski, Theodore, ed. 1973. *Hesse: A Collection of Critical Essays.* Englewood Cliffs, N.J.: Prentice Hall.

Böttger, Fritz. 1974. *Hermann Hesse: Leben, Werk, Zeit.* Berlin: Verlag der Nation.

Dhority, Lynn. 1974. "Toward a Revaluation of Structure and Style in Hesse's *Steppenwolf.*" In *Theorie und Kritik: Zur vergleichenden und neueren deutschen Literatur: Festschrift fur Gerhard Loose zum 65. Geburtstag.* ed. Stefan Grunwald and B. A. Beatie, 149–58. Bern: Francke.

Schwarz, Egon. 1974. "Ein Fall globaler Rezeption: Hermann Hesse im Wandel der Zeiten." *Zeitschrift für Literaturwissenschaft und Linguistik* Heft 15: 50–60.

Tusken, Lewis W. 1974. "The Question of Perspective in Hesse's *Steppenwolf.*" In *Theorie und Kritik: Zur vergleichenden und neueren deutschen Literatur: Festschrift fur Gerhard Loose zum 65. Geburtstag.* ed. Stefan Grunwald and B. A. Beatie, 159–66. Bern: Francke.

Farrer, Edward A. 1975. "The Quest for Being: D. H. Lawrence and Hermann Hesse." Ph.D. diss., Purdue University.

Middell, Eike. 1975. *Hermann Hesse: Die Bilderwelt seines Lebens.* Leipzig: Reclam; Frankfurt am Main: Röderberg.

Hensing, Dieter. 1976. "Nichts ist aussen, nichts ist innen, denn was aussen ist, ist innen." In *Wissen auf Erfahrung: Werkbegriff und Interpretation heute: Festschrift für Hermann Meyer zum 65. Geburtstag,* eds. Alexander von Bormann, Karl Robert Mandelkow and Anthonius H. Tauber, 807–28. Tübingen: Max Niemeyer.

Michels, Volker, ed. 1976. *Über Hermann Hesse.* Vol. 1. Frankfurt am Main: Suhrkamp.

Baumer, Franz. 1977. "Deutschland." In *Hermann Hesses weltweite Wirkung: Internationale Rezeptionsgeschichte,* ed. Martin Pfeifer, 15–38. Frankfurt am Main: Suhrkamp.

Gummerer, Gottfried. 1977. "Italien." In *Hermann Hesses weltweite Wirkung: Internationale Rezeptionsgeschichte,* ed. Martin Pfeifer, 69–84. Frankfurt am Main: Suhrkamp.

Koester, Rudolf. 1977. "USA." In *Hermann Hesses weltweite Wirkung: Internationale Rezeptionsgeschichte,* ed. Martin Pfeifer, 155–71. Frankfurt am Main: Suhrkamp.

Liebmann, Judith K., ed. 1977. *Hermann Hesse: A Collection of Criticism.* New York: McGraw-Hill.

Mayer, Hans. 1977. "Hermann Hesse und das Magische Theater: Ein Vortrag." *Jahrbuch der deutschen Schillergesellschaft* 21: 517–32.

Michels, Volker, ed. 1977. *Über Hermann Hesse.* Vol. 2. Frankfurt am Main: Suhrkamp.

Mileck, Joseph. 1977. *Hermann Hesse: Biography and Bibliography.* 2 vols. Berkeley: U of California P.

Pfeifer, Martin, ed. 1977. *Hermann Hesses weltweite Wirkung: Internationale Rezeptionsgeschichte.* Frankfurt am Main: Suhrkamp.

Watanabe, Masaru. 1977. "Japan." In *Hermann Hesses weltweite Wirkung: Internationale Rezeptionsgeschichte,* ed. Martin Pfeifer, 222–33. Frankfurt am Main: Suhrkamp.

Weaver, Rix. 1977. *Spinning on a Dream Thread: Hermann Hesse: his life and work, and his contact with C. G. Jung.* Perth, Australia: Wyvern Publications.

Freedman, Ralph. 1978. *Pilgrim of Crisis: A Biography.* London: Cape.

Golden, Kenneth Lacoy. 1978. "The Problem of Opposites in Five Fictional Narratives: Jungian Psychology and Comparative Mythology in Modern Literature." Ph.D. Diss., University of Southern Mississippi.

Hollis, A. 1978a. "Political Ambivalence in Hesse's *Steppenwolf.*" *Modern Language Review* 73: 110–118.

———. 1978b. "*Steppenwolf*: The Laughter in the Music." *New German Studies* 6: 15–30.

Jansen, Peter. 1978. "Personalität und Humor: Hesses *Steppenwolf* and Kierkegaard's Humorkonzeption." *Sprache im technischen Zeitalter* 67: 209–20.

Mileck, Joseph. 1978. *Hermann Hesse: Life and Art.* Berkeley: U of California P.

Knüfermann, Volker. 1979. "Sprache und Neurose: Zu Hermann Hesses *Steppenwolf.*" *Études Germanique* 34: 276–83.

Pavlyshyn, Marko. 1979. "Music in Hermann Hesse's *Der Steppenwolf* and *Das Glasperlenspiel.*" *Seminar* 15: 39–55.

Hsia, Adrian, ed. 1980. *Hermann Hesse heute.* Bonn: Bouvier.

Karalaschwili, Reso. 1980. "Harry Hallers Goethe-Traum: Vorläufiges zu einer Szene aus dem *Steppenwolf* von Hermann Hesse." *Goethe-Jahrbuch* 97: 224–34.

Ziolkowski, Theodore. 1980. "Hermann Hesse in den USA." In *Hermann Hesse heute,* ed. Adrian Hsia, 1–24. Bonn: Bouvier.

Neuswanger, R. Russell. 1980. "The Autonomy of the Narrator and the Function of Humor in *Der Steppenwolf.*" In *Hermann Hesse heute,* ed. Adrian Hsia, 233–41. Bonn: Bouvier.

Breugelmans, René. 1981. "Hermann Hesse and Depth Psychology." *Canadian Review of Comparative Literature* 8: 10–47.

Karalaschwili, Reso. 1981. "Der Romananfang bei Hermann Hesse: Die Funktion des Titels, des Vorworts und des Romaneinsatzes in seinem Schaffen." *Jahrbuch der deutschen Schillergesellschaft* 25: 446–473.

Seckendorff, Klaus von. 1982. *Hermann Hesses propagandistische Prosa: Selbstzerstörerische Entfaltung als Botschaft in seinen Romanen von "Demian" bis zum "Steppenwolf."* Bonn: Bouvier.

Cremerius, Johannes. 1983. "Schuld und Sühne ohne Ende: Hermann Hesses psychotherapeutische Erfahrungen." In *Literaturpsychologische Studien und Analysen*, Amsterdamer Beiträge zur neueren Germanistik, ed. Walter Schönau, 169–204. Amsterdam: Rodopi.

Goode, Ruth. 1985. *Hermann Hesse's "Steppenwolf" and "Siddhartha."* Woodbury: Barron's Educational Series.

Unseld, Siegfried. 1985. *Hermann Hesse: Werk und Wirkungsgeschichte*. Revised and expanded version of 1973 edition. Frankfurt am Main: Suhrkamp.

Karalaschwili, Reso. 1986. *Hermann Hesses Romanwelt*. Literatur und Leben, n.s., vol. 29. Cologne: Böhlau Verlag.

Richards, David G. 1987. *The Hero's Quest for the Self: An Archetypal Approach to Hesse's "Demian" and Other Novels*. Lanham, Maryland: U P of America.

Delphendahl, Renate. 1988. "Narcissism and the Double in Hermann Hesse's *Steppenwolf*." *Journal of Evolutionary Psychology* 9: 141–53, 208–17.

Stelzig, Eugen L. 1988. *Hermann Hesse's Fictions of the Self: Autobiography and the Confessional Imagination*. Princeton: Princeton U P.

Baumann, Günter. 1989. *Hermann Hesses Erzählungen im Lichte der Psychologie C. G. Jungs*. Rhenfelden: Schäuble.

Schwarz, Egon. 1991. "Hermann Hesse: *Steppenwolf* (1927)." In *Reflection and Action: Essays on the Bildungsroman*, ed. James Hardin, 382–414. Columbia: U of South Carolina P.

Abret, Helga. 1992. "Schlechte Zeit für Literaturkritik: Hermann Hesse als Literaturkritiker zwischen 1933 und 1938." In *Hermann Hesse und die Politik*, 7th International Hermann-Hesse Colloquium in Calw, ed. Martin Pfeifer, 107–140. Bad Liebenzell: Verlag Bernhard Gengenbach.

Michels, Volker. 1992. "Zwischen Duldung und Sabotage: Hermann Hesse und der Nationalsozialismus." In *Hermann Hesse und die Politik*, 7th International Hermann-Hesse Colloquium in Calw, ed. Martin Pfeifer, 87–105. Bad Liebenzell: Verlag Bernhard Gengenbach.

Muschg, Adolf. 1992. "Hermann Hesse und das Engagement." In *Hermann Hesse und die Politik*, 7th International Hermann-Hesse Colloquium in Calw, ed. Martin Pfeifer, 11–24. Bad Liebenzell: Verlag Bernhard Gengenbach.

Werner-Birkenbach, Sabine. 1992. "Hugo Ball's 'Hesse-Biographie': Zur Wechselbeziehung von Rezeption und Edition." *Hugo Ball Almanach 1992*: 157–236.

Weiner, Marc A. 1993. *Undertones of Insurrection: Music, Politics, and the Social Sphere in the Modern German Narrative*. Lincoln, Nebraska: U of Nebraska P.

Huber, Peter. 1994. "*Der Steppenwolf*: Psychische Kur im deutschen Maskenball." In *Hermann Hesse: Romane*, 76–112. Stuttgart: Reclam.

Index

DATE DUE			
JUN 0 9 1997			
APR 2 8 1999			

CONCORDIA UNIVERSITY LIBRARY
2811 NE Holman St.
Portland, OR 97211-6099